ga

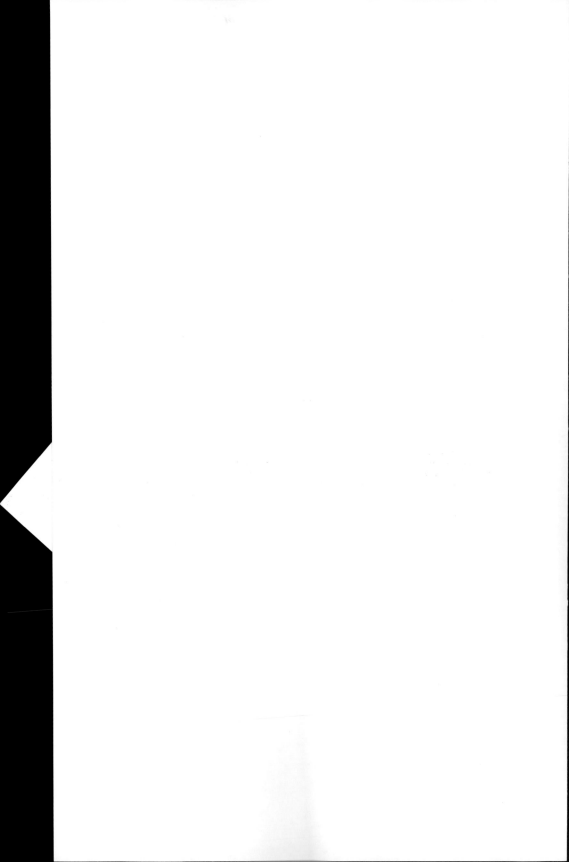

Additional Praise for
Startup Life

"Being an entrepreneur is one of the hardest jobs in the world. Staying happily married is one of the others. Brad and Amy show us how to successfully do both. My wife and I loved this book. Mandatory reading for any entrepreneur who doesn't want to live alone... Forever."
—Dr. Sean Wise, Professor of Entrepreneurship & Strategy, Ryerson University

"Bursting with revealing personal insights, tested strategies and case-studies, *Startup Life* lays out a path to sanity and success for entrepreneurs seeking to build not only a game-changing business, but a vibrant and engaged relationship along the way."
—Jonathan Fields, author of *Uncertainty*

"We've experienced the mix of marriage, children, and several high-growth companies and even now while helping people across the United States develop startups and startup communities the path is similar. While entrepreneurship is critical to drive our economy, navigating it as a family is extremely challenging. Amy and Brad draw on wisdom from entrepreneurs and their own life to provide a phenomenal roadmap for you to maximize the upside and minimize the downside."
—Scott Case, CEO, Startup America Partnership & Leslie Case, Manager SAKR LLC

"Through my work as founder and CEO of National Center for Women & Information Technology, Brad and I have had numerous conversations about issues entrepreneurs, especially women; have around work-life balance. In this book, Brad and Amy cover much new ground in articulating what has worked for them and giving any entrepreneurial couple a framework for thinking about how to integrate entrepreneurial work and life."
—Lucy Sanders, CoFounder and CEO, National Center for Women & Information Technology

STARTUP

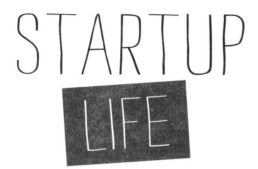

LIFE

SURVIVING AND THRIVING IN A RELATIONSHIP WITH AN ENTREPRENEUR

BRAD FELD
AMY BATCHELOR

WILEY

John Wiley & Sons, Inc.

Published by John Wiley & Sons, Inc., Hoboken, New Jersey.
Published simultaneously in Canada.

For general information on our other products and services or for technical support, please contact our Customer Care Department within the United States at (800) 762-2974, outside the United States at (317) 572-3993 or fax (317) 572-4002.

Wiley publishes in a variety of print and electronic formats and by print-on-demand. Some material included with standard print versions of this book may not be included in e-books or in print-on-demand. If this book refers to media such as a CD or DVD that is not included in the version you purchased, you may download this material at http://booksupport.wiley.com. For more information about Wiley products, visit www.wiley.com.

ISBN 978-1-118-44364-4 (cloth); 978-1-118-51686-7 (ebk); 978-1-118-51685-0 (ebk); 978-1-118-49386-1 (ebk)

Printed in the United States of America
10 9 8 7 6 5 4 3 2 1

To the believers and the empiricists:
those who are willing to love.

CONTENTS

I t was the summer of 2000. The NASDAQ had peaked, and while things weren't yet in free fall, it was clear that Internet-related companies had some major stress in front of them. Brad had spent a week on the East Coast totally maxed out in 18-hour days at numerous companies in which he was an investor. We had a relaxing weekend planned with longtime friends in Newport, Rhode Island, and Brad was looking forward to catching his breath.

A town car picked up Amy at Logan Airport and then swung by an office park in the Boston suburbs to pick up Brad. He came out of the office on his cell phone, dragging his luggage, and somehow managed to get in the car while continuing the conversation. He waved a quick hello to Amy and continued talking. The driver took off on the 90-minute drive to Newport.

About halfway there he finished his call. He hung up, turned to a moderately annoyed-looking Amy, and said a more enthusiastic hello. We chatted for a few minutes and his phone rang again. He answered immediately and launched into another conversation that lasted until we got to our friends' house.

It was late Friday afternoon in Newport on a beautiful summer day. We settled into chairs in our friends' backyard with a drink. Brad pulled a pile of paper out of his bag and set it in front of him. Smartphones weren't very smart in 2000, and Wi-Fi wasn't ubiquitous yet, so he often dragged around a bunch of stuff he had to read and used "downtime" like late Friday afternoon to grind through it.

Amy and our friends chatted while Brad turned the pages on what felt like an infinite pile of stuff to read. Eventually, it was time to head to dinner, so we all hopped in the car and went to a nice seafood restaurant in downtown Newport. Our food had just appeared when Brad's cell phone rang. He answered it, excused himself from the table, and walked outside to take the call. Thirty minutes later he reentered the restaurant to Amy and our friends eating dessert. Amy had a profoundly annoyed look on her face, but Brad figured he would relax on Saturday and Sunday and everything would be okay.

When we got into bed an hour or so later, Brad could sense that something was wrong.

"I'm done," said Amy.

"Yeah, this was a bitch of a week. I've got a couple of companies that are imploding, and it seems like nothing is going right anywhere. I'm exhausted. I'm glad it's the weekend—I'm done with this week also," Brad replied.

"No. I'm done. Not with the week. But with living this way. You aren't even a good roommate anymore. I love you, but I just don't want to live this way. I'm done."

Silence. Even though Brad is a guy, he knew that at moments like this the goal should not be to solve the problem. As uncomfortable as it was, he let the silence sit in the air, partly because he had no idea what to say.

Eventually, Brad quietly responded, "Wow, I've really fucked up to get things to this point. I'm not done, but if you are, then it's on me to try to change. I hope you'll give me one more chance."

Amy did. And a dozen years later, we are happier than we've ever been. Sure, we have our bad moments together, but they are few and far between.

That night in Rhode Island was the nadir of our marriage. This book is our effort to tell the story about how our relationship survived and how we learned to thrive in the very complex and stressful world inhabited by an entrepreneur.

AUDIENCE

This book is for any entrepreneur who wants to be in a successful relationship. It's also for anyone who wants to be in a successful relationship with an entrepreneur. Whether you are already in a relationship, have a family, or aspire to be in a relationship, we hope you can learn and benefit from this book.

If your relationship is in trouble, this book can help. If your relationship is going well, this book can help you make it better. If you are on top of the world as a couple, this book can help you stay there.

While we've aimed this book specifically at entrepreneurial couples, we think the advice, stories, suggestions, and approaches here can apply to any relationship.

We've been together for 22 years. We've had major ups and downs and almost had our relationship end 12 years ago. We've worked hard to get to an amazing place, and have thought and talked hard about it along the way. We've spent many hours talking to our friends, many of whom are entrepreneurial couples, about their relationships. We've learned a lot, made a lot of mistakes, and figured out a lot of things.

Several years ago we decided to try to write it all down so we could share with everyone on the planet, especially as the Startup Revolution that we are so involved in spreads. This is our attempt to do that.

OVERVIEW OF THE CONTENTS

After a brief introduction, we'll explain our philosophy around relationships and cover some specific concepts that we feel are at the core of any relationship. We'll then spend a chapter on communication, which we believe is the foundation that every relationship is built on.

We'll spend a chapter talking about startup company life, followed by the personality of an entrepreneur. We'll then go deep into a set of values that we believe are key to a successful relationship for any entrepreneurial couple.

We'll then spend time on skills, tactics, and tools that we have developed and learned over the years and applied to our relationship. We'll talk about common issues and conflicts, and then spend a chapter on the scary big issues such as illness, relationship failure, and divorce.

We then spend entire chapters on four issues: money, children, family, and sex and romance. Since we don't have children of our own, the children chapter is primarily contributions from entrepreneurial couples who do have children.

We finish up with a chapter titled "Enough."

ADDITIONAL MATERIALS

Startup Life is the second book in the Startup Revolution series. The Startup Revolution web site (*http://startuprev.com*) has links to numerous additional resources, including the Startup Life web site (*http://life.startuprev.com*). This site includes a blog that we regularly update with stories about different approaches to having an amazing startup life.

The first book in the Startup Revolution series is *Startup Communities: Building an Entrepreneurial Ecosystem in Your City*. The Startup Communities web site is at *http://communities.startuprev.com* and includes a blog that we regularly update with stories about startup communities around the world, a discussion board at *http://hub.startuprev.com* for those interested in talking about startup communities, events that Brad will be participating in around startup communities, and resources for anyone interested in creating a startup community.

Come join us and explore, talk about, and help create the Startup Revolution.

ACKNOWLEDGMENTS

We have had an amazing experience writing this book together. We have been talking about it for several years and finally committed to it when Brad agreed with his publisher (Wiley) to do a series of books called Startup Revolution. We started in earnest in June 2012 during a three-month stretch where we spent the entire summer at our house in Keystone, Colorado. Other than a trip to Europe last summer where we spent 60 days together, this was the longest uninterrupted stretch of time we've spent together in our 22-year relationship.

While we had high hopes of writing together side by side all summer, Brad was hard at work on the first book in this series, *Startup Communities: Building an Entrepreneurial Ecosystem in Your City*. We spent some time on *Startup Life*, but the work really didn't start in earnest until the beginning of September. As a result, this book is evidence that you actually can write a book largely in two months in the midst of all the other craziness of an entrepreneurial life. While several of our friends have suggested that our next book should be called *Startup Author: Surviving and Thriving Writing a Book with Your Significant Other*, Brad is going to get to work next on *Startup Boards: Making Your Board of Directors Useful Again*, and Amy is going to finish up her first novel, *The North Side of Trees*.

We have learned from numerous people about how to have a successful and satisfying relationship. Many of them have been entrepreneurs—some of whom we have worked with, many of whom we are close friends with, and all of whom we have incredible respect for. This book is a blend of our experiences and what we have learned from others; we couldn't have done either our relationship or this book without the help, support, wisdom, and friendship of all of these amazing people.

There are a number of contributions throughout this book from friends of ours who are entrepreneurs or are in a relationship with an entrepreneur.

They have been brave, kind, and generous enough to share their thoughts and stories, and we value both their friendship and their contributions. Following is the list, in the order they first appear in the book. Gang, you are awesome—thank you!

Geraldine DeRuiter and Rand Fishkin, Laura and Pete Sheinbaum, Ben Horowitz, Alexandra Antonioli, Jerry Colonna, Heather and Tom Chikoore, Fred and Joanne Wilson, Ellen and Howard Lindzon, David and Jil Cohen, Bart and Sarah Loreng, Paul and Reneé Berberian, Keith Smith, Jenny Lawton, Tim Enwall and Hillary Hall, Ilana and Warren Katz, Sandra and Will Herman, April and Jud Valeski, Mark Florence and Nicole Glaros, Krista Marks and Brent Milne, Ben and Emily Huh, Mariquita and Matt Blumberg, Mark and Pam Solon, Jerri and Tim Miller, and Dave Jilk and Maureen Amundson.

Brad's assistant, Kelly Collins, continues to be a critical part of our work life, tirelessly doing whatever we ask her to do. In addition to being an extraordinary assistant to Brad, she is a good friend to both of us and is always incredibly gracious about helping Amy out with whatever she needs that intersects with Brad's life. Kelly, we don't know how we'd do this without your help.

The team that Brad works with at Wiley, especially Bill Falloon, Meg Freeborn, Tiffany Charbonier, and Sharon Polese, continues to be awesome.

Brad's partners at Foundry Group—Jason Mendelson, Ryan McIntyre, and Seth Levine, along with David Cohen, the co-founder and CEO of TechStars—are a special part of our work life. Thanks for supporting us in our own journey.

Finally, there are many couples in entrepreneurial relationships with whom we have worked and been friends over the years. You inspire us every day to live life to the fullest and extract every bit of happiness out of our existence on this planet.

CHAPTER ONE

INTRODUCTION

Welcome to *Startup Life*, a guide for having healthy relationships while working in the pressure cooker environment of a startup company. There are many powerful myths of the all-consuming nature of being an entrepreneur, and it is indeed difficult to balance your work life and your personal life. In fact, many people think that balance is not even worth trying for because it is a fool's errand. Others say that starting a company is another impossible goal, and it is true that the vast majority of startups do fail. But if you're an entrepreneur who loves your company and also happens to be in love with a particular person, you're not going to be stopped by naysayers or discouraged by the difficulty of the challenge of trying to do two hard things at once. If you're stubborn and committed to creating both a company and a relationship, this book will help you and your partner work together to clarify and communicate your core values, experiment to discover which relationship techniques work for you, and build a long-term life together while you're building your company. If you already have a company and are thinking of adding a relationship to what is already a complex system, or you have an existing love relationship and are considering embarking on building a company, this book is for you.

Our goal with this book is to help entrepreneurs and their partners have a healthier notion of what startup life looks like and to decide together what success means to you. There is a lot of buzz about work-life balance, much of it rather defeatist regarding the possibility of figuring out a sustainable solution. We'd like to counter some of the myths about the necessity of a maniacal work life and the notion that more hours at work increases the success rate of startups. The goal should be to work smarter, not harder, and to be efficient and deliberate about where you spend your time. We want couples to examine their preconceived notions of what the startup life entails, and see whether they can create a path that works for them in the face of powerful and persistent mythologies about entrepreneurship.

We'd like this book to serve as a tool to help people think about what they want their lives to look like and be, in an entrepreneurial environment and in a longer and broader time frame. It can be used as a guide for exploration within an existing relationship, clarifying values and needs, and making it easier to have conversations about difficult topics. It's also optimistic and encouraging about the possibility of starting a relationship while you're already on an entrepreneurial adventure.

It's hard to create a startup company. It's hard to create a healthy long-lasting relationship. It's incredibly hard to try to do both of these things at the same time, or to start one or the other while in the midst of an existing startup or relationship. Both experiences can reveal things about yourself that are surprising, disappointing, changeable, immutable, such as whether you believe people change over time or that there's always room for self-improvement. Or that loving someone means accepting everything about them just as it is.

You will hear us say over and over again that the first principle of relationships, and startups, is communication. Without consistent, effective, honest communication, your relationship situation will be much more challenging. If you have different communication styles, use words as weapons, or expect your partner to be a mind reader, you are going to have to solve the fundamental issues around communication before you can tackle anything else. You can try a wide range of techniques, seek professional help, or enlist your best qualities to have effective communication within your relationship. Any efforts to improve communication are worthwhile, even if results can take time to be visible. We will harp on this notion throughout the book without apology. A commitment to being the best communicator you can be is a good place to start, and to return to, throughout your startup life.

One of our basic premises is that language matters. What you call your relationship matters. What you call yourself in public and private matters. What words you use when to speak to each other matters. The words you use when you talk about your relationship and your work to other people matters.

The second principle we're going to emphasize is core values, and communication is obviously a precursor to figuring out what your core values are. Shared values are what keep you together over time. They are part of what initially brought you together as a couple. You will clarify these values together over time. Being able to articulate your personal priorities will help you direct your energy in the directions that will bring your goals to fruition. Having a mission statement for your company is a fundamental part of keeping the ship headed in the right direction, and having the same kind of alignment with your partner can make for much easier sailing. This book will help you communicate about what your core values are and how to live them.

HETERONORMATIVE LANGUAGE AND PARTNERSHIPS

Our language, rich and varied though it is, still lacks words for life partner or significant other that are more romantic and less businesslike but don't imply or require heterosexual relationships. Furthermore, your business partner and your life partner can be the same person. Throughout this book we will use the word *partner* to indicate spouse, beloved, intimate other, soul mate, or whatever you call the person with whom you're working on a lifelong commitment. We will try to use inclusive language without confusing business partner with life partner. We will use the word *partnership* or *relationship* to mean marriage, cohabitation, and any form of long-term romantic intimate relationship that two people enter into. You'll also hear us refer to this throughout the book as an *entrepreneurial relationship*.

We want to say at the outset that we support all committed relationships, and that we fully support the right of our LGBTQ friends to have the same legal benefits afforded by the marriage contract as we do, even though we're not certain why the government confers any benefits at all. We cared so little about the legal part of marriage that we didn't get a marriage license until three years after we eloped to Alaska. We didn't claim any tax deductions, insurance benefits, or even free spousal rental car privileges during that time, but it didn't change the essential nature of our connection to have a piece of paper from the Boulder County Clerk and Recorder's Office. As part of our premise that language matters, being able to call your husband or your wife those things instead of boyfriend or girlfriend, or partner, is a different level of seriousness in our society. We look forward to the day when people who love each other are able to share all the meanings of the word *spouse*. Entrepreneurs who are in committed relationships and don't intend to get married, whether they're legally able to or not, are also covered by the word *partner*.

OUR PANEL OF EXPERTS

We aren't right about everything. Our path is only one of the myriad ways that people have figured out how to be happy together. We've asked a bunch of entrepreneurs and their partners to share their advice, approaches, and stories of success and failure. We appreciate their willingness to share what are often difficult stories. We are here to say that it can be done, and we applaud anyone who manages to stay together in these parlous times. We're not claiming to have some magic book of wisdom, although our secret sauce can add some spice to your relationship. What we do know is that it takes real dedication, hard work, top-notch communication skills, and a sense of humor to find your particular path together in this world.

We want to prevent lovely people who love each other from ever reaching the point that Rand Fishkin, the CEO of SEOmoz, describes here. We agree with everything he shares about how he and his wife, Geraldine de Ruiter, a travel blogger and writer at Everywhereist.com, are trying to get through the current struggle of building an extraordinary business while having an amazing relationship.

It's pretty obvious to most of the team at SEOmoz, to my wife, and (at long last) to me, that I'm drowning. I rarely get the sleep I need. I've been not quite shaking off a minor cold for seven weeks. My back is not getting any better—I still have to walk with a cane sometimes. I'm in fairly constant discomfort. Sometimes I'm in semiconstant, serious pain. I'm never caught up on my email. And I haven't taken a formal "vacation" (the kind without at least four hours of work in a day) since my wedding in 2008. The longest I've gone without checking email since then was in Ireland, and it was around 40 hours. Hell, we've never even gone on our honeymoon.

There's no doubt that my efficiency should be higher, that my demands on my own time should be lower, and that I can't be the single point of failure on projects and communication that I've been over the last five years of Moz's growth.

My coach, Jerry Colonna, gave me some homework at the end of our recent call. After talking to Jerry, I talked to Geraldine about the problems seriously and in-depth. We talked about how my lack of balance made each of us feel. We talked about ideas for overcoming it. We did that. It felt really good—maybe as good as any conversation we've ever had, even if it was hard. And we came up with some rules we're going to try:

Once every week, on Tuesday, I'm going to come home by 7:00 P.M. and not do any work until the next morning. I've literally never done this before. Tomorrow is going to be interesting.

In the first half of 2013, we're going to take a 10+-day vacation where I will only work 60 minutes each day maximum. There will be a timer.

After a few months, we're going to try limiting work to 60 minutes on one day each weekend.

This is going to be hard, and I'm scared I'm going to fall very, very far behind on my emails and my obligations. But it will be a healthy forcing function.

Hardest of all, I'm going to have to say "no." A lot. To many people that I like and wish I could help. That's going to suck, but it's the only way. I don't expect to find balance, but I do think these rules can help build a separation that I've never had before and that should exist.

Rand Fishkin, SEOmoz, *www.seomoz.com*
Geraldine DeRuiter, @everywhereist, *www.everywhereist.com*
http://moz.com/rand/there-is-no-worklife-balance/

Being happily committed is an achievement and a huge and difficult accomplishment. Some of the habits you need to develop to get there are like flossing your teeth—they are good habits that take only a small amount of time, but you can't make up for the missing days. Others are like preventative medicine that helps you keep your love healthy on a regular basis. Yet others are like regular checkups at the doctor that you do on a semiannual basis, while the rest are profound and deep behaviors that require years of commitment to master.

We are trying to share what we have learned in hopes that it will make it easier for you to have a fulfilling and purposeful life, which we believe needs both work and love to be complete. We hope this books helps people who are trying to build an intimate relationship at the same time they're building their startup company. If we help a single startup relationship, we've succeeded.

CHAPTER TWO

PHILOSOPHY

Conventional wisdom says that entrepreneurs can't have work-life balance. It's repeated over and over that entrepreneurship is an "all-in" experience and the partner of the entrepreneur has to accept that he is playing second fiddle to the entrepreneur's startup.

We completely reject this notion. We reject the idea that the more you work, the better the outcome. We reject that time spent on work matters more than having a fulfilling life. And we reject the notion that an entrepreneur should defer her experience of a full life for "after her business has been successful," especially since that day may never arrive.

We strongly believe that every entrepreneur, whether 21 and working on your first startup, or 57 and a multi-time successful entrepreneur starting a new company, benefits from having room in her life for relationships. Your startup is a part of your life, not your entire life. Both you and your startup will be more successful if you have a full experience on this planet.

The historical notion of retirement reinforces the idea that you work hard until later in your life, squeezing in everything else, and defer your exploration of all the nonwork things until you retire. This construct completely misses the point that you have no idea when the lights will go out. As a result, deferring the experience of a full life until you are finished with work may result in your never getting to live the life you want. The cliché of a businessperson's retiring to travel around the world with his partner and dying shortly after retirement is a sad one, but it reinforces the error of deferring the life part of the equation.

Entrepreneurship is really hard. So are relationships. In the same way that failure should be accepted in startups, it should be accepted in relationships. No one is perfect; mistakes will be made—often. Entrepreneurs are told to "fail fast"—make a mistake, learn from it, pivot, and move on. This doesn't mean quit your startup, but it does mean not to linger on the mistake once you've figured out why it happened and what you can do better the next time. The same is true with relationships: own your mistakes, learn from them, and move on.

Patience, a sense of humor, and willingness to forgive are excellent qualities to cultivate in yourself and to encourage in your partner. There are going to be challenging times in any business and in any relationship; having high but reasonable expectations that your relationship will endure through whatever comes is an important piece of the picture for long-term success.

COMMUNICATION

We are going to say this one over and over again: communication is the most important factor in having a successful relationship.

Knowing this and practicing this can be two very different things, especially in an always on, always urgent environment. We will give you some simple tactics to practice. The hard part is making time to do them. The point is for you and your partner to figure out what works for you, keep practicing those techniques, and try new things if something starts to feel stale or just stops working for either one of you. You can circle back to retry techniques that used to work in the past that have been set aside for any reason. Sometimes we drift away from a habit and find that reinstating it can feel fresh and useful and we wonder why we ever stopped.

We've put the best, most obvious, and sometimes most difficult value first on the list, which is where it should go in your relationship. Communication builds trust, connection, and intimacy, and is absolutely the most vital underpinning to a successful relationship. For some couples, communication is easy, except when topics are difficult. Not being able to talk about unresolved issues, having different communication styles, or being conflict avoidant are common barriers to effective communication. It can be challenging to take responsibility for saying what you want and need. Your partner is not a mind reader, nor can you read your partner's mind even if you think you can. Each of you has an obligation to be brave when it comes to initiating communication and working through issues. Some issues don't ever get completely resolved but come up through a relationship over and over again; issues that seemed resolved can crop up again if one of you changes your opinion or has an experience that steers you in a different direction.

If your relationship is relatively new, you won't have a shared history and track record of successful communication with positive outcomes to rely on. But you also have the excitement and chemistry of newness to offset that. We believe that getting to really know your partner is a lifelong journey, and that you can always learn something new about each other, whether you've been together for months, years, or decades.

A fairly obvious but vital part of communication is humor. A lot of anger or built-up frustration can be defused with humor, but it's also important that the aggrieved partner feels heard and feels like they're being taken seriously. As with many things, timing is important. You'll figure out what works for you, and also discover that there aren't necessarily consistent responses from your partner. Figuring out your rhythm, signals, cues, and nonverbal gestures can take time, and there may be unpleasant learning experiences along the way.

Another crucial area for communication is to talk about expectations, limits, boundaries, and being clear on what is unforgivable behavior to each of you. Addiction, infidelity, and violence are potentially some of the reasons that a partner might state are beyond the point of no return for her. We have a friend who says, at least partly seriously, that a serious religious conversion experience in her partner would be a relationship-ending event, primarily because her partner would be a completely different person than he had been throughout the course of their relationship. The work involved in each of you knowing for yourself what is intolerable, and then having the courage to be clear about it with your partner, is work that will strengthen you as individuals and as a couple.

PRIORITIES

There are times when the highest priority is getting the next product release out the door. Try not to schedule these for Friday afternoons, knowing that you will likely create a scenario where it drifts into Friday night, and then Saturday, and then Sunday, especially if you've already committed to spending time with your partner. Be realistic about the ebb and flow of the work cycle, and make sure that there actually are ebb times.

None of this means there won't be stretches of intense work that dominate everything else for days, weeks, or even months. Communicating clearly when these stretches will happen is critical. In this book, we'll give you plenty of tools for dealing with this, as well as for creating a cadence that can actually work, even in the context of these very intense periods of time.

Knowing for yourself and sharing a commitment with your partner that your relationship is a high priority, and sometimes is the highest priority of all, will make it easier to adapt to intense work times and to make more time for the two of you when there is an ebb time. If your company really has no cycles of lower intensity or you feel like you can never take a week away, that's an indicator that you have work to do to grow your company structure to support healthier lives for you as well as your employees. The actual long-term highest priority is to have a good life, with room for both love and work.

MOTIVATION

Many different things motivate people. Motivation as a psychological topic has been studied since at least the 1970s, and most researchers divide motivation into extrinsic (or external) and intrinsic (or internal). Extrinsic motivation occurs when you do something in order to attain an outcome, like monetary rewards, grades, or gold stars, or avoiding punishment or negative emotions like shame, guilt, or humiliation. Enjoying the task itself rather than working for some other reward drives intrinsic motivation. For some, like Brad, intrinsic motivation dominates. Others, like Amy, are more balanced between intrinsic and extrinsic. Yet others are dominated by extrinsic motivation. Understanding what drives you, and what drives your partner, is critical to a successful startup life.

In the 1980s, Ed Roberts (MIT's David Sarnoff Professor of Management of Technology; founder and chair, Martin Trust Center for MIT Entrepreneurship) determined that some entrepreneurs are driven by the need for achievement while others are driven by the need for independence. In our experience, we've observed that some entrepreneurs are driven by the joy of success while others are driven by the fear of failure. There is an ongoing conversation about what motivates entrepreneurs and whether they're as comfortable with risk as the myths indicate, or whether they're motivated by not wanting to risk a life in a cubicle. If the entrepreneur is motivated by success, the inevitable ups and downs of any company can be more emotionally dramatic than for an entrepreneur who is motivated by creating a lasting enterprise.

Understanding what motivates your partner is essential to having a successful relationship over a long period of time. Assuming that what motivates you also motivates your partner, especially if your partner is an entrepreneur, can create a chasm of misunderstanding between you. We'll give you plenty of suggestions and perspectives on this throughout the book, but like many things, it starts with communicating what you think motivates each of you.

LONG-TERM RELATIONSHIP

Part of the fascinating thing about being in a relationship is that it thrusts a mirror in your face so that you see your own behavior more clearly, which can sometimes be hard to take. The paradoxes and internal inconsistencies in each of us are root causes of all manner of conflicts, and often make our partner feel like they are involved with a Dr. Jekyll and Mr. Hyde character. In Chapter 5 we explore common dichotomies in the entrepreneurial personality, and in Chapter 8 we discuss how common issues and conflicts often arise from the entrepreneurial personality.

We believe that a healthy relationship helps you become your best self. You have an opportunity to feel safe and encouraged by your partner, as well as the reciprocal opportunity to be supportive and encouraging. As part of thinking about what you want your life narrative to look like, consider what kind of story you want to be able to tell about yourself. Being thoughtful, kind, honest, challenging when appropriate, and supportive in hard times are qualities that you want to be able to practice and improve upon. And you want to encourage these qualities in your partner.

Two excellent books on marriage (or committed partnerships) are *For Better: How the Surprising Science of Happy Couples Can Help Your Marriage Succeed* by Tara Parker Pope and *Spousonomics: Using Economics to Master Love, Marriage, and Dirty Dishes* by Paula Szuchman and Jenny Anderson. Both books examine what makes a good marriage and what specific things you can do to ensure that yours is one of the happy ones. *For Better* includes chapters on the science of conflict and the science of sex. *Spousonomics* uses economic principles like loss aversion, cost-benefit analyses, incentives, and metrics to monitor the ongoing health of your partnership.

Reciprocity is a high value in personal and business relationships. This doesn't mean tit for tat counting up who did what, but a general sense that both of you are working at making your relationship as great as it can be. Checking in regularly to find out whether you both feel like you're putting in equal effort or being asked to sacrifice more than your fair share is a fundamental communication habit. As children we were all taught that life isn't fair, but that doesn't mean that a sense of fairness isn't a good virtue to cultivate in your relationships.

If one of you feels that he is doing all the sacrificing, that's not going to be sustainable over the long run. It can be good to clearly articulate whose turn it is to be the supportive one, and if your business has certain cycles of craziness (for example, retail products that must be launched in time for Q4 holiday season), you can plan for that and either buffer some extra time together in advance or schedule something special for the aftermath, or both. We like to use a savings account metaphor for this. You can build up a surplus of togetherness and then drain the account down, and you can do some short-term deficit spending, but you need to balance the books regularly. Our Qx quarterly vacation off the grid, which we discuss in Chapter 7 along with other tactics that we have discovered, fulfills this function for us, as well as restoring sleep and energy for all sorts of adult activities that might feel like onerous tasks when work is particularly demanding.

We believe in thinking long term—like a lifetime. If you want to be in a committed relationship with the same person for decades, you need to have a sense of growing together and creating positive and healthy patterns and habits that will build and persist throughout your life together. We believe in having high expectations for yourself and your partner, but also learning how to forgive and practicing that on a regular basis.

Just as good patterns build over time to create a strong foundation for your relationship, the dark side is that bad patterns accrete as well. Resentment, anger, power, control, and other difficult emotions also become more deeply entrenched with repetition of a trigger and an automatic response. It takes hard work to create positive patterns and attention to when bad habits are developing and address the underlying feelings and root causes of the pattern.

TIME COMMITMENT

How many hours a day can you commit to spending time with your beloved? What about weekly? Monthly? Setting these expectations, communicating about what is a reasonable amount of time to both of you, and trying to meet somewhere in the middle is a good benchmark to set. It's also a way to have data-driven accountability and goal setting, which suits many entrepreneurs' personalities.

We like to keep track both subjectively and objectively. Measuring quantifiable data can occasionally be very useful, especially if you have widely divergent ideas of how much time the entrepreneur is working or how frequently you do fun social activities without staring at your phone the entire time. Although it was never going to be reasonable to think that Brad would work 40 hours a week, there were times when we did track Brad's weekly hours with an upper limit of 80 hours a week. There are 168 hours in a week, minus 80 working hours, minus 49 hours for sleeping 7 hours a night, which still leaves 39 hours for doing fun things together—almost a "normal" work week's amount of time. We also defined work as "any time Brad isn't available to play," so that a conference call from home was still work.

We haven't had to track actual hours together versus hours working in a while, but having real data can be a great starting point for conversations about how much work is enough or sustainable or what the ebbs and peaks really look like. Setting specific measurable concrete goals for your personal life can be just as useful at home as it is at work.

UNCERTAINTY

There has been a great deal of research and writing on what happiness is and how to achieve it. Going through the relationship section of a bookstore or the hundreds of thousands of books that show up on Amazon under the search for "relationship" will keep you busy for a very long time. While many of these cover goal orientation, communication, willpower, and the power of positive thinking, they rarely touch on what is at the core of a startup life: uncertainty. We'll go deep on that throughout this book, how to think about it as a couple, and how to address it constructively in the context of a long-term relationship.

PERSISTENCE

While this may sometimes be described as stubbornness, or can trend into the deep waters of being unwilling to listen and change your mind, the same dogged determination to make your company succeed is an excellent trait to bring to your relationship. Being willing is a vital trait: willing to compromise, willing to change, and, above all, willing to keep trying in your relationship no matter how difficult things may become. Knowing that your partner is willing to do what it takes to make your relationship happy is a great trust builder. You may each have histories full of break-ups, or parental divorce, or just a generalized skepticism about the possibilities of love, and persistence may mean needing to reduce your own readiness to run away. Ideally, you are, or are becoming, or want to become, reasonable adults, in this thing for the long haul.

HAPPINESS AND THE POWER OF HABITS

There is a relatively new body of research on happiness and positive psychology that reveals what actually works to make people happy. Each individual is unique, but there are data showing what creates happiness. Having strong intimate relationships is, not surprisingly, an important factor in overall happiness. While a certain amount of happiness comes from your genetics, there are many things within your control that you can do to be a happier person and to have a happier relationship. Some of the useful books in this area include:

- Martin Seligman's *Learned Optimism: How to Change Your Mind and Your Life; Authentic Happiness: Using the New Positive Psychology to Realize Your Potential for Lasting Fulfillment;* and *Flourish: A Visionary New Understanding of Happiness and Well-Being*
- Daniel Gilbert's *Stumbling on Happiness*
- Sonja Lyubomirsky's *The How of Happiness: A New Approach to Getting the Life You Want*
- Gretchen Rubin's *The Happiness Project: Or, Why I Spent a Year Trying to Sing in the Morning, Clean My Closets, Fight Right, Read Aristotle, and Generally Have More Fun;* and *Happier at Home: Kiss More, Jump More, Abandon a Project, Read Samuel Johnson, and My Other Experiments in the Practice of Everyday Life*
- Charles Duhigg's *The Power of Habit: Why We Do What We Do in Life and Business*

It's important to decide that you do indeed want to be happy and then explore what works for you and for your partner to create a happy life together.

Along with positive psychology research, there are some interesting ideas being developed in neuroscience about the power of habits, willpower, and how we can change our behavior. Creating habits of kindness and automatically linking cues about your partner with actions that show your affection, respect, and love can go a long way toward building long-term relationship satisfaction. Technology can be your friend here. Set automatic reminders to monthly write a love note in your very own handwriting and put it in the mail. Send flowers to him. Buy a book that she mentioned in conversation. Make a habit of doing small things that you're fortunate enough to have someone in your life to do for—showing gratitude is one of the common happiness boosters.

THE 97 PERCENT: CHOOSING WHAT TO CARE ABOUT

We like to say that Brad cares about getting his way on only 3 percent of the decisions in our life. He doesn't want to be involved at all in choosing new couches or curtains; in fact, he pleads not to ever be shown a fabric sample again during his life. He wants more input on where to go on vacation, but doesn't want to be involved in the logistical details.

But on the 3 percent that he does care about, Amy defers to his preferences almost all the time. Sometimes the preferences are small, such as Brad's hating capers or being on boats, and sometimes they're larger, like Brad's not celebrating Thanksgiving or Christmas because he views them as soul-crushing experiences due to all the emotional and societal pressures around them. Some of them are physical, such as Brad's requiring that the couches we have be ones he can lie down on sweaty after a run even though he doesn't care what they look like or want to be involved in picking them out. Or that we have fancy magic Toto toilets that wash and dry you after you do your thing so he doesn't have to shower after going to the bathroom. Yet others are emotional, like Brad's needing 90 minutes of quiet time in the morning to wake up. But beyond this 3 percent, he rolls with anything Amy wants.

Within your partnership, as at your company, being able to effectively delegate tasks rather than needing to be involved in every decision improves efficiency and gives each partner regions of autonomous decision making. Knowing the things each partner really cares about, and being able to accommodate for that, is extremely powerful.

DELEGATING

Often, entrepreneurs are not the best delegators and they need to work hard to develop this skill at work and at home. There are some beneficial aspects of being willing to do everything yourself at a startup company, but you will reach a limit on your time, and possibly your ability, to be an expert in all facets of your business. Divide-and-conquer strategies and shared decisions can help you avoid decision fatigue and are important ways of building a strong team mentality in your company, as well as with your partner. It's a good general strategy to delegate things that can be done by other people and/or that you don't enjoy, and save the things for yourself that you really love or are uniquely qualified to do. In your personal life, the real test of delegation skills can often be found in the laundry room.

When we started living together, Amy thought it would be appropriate to share the housework. She proposed that we create a list of chores where we would alternate weeks doing them. Brad agreed, but suggested that during his week, a woman named Linda, who was already his housekeeper, would take care of his chores. He offered Amy the option to have Linda take care of her weeks as well, which Amy quickly agreed to.

Another great situation to test delegation skills is to remodel, redecorate, or build a house. We've seen friends whose partnerships have nearly come unraveled by the process of remodeling their homes while one of them is also trying to grow their startup. The key is to communicate clearly about responsibilities, trust, and be willing to delegate to each other.

IS A RELATIONSHIP PART OF YOUR VISION OF A GOOD LIFE?

While we're asking hard questions, it's important to look at whether you really do want to be in a relationship at the same time you're creating a company. You may feel some pressure to say that, of course, you want to be in a relationship, but maybe this isn't really true for you. You might want to focus only on building your company, and having casual relationships or wide-ranging dating may suit you best.

There are many societal pressures to conform to a norm that really isn't the norm anymore. Being in a committed relationship can be just another item on a parental or societal checklist of what constitutes your adulthood—an item that's maybe not on your list at all. Bucking the trend toward forming couples in early adulthood may be part of your independent entrepreneurial self. Having some quiet space in your life to listen to what you really want at any phase of your life is a very good idea. With the flurry and demands of a startup work environment, it can be difficult to make time to check in with yourself and see what you really feel. It's absolutely worth doing. There are several methods to try, including meditation, writing, talking with trusted friends, therapy, and being outside in nature. If you're a maverick in your work life, it may very well be the case that you're not part of the mainstream of coupledom. You just need to be honest with yourself about this, and with anyone with whom you do enter an intimate relationship, in case her expectations are headed toward the marriage altar.

WHAT DO YOU WANT YOUR STORY TO BE?

Everyone's relationship has a narrative. As a couple, you're writing a life story together. Every action and experience matters—both good and bad—as part of this narrative. The tone you set early in the relationship often carries through the whole experience.

Let's take the story of Pete and Laura Sheinbaum. Pete is a very successful entrepreneur and is driven by need for achievement. So it won't be surprising that on their honeymoon, Pete and Laura went on a trip to Africa to climb Mt. Kilimanjaro. Following is their story.

Pete and I married on June 25, 2005. We rocked a huge party in a loft in downtown New York City and then waited to take our honeymoon to Africa in August of that same year. I handled many of the wedding details, and Pete planned our trip of a lifetime. It was the perfect combination of romantic, exotic, and adventure. This trip was to be by far our best travel experience, and we are both well traveled. We spent a month bouncing between Mnemba Island off the coast of Zanzibar, safari adventures in the Ngorogoro Crater, and the Serengeti. We snorkeled around reefs crowded with crazy fish; sailed while fishermen hunted octopus at sunset; saw black rhinos, lions, tigers, hippos, and zebras; and even got to witness the elusive wildebeest crossing in Kenya. We dined on spectacular food such as pumpkin coconut soup and slept with baboons playing overhead in a tree house. We were in heaven, in love, and on top of the world.

So why not head to the top of the world—at least in Africa? Pete and I met in Boulder, Colorado, and though we were living in NYC at the time, considered ourselves Coloradans. We hike, we bike, we ski, we run marathons, and we climb 14,000-foot mountains. We are athletes, and our honeymoon would not be complete if we didn't summit Kilimanjaro. The fact that we had been living at sea level for nearly two years and that our most strenuous form of exercise was walking our two dogs in Central Park never crossed our mind. Kilimanjaro would be no problem.

We have a good friend in Boulder who knew a guy who ran treks up Kilimanjaro. We attempted to book our trip with this group and received some basic information: where to meet, how many days, and cost. It was at least a seven-day excursion. All our research stated that it was best to bring your own gear, but if you didn't want to do that, you could rent the gear in Africa. But we trusted the friend's guy, who said that we could rent all the gear we would need, and we packed only basic hiking and beach clothing and opted to leave our heavy boots, heavy jackets, and all other climbing essentials at home. We also had only five days in our itinerary to complete the trek (Pete failed on the logistics front). The guide felt that we could summit Kilimanjaro that quickly, and as they say in Africa, "no problem."

The day we met our tour guide was beautiful and sunny in Arusha, Tanzania. He picked us up in a well-worn jeep and took us to the warehouse where we would be able to rent our gear. We arrived at a dusty back alley of a neighborhood and stared mutely at a pile of very worn camping gear. Nothing could dull our bliss, however, so we dug in, found some gear that would sort of work, and gave our guides the thumbs-up. Let's go!

We stopped at the local butcher, and our guide picked up a couple of chickens hanging in the front window, some popcorn, and about four dozen eggs. No refrigerants or anything, but it was cold at night so "no problem."

Next stop: the trailhead. We were going to hike to the first overnight campsite and make camp. The trail was beautiful and we climbed rigorously through a rainforest. We were quickly above the cloud line and the lighting was sublime. We camped the first night at about 9,000 feet. Pete and I felt great. The guides spoke little English but were friendly enough. Our main guide had been to the summit of Kilimanjaro 40 times, and our favorite guide was Hollywood, who was an 18-year-old kid with a personality that equaled his nickname.

Days 2 and 3 were more of the same. Day 4 was our longest trek. Most guides break our day 4 into two days, but given our abbreviated schedule, we needed to get to base camp at the end of day 4. We hiked for 10 hours and got to base camp around 5:00 P.M. We had a quick dinner and then they put us to bed immediately with instructions to sleep, as we would begin our summit hike six hours later at 11:00 P.M.

Pete had a splitting headache, and I didn't feel great, either. The hike that day had been strenuous. We had gained more than 4,000 feet in elevation and had ended our hike at 15,000 feet. This was higher than either of us had ever climbed before. We were tired and dehydrated and suffering from the elevation. After eating a dinner of popcorn, we attempted to sleep. The other groups camped at base camp took at least two days to acclimatize. There was a party feeling at the base that made sleep difficult (not to mention the vocal sexual exploits of the couple in the tent next to us). We woke at 10:45 P.M. weary and ill.

It was dark and very cold, and I was exhausted before we even started. Having never climbed to such an elevation, we were caught unaware of the timing of the start. We started up the mountain, single file, looking only at the small globe of light a few inches in front of our feet as we staggered up the mountain. Two in a long line of guided tourists. The pace was intentionally slow and deliberate. My pace became even slower after a couple of hours, and decidedly less deliberate. I was really sick. Someone had drilled a screw between my eyes and my insides were emptying out. Not pretty. Our guide told me, "Vomit, you feel better. We go on. No problem!" There was no way I was going to be able to continue. In the back of my addled mind was the story of the person who died on the summit the day before of altitude sickness. While I am not a quitter, I was aware enough of my physical state to know I needed to get off that mountain and fast. I had altitude sickness. We were only 1,000 feet from the summit, however. I urged Pete to continue. In fact, I begged him to continue. At least one of us would summit.

Of course, Pete is pretty competitive and wanted more than anything to summit. So did he head up and leave me to descend 3,000 feet with one of our non-English-speaking guides, in the dark, the puke still fresh on my lips?

No summit.

When I asked Pete what was going through his mind at that time, he was pretty clear in his thinking. He said yes, there was a flash of quickly bagging the summit and returning right to my side, but that thought passed quickly. While his intentions and care are always in the right place, he quickly realized that leaving his one-month bride puking on the side of an 18,000-foot mountain, freezing cold in the middle of the night, was pretty much the biggest lose-lose scenario of his life. He imagined returning to the States and telling the story of satisfying his ego while his wife was very much out of sorts.

Even though he felt strong enough to continue, he said there was absolutely no way was he leaving my side. I continued to argue weakly and lost. Deep down, I was happy to have him with me. I felt guilty for making him stay with me when I was sick, but ultimately I was relieved to have my husband with me. We made our way down the mountain, rested at the base camp for only about an hour, and then hiked the last 15 miles out so we could spend the night in the nearest town. We needed showers, a bed, and real food. While I felt terrible that Pete did not summit, his consistent response was that of all the wonderful things we experienced on our honeymoon, had he left me, our only memory would be that he made it to the top of Kilimanjaro without me. We started together and needed to finish together—summit or no summit.

That is the best indicator of our marriage. He supported me when I needed support. He continues to do that every day. I try hard to do the same. That example of being a team in good times and bad carries us through challenges such as the ups and downs of startups, young kids, and aging parents.

Someday, Pete and I will go back. We'll bring our gear. We'll bring our kids. We'll make it to the top. But ever since we started our journey together in life, we've been fortunate to be able to summit many things together, even if Kilimanjaro wasn't one of them.

Laura Sheinbaum, Boulder Housing Partners
Pete Sheinbaum, LinkSmart, *www.linksmart.com*

While claims about what makes us uniquely human keep getting revised in the face of new research showing animals using tools and language, our ability to construct a coherent narrative underlies our experience as humans. Fred (*www.avc.com*) and Joanne Wilson (*www.gothamgal.com*), who recently celebrated their 25th wedding anniversary, blogged that they had each heard all of the other person's stories a thousand times. If you share many experiences, you'll have many of the same stories, although each of you will have their own perspective on an event.

What kind of story do you want other people to tell about you? While some of us are incredibly intrinsically motivated, many people do care what other people think of them. This can be a positive force for you to craft a life that results in a positive narrative. You can decide what kind of story you want to be able to tell about yourself. Did you behave well? Do you behave kindly? Is your behavior in alignment with your value system?

It is also important to examine the narrative or mythology you have about entrepreneurship. We've all heard the cliché that no one says on their deathbed that they wish they had spent more time at the office.

Several insightful books have been written by people with terminal illness, including Randy Pausch's *The Last Lecture,* and *Chasing Daylight* by Eugene O'Kelley, about how remembering your mortality shapes your priorities, and over and over again people write about cherishing relationships.

As a conscious adult, you've spent time thinking about what constitutes a good life for you. This is a question that's worthwhile to keep asking for yourself, and your partner, throughout the life cycle of your company, your relationship, and your life.

CHAPTER THREE

COMMUNICATION

earning how to communicate effectively is essential for any successful relationship, but it's especially important in the context of an entrepreneurial couple. For the entrepreneur to be successful at work, she must be excellent at communicating. She must also be excellent at communicating if she wants to be successful at home. The communication style, the requirements, and the pressures surrounding it are often very different but equally important.

Tactics as well as broader philosophical approaches can address these differences. The tactics can cover positive situations and negative situations, your daily routine as well as long arc discussions. Learning how to communicate effectively when you are fighting or melting down is just as critical as learning how to communicate when everything is going fine but you are both running at full speed in different cities.

While the ideas in this chapter apply to any couple and may cause you to feel that you've entered into reading yet another relationship book, we've tried to focus and explain aspects of communication that we think apply and take into consideration the unique characteristics of the life of an entrepreneurial couple.

APPOINTMENTS

We are huge believers in making appointments with each other. Our lives are incredibly busy and full. We have time for a myriad of appointments, especially in the work context, but we used to find that we never had time for each other. This is common in an entrepreneurial relationship.

Many years ago we started making appointments with each other. This started off as short 30-minute slots of time that were scheduled to talk about or work on a specific thing. Over time, they evolved into a broader rhythm.

You'll see examples of them throughout this chapter in regularly recurring things like Four Minutes in the Morning, Life Dinner, or our Sunday Post-Game Analysis, where we chat briefly about the previous week and the upcoming week before we go to bed on Sunday nights.

We like to view appointments with each other as opportunities rather than obligations. Rather than viewing them as a "duty," which we both think of as a four-letter word, we look forward to these chances to spend time together even though they are scheduled and not spontaneous. Following are a few examples of recurring appointments.

FOUR MINUTES IN THE MORNING

One simple thing that we do that connects and grounds us each morning when we are physically in the same place is to spend four minutes together, making eye contact, and chatting casually about what the day's schedule is and when we might see each other again. We've been doing this for so long that Brad thinks we made it up, but Amy thinks it might be from John Gray's 1993 book *Men Are from Mars, Women Are from Venus: A Practical Guide for Improving Communication and Getting What You Want in Your Relationships*. Four minutes is a small enough amount of time that it doesn't unduly burden your busy morning, and is long enough that we often run out of things to say and just look out the window and snuggle with our dogs. You can set a three-minute egg timer and watch the grains fall and spend a little bit more time together, and there's your four minutes. Try to make it a time to really connect and not to go over your To-Do Lists or talk about big ongoing or unresolved conflicts.

With Skype or Google Hangouts, we also do pretty well having Four Minutes in the Morning when we're apart, and the visual connection is nicer than just a phone call, even though nothing beats beginning our day together. And when one of us is running around already (usually Brad), we still make sure to at least get our four minutes via a phone call.

A GOOD-MORNING AND GOOD-NIGHT CALL

Given that the entrepreneurial life often involves large amounts of travel with long days and business dinners and late nights, it's still worth making an effort to have a good-morning and good-night phone call when one, or both, of you are on the road.

No matter where we are or what we are doing, we always try to start our day with Four Minutes in the Morning and end it with a good-night call. The morning calls are usually easy as we both get up early enough to be able to do it before the fullness of the day begins. Evenings are often harder, so Brad is always aware when it's approaching 10:00 P.M. in Amy's time zone and makes a concerted effort to take a break from whatever he's doing to say good night.

Sometimes time zones make one or the other calls impractical, but knowing that you're going to hear an "I love you" at least once a day is a happy thing.

LIFE DINNER

We explicitly schedule a time to tackle more challenging or difficult topics once a month. It's easy to set a recurring calendar appointment for the first of the month, or the first Saturday of the month, or whatever is easiest for your schedules, for Life Dinner. We think regular date nights are important, but Life Dinner is different from a night for focusing on romance and fun, although it also can contain those elements. Life Dinner is when we talk about goals for the upcoming month and assess the previous month, give constructive criticism and feedback, and make time to clear out any unexpressed unhappiness or lingering unresolved issues. It's essentially a two-way performance review, with a nice meal to foster deeper conversation. We've been doing this for about a dozen years, and we really notice when we miss one because it contributes to feeling like we're drifting apart or aren't still putting energy and effort into our relationship. Knowing that there is a time and place set aside when hard talk is on the agenda makes it easier to defer those conversations during our limited talking time during the rest of the month.

HONESTY AND RESPECT

Honesty is a basic aspect of good communication and healthy relationships. You need to feel safe to be honest with your partner, but you each also have to do deep digging into your own selves to honestly know what you're truly thinking and feeling before you can share with your partner.

Honesty is certainly a virtue, but it can also be used as a form of power or to hurt your partner or to abdicate responsibility for the impact your words can have on each other. "I'm just being honest" can also be a way of saying "I don't care about whether my words are hurtful or unkind." We don't recommend this strategy. Honesty is what builds trust, but kind honesty is preferable to brutal honesty.

Learning how to deliver criticism in a constructive way is especially important. The phrase "constructive criticism" is often used, but rarely followed, as criticism is often part of the power dynamic around honesty. While there are certain contexts, like Brad's partnership at Foundry Group, that value complete directness and brutal honesty, that is a culture norm in his work context that we don't carry over into our personal partnership.

We make great efforts to deliver constructive criticism in a safe environment. We try to be direct yet kind, and encourage growth and change rather than just dish out criticism. We each make sure we can take the equivalent amount of criticism to what we dish out, so the feedback and context is balanced and it never drifts into a way for one of us to hurt the other.

Lying is not acceptable to either of us. Even little white lies or lies of omission aren't okay. Instead, we try to offer up feedback in a direct, friendly, and polite way. We incorporate this into our normal communication patterns—if you spend time with us, you will hear each of us regularly say thank you to the other and acknowledge kind deeds. You will also hear us disagree, but always politely and with substance, and rarely delivered in a hurtful way. Sure, we make mistakes, but when we do, we call ourselves out, own them, and apologize for them.

While this may seem excessive, we've learned over a long period of time that deeply felt mutual respect is a foundational element of our relationship. Being in a committed relationship may feel like it gives you the freedom to be your worst self. A way to avoid this tendency is to always communicate with each other with respect. You may lose your temper and say unkind things, and then have to apologize and ask forgiveness, but your goal should be to try to use language that shows your positive feelings.

One lesson learned is to not hold a grudge or stay mad long after an incident. Several happiness studies indicate that deep-seated resentments and grudges are some of the most corrosive emotions in a relationship. It's better to express your anger in the moment and move past the conflict than to cling to feelings of injury for long periods of time.

LANGUAGE, TONE, AND FAIRNESS

Words matter. Language is how we are human. The way you talk to each other creates relationship patterns over time. It takes at least five positive interactions or actions to counteract a single negative exchange. It takes 1,000 positive interactions when interacting with your mother-in-law (*www .bakadesuyo.com/is-5-to-1-the-golden-ratio-for-both-work-and*).

It's worth paying attention to the words you choose. Create habits of expressing yourself in a loving manner, even when talking about tough topics. At Feld Technologies, Brad's first successful company, one of the company's precepts was "No thinly disguised contempt" for customers or co-workers. We think this is an excellent precept to practice in your entire life. If your tone says to your partner that you think he's not worthy of your respect, it's hard for him to continue to make an effort to communicate with you.

When you're making time just to communicate with each other, it's important to take turns and not interrupt. Amy is a big practitioner of interrupting in casual conversation, and has lots of female friendships where interrupting is part of the fun of just letting fly with whatever you're thinking. However, when the conversation is about really connecting with your partner, don't interrupt. Listen until your partner is finished, and then take a deep breath to make sure she's done and that it's your turn. Getting additional oxygen to the brain is a nice side effect of taking a deep breath, and then it's your turn to talk.

Don't bring up charged topics at bedtime. Your bedroom should be a sanctuary and a safe haven from the demands of the world. When you're in bed and your partner is dozing off to sleep, even though it might feel like a ripe opportunity to take advantage of his vulnerability and go in for the attack, that really isn't effective or kind. Use one of your regularly scheduled Life Dinners instead.

Thinking in black and white and absolutes can be a barrier to effective communication and connection. The words *always* and *never* are particularly loaded. Your partner may feel attacked and become defensive and less able to hear what you are trying to say. As a result, you end up constructing a narrative that's less subtle and nuanced than every partnership deserves.

If you're struggling to understand your partner's point of view, you can elicit deeper conversation with open-ended questions like:

- *Can you tell me more about _____?*
- *How can we make things better?*
- *What are you saying?*
- *What can I do differently?*

Don't be afraid to ask for what you want from your partner. This is deceptively simple since it first requires you to know what it is that you want. Be specific. Ask your partner what he wants. Listen, even if it's hard to hear that he is disappointed or even slightly less than thrilled with some of your behavior. The notion of accepting your partner just as they are doesn't mean you can't ask for changes in behavior or ask for what you need. It doesn't mean you're trying to control your partner, although that may be happening and is worth addressing also.

Over time, we've discovered that it's okay to want attention and ask for attention. Each of us have different daily pressures, and Brad often spends a lot of time in the spotlight and paying attention to all kinds of things going on around him. When he's home, he's often fried and just wants to chill out. But there are days where Amy has been home alone hanging out with the dogs, who give her plenty of attention, but not the same kind that Brad can provide. Rather than be annoyed with Brad when he is lying on the couch in a semicomatose state, if Amy wants attention, she often asks for it, usually in a playful voice to "Pay attention to me, me, me!"

Be ready to accept that your partner has the right to say "no." A freely given "yes" is always preferable to an act done via coercion, guilt, or the threat of punishment. The only way to get a freely given "yes" is to accept that "no" means "no" in whatever context it is given.

Although most of us were taught as children or have learned through our own experiences that life isn't fair, it's worth striving to create and maintain a sense of fairness in your partnership. Feeling that someone in the world really makes an effort to treat you fairly can bolster your own efforts to behave fairly to your partner and to all the other people you encounter. Emotions are contagious both in positive and negative ways, so try to use words that convey your true value system.

DRAMA

If you are the partner to an entrepreneur and need drama, join your local theater company. Your partner already has enough drama in his entrepreneurial life and doesn't need more in his personal life. While the occasional fight can lead to amazing make-up sex, if arguments become a way to connect or have intimacy, you will eventually wear each other out.

Some of us tend to be scorekeepers—we care about being right, and either like to win or hate to lose (or both). All of these ways of thinking can be limiting in a relationship. It's not a zero-sum game, and if you don't feel joy from encouraging and supporting your partner, but feel a burden or obligation or duty or debt, that's a warning sign. If you win at the expense of your partner, you're not really winning.

While drama is inevitable in a relationship, we believe strongly that only one of us can have a meltdown at any given time. When one of us notices that the other is having a meltdown, the observer of the meltdown goes into hyperrational, supportive, meltdown management mode. Following is Brad's story of how each of us handled the other's meltdown.

Amy and I have been in Paris for four days. We've each had two meltdowns—one minor and one complete, total, and extreme. Fortunately, they were at completely separate times. In the case of travel, especially international travel, at least one meltdown per partner should be expected. Over the years we've learned how to manage the other partner's meltdown.

Amy's major meltdown resulted from lack of food. I'd had a minor meltdown the day before on our first trip to the grocery store, and Amy's solution to this was for us to pay and head home well before we'd finished stocking up on food. I took a nap in the afternoon and headed out for a predinner run. I left the apartment at 6:30 P.M. for a 90-minute run through the Bois de Bologne. When I returned at 8:00 P.M., I could tell something was wrong. I usually stretch and mess around for 15 minutes after a run before hopping in the shower; this time after three minutes Amy was all over me.

"Hurry up—I'm hungry."

"Okay, just give me a minute to enter my running data."

A few minutes pass.

"Get your ass in the shower—I'm starving and there's no food in this apartment."

At this point I realized that Amy was hungry and that if we didn't address it soon, Armageddon was sure to follow. Five minutes later, after a quick shower, I had my shoes on and was ready to go. Stupidly, I announced my intentions by saying, "Okay, I'm ready. Where do you want to go?," which generated a predictable, "How do I know? Let's just go."

We marched down the six flights of stairs as I made nice cooing noises to Amy. At this point I realized a meltdown was in process, and I shifted into super nice extra helpful husband mode. When we got out to the street, I said, "Let's try the place down the block." My goal at this point was to find an acceptable place to Amy as quickly as possible. She didn't like the first place we found, so I tried again.

"How about the place across the street?"
"Which place?"
"The one right there—Do Re Mi."
"How do we get in?"

At this point I made another mistake. I went searching for the entrance without telling Amy what I was going to do. When I realized I had gone the wrong way, I turned around, only to see the love of my life in a full-blown meltdown. Tears were in the corners of her eyes as she said:

"I hate this. I hate this. I hate this."
"It's okay, Sweetie. I'll figure out how to get in the restaurant."
"I hate this. I hate this. I hate this."
"See, look—all we need to do is take a seat."
"I hate this. I hate this. I hate this."

We took a seat and I waved the waiter over. Of course, I speak no French, and the waiter didn't seem to speak English. But he brought the menus and we eventually managed to order. During the entire process, I tried to take charge while being calm and soothing to Amy at every step of the way.

Thirty minutes later, when we finally had some food in us, the meltdown was over. Amy looked at me and said, "Wow, I was completely insane." Fortunately, it was with hunger, not with rage, and we got through it.

My major meltdown happened as a result of the insanity of trying to get a SIM card working in Paris. We'd been trying for the previous two days to get a SIM card for my Nexus S phone. I'd gotten a lot of suggestions in advance via a blog post that I had written and, after two days, wasn't making any progress. On day 3, we tried one more time at the SFR store and ended up feeling like we had made progress. At least this time we'd ended up with an actual SIM card.

At each place, Amy had to do all of the work as none of the store clerks that were helping us spoke particularly good English. She tried her hardest to communicate what we wanted in French, in spite of hearing "no" many times. Now, for perspective, Amy hates this kind of technology experience. Her idea of hanging out in the SFR store is akin to my idea of hanging out in the Prada store. In other words, no fun was being had by anyone.

We victoriously claimed our SIM cards and headed home. I was pretty tired at this point, but after three days of trying to get the right SIM card, I was determined to get my phone working. We got home, walked up our six flights of stairs, and I sat down at my computer to activate the SIM.

I put the SIM in my phone and went to the sfr.it web site. Of course, it was all in French, and there was no English version. Google did an okay job of translating the web site into English, but I had no idea what to do next.

"Amy, can you give me a hand?"

"Sure, what's up?"

"I can't figure out what to do to activate this f*&^%$# SIM card."

Amy came over and very peacefully said, "Let me take a look." She made a few suggestions that I tried, but they didn't work.

"Piece of shit SIM card."

"Brad, it's okay, we'll figure it out."

"I just wasted €30 on a SIM card that doesn't work."

"Sweetie, we'll figure it out. Let's just keep trying."

We kept trying. I ended up in an infinite loop where I needed a password to log in, but I didn't have a password, but when I tried to recover my password I was told that my account number wasn't valid."

"Oh, f&^% it. I just won't use a phone over here. I hate the phone anyway."

"It's okay. We'll go back to the store and try again tomorrow."

"No, we won't. I'm never going back into that store again."

"Can I get you anything to eat?"

"No. I'm not hungry. I just want my phone to work."

"How about we take a nap?"

At this point I vigorously shook my head, which resulted in the very loose screw holding the earpiece on my glasses finally coming out, which resulted in my glasses falling off my face, which resulted in my not being able to see anything.

"F%^$ it. I'm going to go take a nap."

As I got into bed, Amy appeared next to me, snuggled up to me, and made nice soothing sounds as I fell asleep.

You'll notice a consistent pattern in each meltdown story. One of us melted down. The other, rather than react, went into a super calm, let me try to help, or at least be really nice mode. We call this "soothing the bear."

When the meltdown starts, our inner bear appears. This bear can be ferocious—more aggressive than the mother bear protecting her cubs. The inner bear starts off slowly, thrashing a claw around. If the claw strikes anything, it accelerates. When confronted with the partner's inner bear, stay calm, be tranquil, and make quiet, soothing, happy noises.

If the bear continues to be wound up or provoked, it'll just get madder. If kids aren't around, the words *fuck* and *shit* are often a good signal this is happening. As the bear's partner, just stay cool. Don't criticize, don't escalate, and don't react. You know you are confronting a meltdown, but you also know that it will pass. Your goal is to wait it out while doing what you can to create a calm, safe environment.

Eventually, the meltdown will peak. This is the moment when tears appear or yelling at inanimate objects begins. Assuming you haven't escalated, it's unlikely that any anger will be directed at you. However, this is the time to be most careful. Your next move should be as supportive as possible of whatever the bear wants to do next.

Meltdowns ultimately end. Let them.

Amy Batchelor, Anchor Point Fund, *www.anchorpointfund.org*
Brad Feld, Foundry Group, *www.foundrygroup.com*

ANGER MANAGEMENT

Unaddressed issues can lead to anger, resentment, frustration, undermining each other, and other problematic behaviors. Not surprisingly, the solution to not having negative emotions build up over time is to talk about the feelings and the underlying sources of the dissonance. How each of you expresses anger can be a gigantic and scary source of conflict, and figuring how you come to healthy resolution of anger is an important part of building your long-term happiness.

Different communication styles are especially challenging when it comes to anger. If one of you immediately escalates into a mutually assured destruction thermonuclear war type of attack, it's unlikely that your partner is going to feel comfortable initiating conversations about things that she is concerned about. This was never really our approach, although Amy is much more likely to push things in this direction. Given that we recognized it, whenever Brad observes Amy going thermonuclear, he immediately backs off and initiates détente.

Often, anger gets muddled up with other emotions or is easier to express than underlying hurt. The fires of righteous indignation can feel very energizing and exciting, but are often layered over fears of inadequacy or abandonment. Some people are just more even-tempered than others, but even the most choleric among us can find better ways to express anger than screaming, temper tantrums, or explosive rage. Exerting some self-control while you're feeling strong emotions takes some energy, but it's worth doing; both you and your partner will feel better.

In a relationship with a hyperrational engineer type of entrepreneur, it can be maddening to have him try to solve your problem or figure out what has caused you to be angry. This is especially vexing when the gender dynamic around solving a problem versus providing empathy is tossed into the mix. Try to recognize when this is going on and shift into empathy mode to calm the savage beast, rather than problem-solving mode, which will likely just inflame things.

It is almost always better to clear the air than to let things fester. Try to say what you're feeling when you're feeling it, or if you're very angry, wait until you can talk about things calmly. However, being angry may be one area where there can be too much talk, and action can be more helpful. Stop talking and go hiking or hit some tennis balls. Take a kickboxing class— alone. Agitation can be exacerbated by trying to sit still and speak calmly when you're just not in a physical state to do that. There are times when it's good to move the body and come back to talking when you feel calm and safe at a later time. But don't forget to clear the air.

FIGHTING FAIR

A key to effective communication is to choose a time and place to talk when both partners are rested, ready, and relaxed, and to do this on a regular basis. If one or the other of you is exhausted, still wound up from the workday, or processing some other emotional event, it will be much more difficult to have genuine connection. This is especially true in the context of anger.

We each have different personalities around anger. Amy is afraid of other people being angry, disappointed, or unhappy with her. She's still working on not being an approval-seeking people pleaser and has accepted that it is a lifelong journey. In contrast, Brad doesn't really care what other people think about him and rarely reacts when someone is angry, disappointed, or unhappy. Instead, he focuses on what is going on and tries to be helpful and constructive in the context of the situation.

You can imagine that our early fights were entertaining in the context of these differences. For Amy, fear, anger, disappointment, and unhappiness are all bundled up in one context, so when one of those things happens, her emotions spike and she gets angry. When provoked or fearful or scared, she escalates. And if attacked in response, she escalates again. Our metaphor for this was global thermonuclear war, and we quickly learned that, as in the movie *War Games*, "the only winning move is not to play." As a result, Brad never escalates in the situations. Instead, he hugs Amy, makes funny sounds, jumps up and down and laughs, and basically signals that it's okay and we should calm down for now.

Note that Brad doesn't say, "Calm down." He doesn't say, "Don't be angry." He doesn't try to shut Amy down. Instead, he plays chess instead of thermonuclear war, takes a different approach, and shifts the emotion. We don't ignore the conflict or whatever made Amy angry; we wait until the emotions have cooled and then discuss what happened.

During these conflict situations, we've learned to use "I" language instead of blaming "you" language. Saying "I am angry," rather than "you make me angry" keeps the conversation going and reduces your partner's feeling defensive and clamming up or striking back. Making "I" statements also serves to keep responsibility centered in the right person and forces the angry person to be honest about how she is really feeling.

We try to cover three things in our "I" statements: what's happening, how we are feeling, and why we feel that way. For example, "When you are late, I feel worried because I am afraid you've had an accident." Notice that this is communicating clearly the root cause of the anger, which is fear that something terrible happened. By using the word *because* and following it with *I*, your partner won't feel blamed, become defensive, and shut down.

We've learned to address one thing at a time. By focusing on a single issue that is causing anger and conflict, we don't conflate what is going on and make a difficult situation more complex. To be able to do this, we work to resolve any conflicts in a short time period and not bring up the same issues over and over again. However, when we find repeating patterns, we pay extra attention to them, especially when they cause resentment, frustration, mistrust, and anger. Unresolved problems just grow like mold in the dark.

Some of us have good models from childhood about how to resolve the conflicts that arise in any relationship, and some of us don't. Your relationship with your partner is an opportunity to develop new habits that are good, constructive, and work for both of you, rather than repeat old models that you experienced as a child. Don't be afraid to be explicit about these with your partner, especially if you find you are repeating bad habits that are deeply engrained. Learn to apologize, ask for forgiveness, and accept apologies, especially in this context.

When we were first living together and working at the same startup company, Friday night would often be the first time we had been together all week, with Brad's frequent out-of-town travel. Amy would want to have some connection and talk about our relationship, while Brad was just exhausted and didn't want to talk at all. Although neither of us is quick to anger, these conversations would almost always deteriorate into bickering and frustration, which didn't help either of us feel good. We often had social commitments of some sort—dinner, movie, or an evening out with friends—and Brad was often late or distracted from the week and still in the process of shifting gears. Amy was also often tired from her work week and low on reserves of patience.

It took us an inordinately long time to figure out that we weren't fighting about our relationship, but that we were merely tired and that the end of a long week is just not a good time for intense communication. It sounds so simple now, but at the time it often felt like a weekly crisis. We changed the underlying pattern to dinner and a movie with only minor chitchat and no probing relationship queries from Amy until later in the weekend when we were both rested and ready. By doing this, we stopped having Friday night fights.

It's easier to defer needing to communicate to a better time if trust is developed that there will be a time for talking, and soon—not that the important business of communication will always get moved down the priority to-do list behind other urgent but not important items. We did commit to catching up about what was going on in our lives every weekend. Having this consistent weekly commitment was the basis for our being able to defer going deep on things on Friday nights.

Following is an example of how Friday night fights start from Brad's point of view. This happened recently, which is a good reminder that you have to keep practicing these techniques over time and that some of the underlying issues never really go away.

Friday night at 6:20 P.M., Amy called me. My first thought was "Fuck—I screwed up." I answered the phone as I was walking down the stairs to the front door of my office building.

Me: "Hey there."
Amy: "I hope you are almost to Keystone."
Me: "Er, um, I'm just leaving my office now."

Silence.

I expect you've had a conversation that started that way and you know where this is going. Earlier in the day, I had told Amy that I thought I'd be in Keystone, which is 90 minutes from my office, around 6:30, and suggested that we do dinner and a movie. Unless I had magically invented a teleportation device, I was going to be about 90 minutes late.

I apologized. Amy appropriately was pissed off. She expressed her frustration. I apologized again. Then she dropped the bomb—she was dressed up and ready to go out to dinner and see a movie that I had promised her earlier that day. Date night ruined.

I apologized again, told her I knew I'd blown it, and got in my car and headed to Keystone. I'd had a long, intense week (like most of my weeks) and felt crappy and demoralized. What I hoped was going to be a great, relaxing weekend with my favorite person in the world had started off completely wrong, entirely due to my not prioritizing us.

Twenty years ago, I bought a statue of Abe Lincoln, the Lincoln Memorial version, and put it in the middle of a bookshelf in our shared apartment. We were in our mid-20s at the time, and we committed to "let Abe moderate our Friday night fights." Since he was a speechless inanimate object, his actual utility was to remind us of civil wars and great peacemaking. We quickly agreed not to have high expectations for our Friday nights as communication time. Instead, we would use them as a chance to wind down from the week, reconnect, and get aligned for a nice weekend together.

Here's how this recent developing Friday night fight described above was avoided.

About an hour into my drive, Amy called. She apologized for being so upset earlier. She was happy and cheerful, told me she couldn't wait to see me, and was just disappointed that my work had overrun my good intentions. I apologized again, but felt deep relief since I knew that we were back to a good place. I'd still screwed up, but at least we'd now have a chance to get things started on the right foot.

When I arrived in Keystone, I consciously made sure that I didn't rush to check my email. We said hello, I played with the dogs as they greeted me, and then made two cups of tea and we sat down on the couch together. We spent the next hour catching up with each other on the week, just talking about what we had done and what we were thinking, all the while playing with our dogs. By about 9:30 we decided to call it a night. While not dinner and a movie, we started the weekend off right.

We still have our statue of Abe Lincoln. The tactic of waiting for a good time for real talking has served us well for many years.

CONFLICT AVOIDANCE

Although it may sound idyllically happy to be a couple that "never fights," it's almost always a sign of avoiding talking about troubled topics and not the result of complete accordance and unity with each other. It takes courage to express unhappiness and to bring up issues that may feel more natural for you to sweep under the rug. An advantage to having frequent open communication times is that you develop good patterns of addressing conflict in a healthy way before things really build up to an ugly stage.

It is much better to say, "I feel angry," than to yell or scream; it's also problematic to never say that you do indeed feel angry. If you feel afraid of your partner's anger, that may indicate either that your partner is indeed scary, or that you don't know what healthy expressions of anger look like. Adverse childhood experiences of growing up in a household with major stressors such as alcoholism, mental illness, incarceration, violence, or poverty can have very long-lasting impacts on personality and the way that you deal with stress as an adult. (See *www.acestudy.org* for more on this topic.)

One of you may feel that he or she is risking rejection and abandonment by saying that they're unhappy, and try to hide these emotions. On a long ago *Simpsons* episode, Marge tells her daughter Lisa to "just push those bad feelings down into your toes and bring up a big smile." Admittedly, *The Simpsons* is a cartoon, but that particular method of coping is practiced by a lot of adults who didn't grow up in environments where anger was dealt with in a healthy way. It can be hard to learn that disagreement doesn't mean that your relationship is in danger. If you're a person who thinks that being angry or upset is not such a scary thing, it may fall to you to model healthier behavior for your partner.

LISTEN

Listening is the other side of communication from being honest about your own feelings and clearly expressing your needs. It may be the case that one of you does most of the talking and needs to practice really listening once in a while. You may again find a three-minute egg timer to be all that you need to give the quieter person a chance to talk. Take turns. Turn the timer and keep quiet if it's not your turn. Try to just listen. Don't be preparing your rebuttal or counterargument while your partner is talking. Try to feel empathy for what she is feeling. Pay attention to your physical response to what you're hearing. Is your stomach tight? Is your neck stiff? Is your jaw tense? Take some deep breaths, relax, and keep listening. It can be very hard to hear difficult truths from your partner, but it is crucial to honest communication and trust that each of you regularly has a safe opportunity to speak.

If you're the quiet one, just knowing that you have a three-minute chunk of time to talk without being interrupted or questioned or argued with can bring a sense of freedom and relief. It can also be that three minutes is a long time to share your feelings, especially if you haven't had a lot of opportunities to do the talking. Sharing some silence together can be a very intimate experience while that egg timer runs out. Be sure to have a nice long hug at the end of your talking and listening sessions.

GEEZ, DO WE HAVE TO TALK ABOUT OUR RELATIONSHIP AGAIN?

You may also reach a point where you've rehashed your core issues again and again and you're either not making progress, one of you is feeling nagged, or you feel that you can't do anything right. This is another benefit of having regularly scheduled times to talk about challenging things—then you don't have to talk about them the rest of the time and can do some fun couple things together or with friends and share some experiences instead of just relying on words all the time. Gestures count, too, and a hug at the right time or flowers or the gift of a pair of zany socks can shift the dynamic into a lighter place.

You might also agree to take a vacation from talking, with the understanding that there are unresolved topics that aren't going to be settled today, or tomorrow, or this week, but that you're willing to come back and talk about them again until they're resolved. It's a long haul, this relationship thing.

LOVE TALK

Don't be afraid to be smarmy. Some of us grew up in environments where not a lot of physical affection was shared and feel stomach-clenching anxiety and embarrassment at giving and/or receiving expressions of love as adults. Some of us may be trapped by testosterone-poisoned self-images of manly men not saying silly things or showing silly emotions like deep and abiding love. Being in a loving partnership is one of the best paths to grow beyond your past and your limitations as a human. Be grateful that you have a person to do smarmy things for and with. Practice showing your love in big and small ways, and use love talk with your partner since he is the only person you get to use those words with. Develop your own secret silly language together. When Brad and Amy first started dating, one or the other of us mistyped *love* as *kive* by shifting the right hand one space on the keyboard when sending an email, and *kive* has persisted as a personal code word. In fact, it's engraved on the inside of one of Amy's anniversary gift rings. In the poem "Desiderata," Max Ehrmann wrote, "Neither be cynical about love; for in the face of all aridity and disenchantment, it is as perennial as the grass."

If showing your love doesn't come easily or naturally to you, there are books that can help. We're fond of the series of books by Gregory J. P. Godek, which include:

- *1001 Ways to Be Romantic*
- *1001 More Ways to Be Romantic*
- *10,000 Ways to Say I Love You*
- *Romantic Questions: 264 Outrageous, Sweet, and Profound Questions*

Your partner can say whether she finds certain things to be romantic or not, and you can use your creativity to discover new and personal ways to show your love.

PROFESSIONAL HELP

In some difficult phases of our relationship, we considered getting help from a therapist. Amy pointed out that if Brad were able to commit to and actually attend an hour-long appointment each week, many of the underlying issues around prioritizing and time management would be solved whether any actual therapy happened. We never did meet with a professional, but that doesn't mean we don't advocate that option. We've both individually sought counseling to get through difficult phases of our lives, and have both found therapy, particularly if you're not emotionally expressive or verbal, to be incredibly helpful.

A therapist can help you articulate what is true for you as individuals and within your relationship. If you come with a lot of baggage, counseling can help you clean out those steamer trunks from the past and be clearer in your current relationship rather than reliving past patterns.

VIOLENCE

We've been fortunate that we've experienced very little violence in our lives, and none in our partnership, but we have had friends who have had violent interactions in their relationships. In one situation, we discovered a long-term pattern of physical abuse; in another, there was a consistent pattern of verbal abuse that walked up to the line of physical abuse. These are terrifying in the moment as well as having the potential to create long-term damage, both physically and emotionally.

If your partner ever commits any act of violence or physical expressions of power and control, you should seek help immediately from the police, a domestic violence shelter, or friends or family—just get out of the immediate unsafe space. Domestic violence and abuse warning signs include the following.

If one partner:

- *Embarrasses the other with put-downs.*
- *Acts in ways that scare the other partner.*
- *Controls what the other does, who they see or talk to, or where they go.*
- *Stops the other partner from seeing friends or family members.*
- *Takes the other partner's money or Social Security check, makes the other partner ask for money, or refuses to give money.*
- *Makes all of the decisions.*
- *Tells the other partner that they're a bad parent or threatens to take away or hurt their children.*
- *Prevents the other partner from working or attending school.*
- *Acts like the abuse is no big deal, it's the victim's fault, or even denies doing it.*
- *Destroys property or threatens to kill family pets.*
- *Intimidates with guns, knives, or other weapons.*
- *Shoves, slaps, chokes, or hits the other.*
- *Threatens to commit suicide.*
- *Threatens to kill their partner.*

We sincerely hope that none of you finds yourself in a relationship where violence occurs, and cannot encourage you strongly enough to seek immediate help if you do. The toll-free number for the Domestic Violence Hotline is 1-800-799-SAFE(7233), and online resources are available at *www.thehotline.org/get-help/.*

CHAPTER FOUR

STARTUP COMPANY LIFE

reating and growing a company is extremely difficult. As an entrepreneur you have choices about the kind of environment you want to work in, the culture you're creating for your team members, and the tempo of your work. While you don't have complete control over culture since this is a collaborative endeavor, as the founder you have great influence over this aspect of your business. It's worth thinking hard about your core values, how you communicate and implement them, and how you live them.

STARTUPS ARE HARD

There will be times as an entrepreneur when your schedule will be insane. Startups are extremely hard and unpredictable, in times of success and failure. These crazy stretches can last for a while, but they shouldn't, and can't, be indefinite.

As the creator of your company, you will likely feel more emotionally attached and committed to the success of your company than other people on your team. Even if you find exceptionally energetic employees, you will likely be the person waking up in the middle of the night, worrying. Ben Horowitz, a partner in the venture capital firm Andreessen Horowitz and a very successful entrepreneur who previously cofounded Opsware, describes this brilliantly in his blog post titled "The Struggle."

The Struggle is when you wonder why you started the company in the first place.

The Struggle is when people ask you why you don't quit and you don't know the answer.

The Struggle is when your employees think you are lying and you think they may be right.

The Struggle is when food loses its taste.

The Struggle is when you don't believe you should be CEO of your company. The Struggle is when you know that you are in over your head and you know that you cannot be replaced. The Struggle is when everybody thinks you are an idiot, but nobody will fire you. The Struggle is where self-doubt becomes self-hatred.

The Struggle is when you are having a conversation with someone and you can't hear a word that they are saying because all you can hear is The Struggle.

The Struggle is when you want the pain to stop. The Struggle is unhappiness. The Struggle is when you go on vacation to feel better and you feel worse. The Struggle is when you are surrounded by people and you are all alone. The Struggle has no mercy.

The Struggle is the land of broken promises and crushed dreams. The Struggle is a cold sweat. The Struggle is where your guts boil so much that you feel like you are going to spit blood.

The Struggle is not failure, but it causes failure. Especially if you are weak. Always if you are weak.

Most people are not strong enough.

Every great entrepreneur from Steve Jobs to Mark Zuckerberg went through The Struggle, and struggle they did, so you are not alone. But that does not mean that you will make it. You may not make it. That is why it is The Struggle.

The Struggle is where greatness comes from.

Ben Horowitz, Andreessen Horowitz, *www.a16z.com*
http://bhorowitz.com/2012/06/15/the-struggle/

It can be exhilarating to push to a deadline, ship a release, or reach a major milestone as a business. The feeling of satisfaction for a mission accomplished is hard to beat. But it's fleeting—once the milestone has been reached, the struggle begins anew. The phrase "everything will get easier once we get past this one issue in the business" has been uttered over many dinner tables, in many bedrooms, and over many phone lines. It's a fantasy—it might be easier for a little while, but it'll get difficult again soon. Very soon.

A VISION

As a founder, you get to create the vision for your company. But you also get to define a vision for the culture, for the kind of people you want in your company, and even your own relationship with the company, including what you want the environment to look like on a typical day.

Ideally, your culture will reflect your values as a person. It's challenging and unsustainable to have one set of values in your personal life and a different set of values in your entrepreneurial life. The intellectual and emotional dissonance between the two will overwhelm most people.

If you start with the same values you share with your partner, around things like trust, commitment, respect, and communication, you'll be off to a good start. Defining these values clearly, codifying them like Rand Fishkin and the team at SEOmoz does with TAGFEE (*http://moz.com/rand/ diving-deep-on-tagfee/*), and then living them consistently every day is key. If someone on the team doesn't share these values, set them free to go find a company to work for that has values they share. And if these values are inconsistent with the values you share with your partner, explore why this is the case.

A RHYTHM

Companies have a rhythm. There are weekly meetings, monthly goals, quarterly financials, and annual plans. These rhythms tend to frame the tempo in which work gets done in a startup. But they rarely sync up with the rhythm of an individual entrepreneur's life.

There are a lot of myths about what is required to create a startup. Many founders embrace these myths and work like a relentless machine, sacrificing everything else in the service of their company. And then they break. It's more productive to establish a rhythm that encourages extreme effort followed by rest and recovery. We are not yet machines, although that day may yet come as the singularity approaches.

In this book, we've come up with lots of tactics for creating a rhythm, many of which we explain in Chapter 7. Things like an off-grid vacation, where you literally go off the grid with no cell phone, Internet connectivity, or communication with your office during your vacation. Just you and your partner, focusing 100 percent of your energy on each other. And once you've realized the power of this, you might institute it across your entire company, just like Bart Lorang did when he rolled out Paid PAID vacation *(www .fullcontact.com/2012/07/10/paid-paid-vacation/)* to everyone at FullContact.

Time alone is another important part of a sustainable rhythm. People and stimuli surround entrepreneurs all day long. They are pulled in many different directions. There is an infinite amount of work to fill up all the available time. The first thing that gets sacrificed is time alone. Are you a runner? I'll just do a little more email instead of going for my run today. Do yoga? Crap—I don't have time to drive to the yoga studio before class starts. Like to read? I really need to catch up on my email. Quiet time alone in your backyard? I'll just make one more phone call.

The endless chaos of a startup often crowds out creative time. Many entrepreneurs were great creators or inventors. Early in the life of the company they were the ones who came up with the original idea, wrote the first lines of code, or built the first prototype. But now they are consumed by manager activity. Every day is scheduled. Meetings blur into phone calls blur into conferences blur into sitting on the toilet catching up on email as you go to the bathroom.

The last thing in line is family time. Your partner and your family never see you. Even when they do, they aren't prioritized—the constant checking of email on the smartphone, a quick "I just need to take this call," or an absent-minded, glazed look at the dinner table when everyone around you knows you are thinking about something else.

A FAMILY

You've heard it many times: "We treat everyone here like family." The metaphor of a company as family is one that has been around for a long time. While it works sometimes, it's not always effective.

Remember that many families are very dysfunctional. While the family as a whole may work, there are many aspects that don't. Parents fight. Children do bad things. Punishments are ineffective and generate more bad behavior. Rather than address and resolve conflict, many things are left to simmer, requiring years of therapy as an adult to resolve.

A business is often much more dynamic than a family. Imagine the typical family—partners get together, have a few children, and then nothing changes until a parent dies, or a divorce happens, or one of the children gets married. Long periods of time can pass without structural change, while in a fast-growing company you can have new people joining on a weekly basis.

Are you sure you want everyone in your company to feel like part of a family? As an entrepreneur, you get the chance to define the culture of the company from the beginning and, as the business grows, evolve the culture to fit your vision of it. Be deliberate about it and choose what you want it to be like, rather than defaulting to a phrase that probably means something very different to each person in your company.

INCORPORATING YOUR PARTNER

When you are tossing and turning in bed at 3:00 A.M. dealing with a vexing issue about your company, it's likely that your partner is feeling your anxiety, even if he is asleep. It's especially true when he is looking at you across the table in a fancy restaurant on a night out and your mind is somewhere else.

At one extreme is the entrepreneur who doesn't share any details with her partner. "My work stays at the office" is a cliché that is often stated but rarely true for an entrepreneur, especially now that the physical and temporal boundaries between home and work have been blurred by technology and ever-present, always accessible communication.

At the other extreme is the entrepreneur who shares every last detail with her partner. Life is all about work, and the entrepreneur's experiences become the center of every conversation. This is just as unfulfilling to your partner as knowing nothing; he has an identity and a life as well. Following are some thoughts from Alexandra Antonioli, who is one year into a relationship with an entrepreneur.

Like it or not, his or her business will become your new stepchild. When dating an entrepreneur you enter a relationship in which your girlfriend or boyfriend has already birthed a company that they love very much. They worked hard and spent time and energy, perhaps devoting years to growing their company. To you the company may not be so pretty or interesting, but to your significant other the company is part of him or her. Similar to a having a stepchild, they may not want to introduce you to the company or tell you a lot about it at first. Alternatively, they might talk about their company all the time.

Either way, it may take time to understand what your entrepreneurial significant other actually does for a living. However, one thing I found is that sharing and being open about your own life can build a foundation of trust, and communication may become easier for both people. If talking is difficult at first, written communication may be more effective. Entrepreneurs use email and social media constantly. I enjoy sending my boyfriend articles, pictures, or short messages to stay in touch during the day. In return, I get business articles, hear updates about the progress he's made with his company, and receive a better understanding of what his life is like.

Alexandra Antonioli

Incorporating your partner into the mix correctly is important. However, recognize that this is bidirectional. An entrepreneur who isn't engaged in any way in her partner's life will also have an unsatisfying relationship. Balance is key. Recognize that there are two partners involved.

ENTREPRENEURIAL HELP

Friends and family may not understand your journey despite your best efforts to include them and share what's happening in your life. You may find your entrepreneurial community peers to be a life-long source of support, encouragement, and wisdom. Brad has been a member of two chapters of the Young Entrepreneurs Organization (Boston and Boulder). YEO, now called EO (*www.eonetwork.org/benefits/Pages/Forum.aspx*), is one of the peer-to-peer entrepreneurial groups where an entrepreneur can find people on the same challenging and rewarding path.

There may be other formal and informal entrepreneurial groups in your community where you can connect with peers. In the Boulder/Denver area, these include Boulder Open Coffee Club, Boulder Open Angel Forum, Boulder Denver New Tech Meetup, and several groups at the University of Colorado, including Silicon Flatirons Entrepreneurship Initiative (*www.siliconflatirons.com/aboutUs.php*). You may believe that you don't have time for extraneous activities, but connecting with your community of peers can be invaluable.

Another source of help can be professional coaching. A close friend of ours, Jerry Colonna, is an entrepreneur, former venture capitalist, and professional executive life coach who blogs at The Monster in Your Head (*www.themonsterinyourhead.com/*) and leads online workshops at Cojourneo (*http://cojourneo.com/*). Jerry, also known as the Yoda of Silicon Alley, writes beautifully about what happens when you overidentify yourself with your work and the company you are creating.

His anxiety was high. So high, in fact, that—at first—he wasn't even aware of it. But I could hear it in his voice, feel it in my chest, as he spoke to me over the phone.

"What's going on with your breathing?" I asked, "I can hardly breathe listening to you. Even more, your voice is way up in the back of your throat. Slow down and tell me what's going on."

He assured me that everything was great. The meeting he'd just come from was very promising; the potential client—a large consumer products company—was going to make a large ad buy, and his company, my client's company, was going to land the deal.

"Okay," I said, probing, "but what if you don't land the deal."

The balloon burst.

"Well, then we're fucked. If we don't get this deal, then there's no way we're going to make our numbers."

"But you'd nailed the last quarter. Doesn't that count?" I said.

Silence.

"What happened?"

Turns out they hadn't made the fourth-quarter numbers. Both the top and bottom lines were off; expenses were up 10 percent over where they expected but, even worse, revenues were off by 40 percent. Forty percent.

He took a breath—maybe his first during the whole call—and he told me that the board had told him that if the company doesn't make the first-quarter numbers, his job was on the line.

"So?" I asked in my annoying coachlike way.

"So?!? So I'll be out of work!"

"You get job offers all the time—is that what you're really worried about?"

He paused again. "No. I guess I'm worried our business model is wrong."

Again, the annoying, "So?"

"And if our business model is wrong, then I'll have wasted the last three years of my life." He was nearly shouting.

He paused again, his voice deepening as his breath steadied and the emotions rose.

"And worse than that," he said, "I'll be tagged with this failure for the rest of my life."

The rest of his life defined by a missed quarter?

Few people understand just how difficult it is to be an entrepreneur.

David Whyte—a brilliant poet who, among other things, speaks to and consults with large corporations, describes well an aspect of why the burden is so keenly felt:

There is an ancient Chinese story of an old master potter who attempted to develop a new glaze for his porcelain vases. It became the central focus of his life. Every day he tended the flames of his kilns to a white heat, controlling the temperature to an exact degree. Every day he experimented with the chemistry of the glazes he applied, but still he could not achieve the beauty he desired and imagined was possible in a glaze. Finally, having tried everything, he decided his meaningful life was over and walked into the molten heat of the fully fired kiln. When his assistants opened up the kiln and took out the vases, they found the glaze on the vases the most exquisite they had ever encountered. The master himself had disappeared into his creations.

How many of us create companies, create products where our blood and bone fuse with the glaze to create something so exquisite as to never have existed before? How romantically seductive is the image of giving one's all to the fire? After all, as Whyte says:

Work is the very fire where we are baked to perfection, and like the master of the fire itself, we add the essential ingredient and fulfillment when we walk into the flames ourselves and fuel the transformation of ordinary, everyday forms into the exquisite and the rare.

I have to understand this viscerally if I'm going to be of service to my clients. But I have to be mindful, too, of the cost. In disappearing into the kiln, the potter created the most meaningful thing possible. But in the end, he ceased to exist.

Jerry Colonna, Executive Life Coach, *www.themonsterinyourhead*

Regardless of what source of support and connection you find, we encourage you to seek out your community of peers so that you can be reminded that you are not alone on your entrepreneurial journey.

CHAPTER FIVE

PERSONALITY

Entrepreneurs have mythical qualities in American culture, some of which may or may not be true for you. There are many different archetypes of entrepreneur, such as the charismatic leader, the technical wizard, the tireless salesman, the relentless evangelist, and the absent-minded visionary. Often, aspects of these archetypes are combined and blended with personality types that span the spectrum from deep introvert to effusive extrovert. In this chapter, we will explore some of the complexities and dualities of entrepreneurial personalities.

Most people aren't completely aware of their own personalities, let alone the personality of their partner. This is made more complex in a relationship with an entrepreneur as the blended archetypes tend to evolve over time and respond to various pressures and specific context.

In this chapter, we explore some of the specific aspects of the entrepreneurial personality. While these are broadly applicable outside the entrepreneurial context, our goal is to set the stage for a deeper exploration of the key aspects a couple should explore together.

DEFINING INITIAL CONDITIONS

Ah, the passion and excitement of a new relationship! Combine that with starting a new business, and do you have an aphrodisiac cocktail or oil and water? Can you really mix the intensity of starting a new business with falling in love? Unfortunately, there isn't a one-size-fits-all model for this topic. Just as every company is unique, so is every entrepreneur's romantic situation. A thoughtful approach can help both coexist and maybe even thrive together.

Similar to your business, some well thought out goals and objectives for your love life are critical to helping your personal and professional lives mix. As unromantic as that sounds, it is important to be honest with yourself about where you are in your life. Are you just starting your career and are more interested in your business than the distraction of a serious relationship? Or are you looking for a more permanent relationship to change your work-life balance and perhaps even start a family? Taking some time to think through what an ideal balance is for you between your company and a relationship will save heartache later. Are you willing to forgo some of the late-night work hours to build a new love, or is just enjoying dinner every once in a while with a good friend the extent of what you are looking for? Some areas to think about are your ability to spend time and emotional energy on a relationship. As with your business, based on your goals, you don't want to underinvest or overinvest. Find the right balance for you.

Wherever you end up in your goals for your love life, understanding ends up being an important factor for success. Your partner's respect for your occupation and support are critical. Entrepreneurs are a different breed, and choosing your partner wisely will have a huge impact on successfully juggling two high-intensity activities—your company and your romance. As the pressures of your work ebb and flow, a partner who can understand and respect that will undoubtedly help enhance your romance. Understanding, though, is a two-way street. Taking the time to understand your partner's needs and supporting them with their career, personal goals, and emotional needs ends up being just as important. Deeply understanding each other leads to a stronger connection, clear expectations, and less stress. And who knows—your partner may end up being an accelerant for your business. You could be more focused, confident, and creative at work!

Entrepreneurs are in the challenging position of having the pressures of making very real, lasting decisions for their business, yet having very few people that they can confide in. Often, a new romantic partner seems like an excellent outlet for those discussions; however, this can be tricky. Entrepreneurs deal with highly confidential information, and sharing that casually may violate confidences, while at other times, not sharing key information may lead to your partner's feeling excluded. Your partner is also inherently biased, so if you are looking for an independent perspective, your part-ner may not be the best place to look. There is also the other side of this issue, where you share your private life within your company. Many small companies are tight-knit groups. Do you share a new romance with your colleagues and co-workers? This can also be a difficult situation for your partner if he is friends with others in the company and you are their boss. The variety of connections and relationships can make for awkward situa-tions for you, your partner, and your colleagues. Striking the right balance of sharing and disclosing information during a new romance is a difficult task. Take your time, talk openly about the issue, and find the right balance for you and your partner.

INTROVERT VERSUS EXTROVERT

While entrepreneurs are commonly thought of as extroverts, many are actu-ally introverts who happen to be highly functional in a group context. This is a result of the demands on most entrepreneurs to be publicly visible lead-ers of their companies and interact with a wide variety of people, such as employees, customers, partners, and investors, on a regular basis. Often, the entrepreneurial couple finds itself in a public setting and the center of atten-tion at a company-related event. Even for the most extroverted entrepreneur, this can be tiring.

The balance between the partners matters a lot. Both of us are self-described introverts who are effective in a public setting. Brad often behaves like an extrovert, but Amy knows the endless pressure on him to be avail-able in public wears him down. Often, when Brad "runs out of extrovert," he crashes and needs to completely recharge. As a couple, we understand this, and Amy gives him space.

In contrast, Amy is less comfortable, or even interested, in engaging publicly. Rather than pressure Amy to participate in public-facing busi-ness events, Brad lets Amy choose what she wants to do. There's no pres-sure to be a visible partner; instead, by leaving it up to Amy, and giving her permission to show up only when she wants to, Brad creates a context that is reflective of and sympathetic to his occasional need to hide in order to recharge his batteries.

INTRINSIC VERSUS EXTRINSIC MOTIVATION

As with the introvert to extrovert spectrum, entrepreneurs are on a spectrum from intrinsic to extrinsic motivation. Extrinsically motivated entrepreneurs are highly motivated by praise, recognition, and positive feedback. In contrast, intrinsically motivated entrepreneurs are motivated by learning, intellectual breakthroughs, or specific success.

Confusing intrinsic and extrinsic motivation is common. Brad is far out on the intrinsic motivation spectrum. When someone gives him praise or positive feedback, he hears it and is gracious, but it has little to no impact on his motivational structure. However, if he learns something, it's incredibly motivating to him. Amy shares this thirst for learning, but appreciates a pat on the back and gold stars a lot more. The absence of this is demotivating to her, but too much praise is also demotivating, as she interprets it as insincere and subsequently devalues it.

In your partnership it's helpful to understand each other's motive structure because it improves communication by making it easier to give the right kind of feedback that your partner can hear and appreciate.

NEED FOR ACHIEVEMENT VERSUS NEED FOR INDEPENDENCE

Entrepreneurs tend to fall into one of two categories: those with a need for achievement versus those with a need for independence. Ed Roberts, in his seminal book *Entrepreneurs in High-Technology: Lessons from MIT and Beyond*, finds that entrepreneurs with a need for achievement tend to be more successful than those with a need for independence, but that both traits are key characteristics of entrepreneurs.

But independence cuts both ways. Lura Vernon, wife of serial entrepreneur Todd Vernon, has a strong recommendation for the entrepreneur: marry somebody who can be independent. Before they were married, Lura worked at NASA at the Dryden Flight Research Center and was an actual rocket scientist. Her thoughts about independence in an entrepreneurial relationship follow.

When I first married Todd, he worked 24/7 on the things that he had a passion for, which included making money. That was my first inkling that I had married an entrepreneur-in-the-making. Turned out that I was right. Todd has started multiple companies and had periods in between where he was home full time. I've listened to him rant and rave about the stupid decisions investors are making, CEOs are making, and boards are making, and I've been regaled with tales of crazy employees. It's had its ups and down, and it has never been boring!

Here's my advice to the entrepreneur: marry somebody who can be independent. Sometimes, you're going to be gone, either physically, as on a business trip, or emotionally, because you're making million-dollar decisions. Your spouse needs to be able to make a go of it on her own. But that independence is a sword that cuts both ways—if she's so independent, she'd probably rather be alone than in a bad relationship. If you marry an independent personality, you'd better be able to BRING IT when you are with her. You need to be worth her doing your laundry, doing your dishes, and raising the kids. Jump in and help out when you're around, listen to her talk about her day, whether it's about kid spit-up and dog puke, or about her day working at NASA (or both!), and try to respect her time when you can.

Here's my advice to the person who marries the entrepreneur: accept him for who he is. I spent many desperate mornings trying to get my husband to help out in the mornings. To this day, I don't know why that was impossible, but I'd ask him to find the shoes and put them on our daughter, only to come downstairs to find them cuddled on the couch watching the Teletubbies. The shoes were nowhere in sight. Once I accepted that he was *no* help in the mornings, but was great at baths and story time before bed, everybody's life got a lot easier!

Also, for any marriage, for anybody marrying an entrepreneur, hair stylist, or dog trainer, my advice is to keep your sense of humor at all times. When your bouncing little bundle of joy crashes her car for the second time, it's best to think of it as a way to get to know your insurance claims adjuster in a more personal way, because who doesn't want to get to know that guy? And when you go on vacation in the Cayman Islands and there's a hurricane, who doesn't want to play canasta indoors during your dream vacation? A sense of humor can go a long way to keeping a relationship fresh and fun.

Lura Vernon, Mom, @luraellen
Todd Vernon, Lijit, *www.lijit.com*

RISK VERSUS SAFETY

While entrepreneurship is often viewed as a high-risk endeavor, many entrepreneurs have a strong desire to minimize risk in nonentrepreneurial aspects of their lives. Safety in relationships, family dynamics, and external activities are found as often as entrepreneurs who fit into the classic adrenaline junkie personality.

Risk may also be defined differently for entrepreneurs, who would rather take personal financial risks than risk getting hurt in a relationship. The entrepreneur's partner often struggles to understand this view, and it's never more challenging than when it is around money, especially early in a relationship. Following is an explanation of this dynamic by our friend, Alexandra Antonioli, who has been a relationship with an entrepreneur for a year.

Money is a hot topic issue in almost all relationships, whether they are with your romantic partner, your girlfriends or guy friends, your parents, or your siblings. The most interesting element about money and the entrepreneur is that it can be more challenging to understand how they feel about it when you are the significant other.

A person who has always worked a salaried position from 9 to 5 arguably does not view money in the same way as the entrepreneur. For these people (like myself), money is there at the beginning of the job and we know how much to expect on a month-to-month basis. It's stable.

Conversely, money to the entrepreneur is much more dynamic. Money is raised, money is earned and lost, all while people are being hired and fired. These are all decisions that are made by the entrepreneur, and it can be challenging, stressful, and frustrating for people in these relationships.

Alexandra Antonioli

MALE VERSUS FEMALE

The differences between men and women are a vast and juicy topic. Whole sections of bookstores and university libraries are filled with opinions on this matter. Neuroscientists are searching for physical differences between the brains of men and women, and there's a lot of controversy and conversation here. In our experience, there are differences in style even if we haven't yet found the exact structural brain differences to explain it yet.

Following is an example from our own life a few months ago.

It's morning and we are together in a hotel room. Brad is in front of his computer grinding through emails and obsessed about a product launch that is happening today. Amy is sitting on the bed in her bathrobe reading the *New York Times*, one of her favorite things to do when we are on the road.

Our brains are in two very different places. Brad is very deep on a specific and narrow set of things. Amy is broad—reading every article and every page of the newspaper. Brad is diving into his issues; Amy is scanning across the surface. Brad's brain is in engineer/problem-solving mode. Amy is enjoying being in liberal artist mode.

Our conversation at this moment could be a total mess. In addition to the different worldviews, toss in gender, the need for Brad to have 90 minutes of quiet time by himself as he wakes up slowly, and Amy's desire for interaction when we are together before Brad races off for the next 12 hours of work, and all of that creates an obvious potential tension.

Yet we coexist happily. We've learned that we just want to physically be together. We don't feel the need to be in joint problem-solving mode. We relish the silence and the nonverbal communication. We let our different approaches mingle at the edges in these moments and just enjoy being near each other.

ENGINEER VERSUS POET

These behaviors exist along a continuum. We prefer to call the ends engineer and poet to reduce judgments about which one is better. Engineers and poets have different worldviews and communication styles; the engineer is systematic, literal, logical, and rational, and the poet is metaphorical, relational, open-ended, and emotional. Both of us have aspects of each, but usually one modality is dominant. If the two people in a relationship are at extreme ends of the gender communication style spectrum, you'll need to work on some techniques to know what each of you needs in a particular communication moment. These are

archetype labels that we've found to be useful when trying to figure out the mysterious spaces between how different people see the
world differently. Sometimes these align nicely with male/female
gender differences and sometimes they don't. Of course, there are
female engineers and male poets (Byron, Keats, and Shelley, anyone?) Working with these labels can be less freighted with judgments
about rationality being superior to emotion or men being emotional
idiots or those sorts of disagreements. It may be easier to describe
your and your partner's differences in perception and processing
by using names that don't stir up entire eras of gender psychology
debates and whether facts trump feelings or whether women simply aren't biologically equipped for math, engineering, and science.
(Thank you, Larry Summers.)

RIGID VERSUS RESILIENT

There are going to be down times. Shit happens. Failure is an inevitable part of life and startups. The real question is how you and your
partner deal with what comes after. How do you recover? How do you
support each other during a down cycle, especially if that cycle lasts
a long time?

While it's important within your business to focus on your mission,
it's unrealistic to think that we are not humans impacted by macro events:
Internet bubble crash, 9/11, major illness or death in the family, business
failure, or your own sickness or injury. One of the potential drawbacks of
the engineer worldview is that rule-based systems don't have rules for every
possible situation that can arise and aren't necessarily as adaptive as a flexible
growth orientation in complex systems. Your own attitude about whether
you can continue to grow and learn throughout your life or whether intelligence is a fixed condition impacts your ability to recover and learn from
tough experiences.

Helpful and interesting books on this topic include:

* *Mindset: The New Psychology of Success* by Carol Dweck
* *Resilience: Why Things Bounce Back* by Andrew Zolli and Ann Marie
  Healy

PROBLEM SOLVING VERSUS EMPATHY

There's a delightful scene in the movie *White Men Can't Jump*. In it, Billy Hoyle (played by Woody Harrelson) and Gloria Clemente (played by Rosie Perez) are in bed together. Gloria says to Billy, "Honey, I'm thirsty." Billy gets up without saying word, goes to the kitchen, fills up a glass of water, brings it back to the bed, and gives it to Gloria. As Billy is crawling back into bed, Gloria tosses the water in his face. Startled, Billy says, "What?!" A long conversation ensues, which can be summarized as, "Honey, when I say I'm thirsty, I don't want a glass of water. I want empathy. I want you to say, 'I know what it's like to be thirsty.'"

In our relationship, this scene has become shorthand for understanding whether a situation requires problem solving or empathy. When Amy states a problem or brings up an issue, Brad's natural tendency is to kick into problem-solving mode. Often, Amy just wants empathy, but instead of struggling to communicate this, she'll often just say, "Honey, I want a glass of water." This is the signal to Brad that Amy doesn't want her problem solved, but instead wants empathy and connection.

Sometimes you just want to feel like someone hears and understands you and that you're not crazy or alone in the absurd and indifferent universe. Ideally, your partner can provide either problem solving or empathy in different contexts, and it's helpful if you take responsibility for communicating what mode you're in.

OPTIMIST VERSUS PESSIMIST

Entrepreneurs tend to be whole-hearted, wide-eyed optimists. There is plenty of research about how optimists are happier and live a longer life, such as a new study in the journal *Aging* recently described in the *Huffington Post* (*www.huffingtonpost.com/2012/05/29/optimism-longer-life-longevity-genes-personality_n_1553967.html*).

Being overly optimistic can show up in odd places, like Brad's belief that the commute time from our house to his office is zero, when empirically it's more like 30 minutes. We've found that questioning the optimistic partner in these moments, such as asking, "Brad, how long do you think it takes to get to the office?" is much more effective than simply asserting that the person is fantasizing. Providing a dose of realism is often more effective when the overly optimistic person comes to their own conclusion.

PUBLIC VERSUS PRIVATE

In this era of diminishing boundaries between private and public, decisions about what to share with your online audiences can be challenging. It's not uncommon for the two people in a relationship to have different notions about what's private and what's appropriate to share with people you've never met in person. An important goal is for each person to feel that they have control over what information the other person shares about them. We have implemented a veto power method since one of us is more private than the other. Amy limits her Twitter followers to people who seem like they're real people, while Brad has no restrictions on his 100,000+ followers, many of whom Amy believes to be fake employees of dating services.

We're on the cusp of the societal transformation to the digital world, and some people are happy to share their every footstep (Fitbit), location (Foursquare), or workout session (Runkeeper), while others don't want a permanent digital footprint and avoid social media. Resolving these differences in a relationship comes down to communication and clarity about what each person wants, expects, and needs. We've had a few instances where things were shared that one person didn't want to be shared, and once again the fine art of apology can be put to use.

With an entrepreneur, it's also often difficult or not even desirable to separate a business online persona from a personal self. If you blog for your company and 100,000 subscribers "know" you through that lens, your partner obviously knows a different, more complex and multilayered you than is conveyed on any web site, but many business contacts will feel connected to your online self.

The constructed self can be a protective mechanism in what is an essentially public role as the founder of a company. You can deliberately choose a persona to bear the slings and arrows that inevitably come in the online world rather than exposing your tender belly to the trolls and haters that have nothing better to do than say mean things online. Amy actually gets more upset about unconstructive and harsh comments on Brad's blog than Brad does, so recognizing your partner's reaction is important. Companies being started today need to use the vast array of social media tools available to them, but you also need to work together with your partner to see what feels comfortable in terms of exposure to the online world, which has its fair share of aggressive anonymous haters.

ONLINE VERSUS OFFLINE

An entrepreneur, especially in the early stages of his company, lives an always-on life. Work is always top of mind for the entrepreneur, email streams in endlessly, the phone is always ringing, and demands from other people are ever present. Heather Chikoore, wife of entrepreneur Tom Chikoore, gives an example of this from her wedding day, along with her view of why it's worth it.

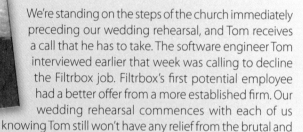

We're standing on the steps of the church immediately preceding our wedding rehearsal, and Tom receives a call that he has to take. The software engineer Tom interviewed earlier that week was calling to decline the Filtrbox job. Filtrbox's first potential employee had a better offer from a more established firm. Our wedding rehearsal commences with each of us knowing Tom still won't have any relief from the brutal and totally unsustainable schedule he's been keeping. An entrepreneur in the startup world wears all hats all the time. Tom was CTO, network administrator, human resources, and many other roles all at once. It didn't matter that he was about to get married—he had to keep business moving no matter the time or place.

But it's totally worth it. Three years after starting Filtrbox, Jive Corporation acquired it. The financial payoff is obviously a huge reward. But equally as satisfying is knowing that Filtrbox employed over 14 people before it was acquired and even more after the acquisition. I attended the last Filtrbox Halloween party with our new baby the year Filtrbox was acquired, and was struck by how many people I didn't know. There were kids everywhere. Kids whose moms and dads *did* accept a job offer at Filtrbox and were part of building the business. It was quite the change from three years earlier when the company gathering was in the CEO's backyard with just a few people whom we all knew.

To our credit, Tom and I are making it work because we accept the challenges of entrepreneurship and we work on the fundamental elements of all successful marriages. We are honest with each other, we are learning how to communicate better, and we take our marriage vows seriously. On good days, we give each other the benefit of the doubt and assume best intentions when dealing with conflict. On bad days, like most people, we don't. That's the key—remembering that each of us is equally as committed to making our marriage work despite the challenges entrepreneurship brings to the relationship.

Heather Chikoore, Colorado Legacy Foundation
Tom Chikoore, Motion Nexus, *www.motionnexus.com*

We give lots of suggestions about how to deal with the challenge of this always-connected life in Chapter 7.

MODERATION VERSUS MANIAC

The entrepreneurial personality can be identified in the wild by a characteristic known as having ants in your pants, or an inability to sit still. Entrepreneurs are noted fidgeters. The positive side of this is energy to do lots of work and create things in the world. The downside is an inability to relax and let go and calm the mind and not be stressed out all the time. There are phases in your startup company's life where you really will need to work like a maniac and draw down your partner's account of patience, support, encouragement, and kindness. But when that phase ends, you will need to put extra energy into restoring the balances in those accounts.

An area where this can cause additional time management conflict in your partnership is around extracurricular activities like fitness and exercise, time-consuming hobbies, or being a sports fanatic. Brad is running a marathon in each of the 50 states, which is obviously a large time commitment outside of work. Some entrepreneurs are also fitness maniacs, since significant exercise is a nice switch from typing at a computer all the time, but still takes time away from your partner and family. You may not enjoy your partner's hobbies. Brad is the football "widow" in our house and doesn't enjoy watching television very much anyway, and really doesn't enjoy watching football. One of our first-of-the-month gifts a couple of years ago was Amy not watching football on Sundays in October as a gift to Brad. On the other hand, many Sundays are about long training runs as Brad prepares for yet another marathon. You need to sort out what a maniacal, work-focused entrepreneur does to downshift and relax and make sure your partner is okay with your nonwork time allocation, too.

SHORT TERM VERSUS LONG TERM

Companies often have short attention spans based on quarterly revenue numbers or other financial metrics. Entrepreneurs can have short planning horizons, too. We believe it is crucial to develop long arc thinking in both your company and your partnership. Things that seem utterly devastating today will blur into memory 10 years from now. Conversely, long patterns of good communication, kind deeds, and shared experiences of both good and bad times help build a foundation for a shared lifetime together.

We've been friends with Fred and Joanne Wilson for almost 20 years. Fred is an incredibly accomplished venture capitalist, having started two very successful firms, most recently Union Square Ventures. Joanne had a number of entrepreneurial experiences early in their relationship, spent 20 years focusing most of her energy on managing their family, which included three kids, and is once again deeply involved in the entrepreneurial ecosystem through her angel investing, tireless advocacy for women entrepreneurs, amazing blog Gotham Gal (*www .gothamgal.com*), and mentorship of a wide range of entrepreneurs. Following is how Fred and Joanne think about their relationship over a long period of time.

When Brad and Amy asked us to write about "her turn, his turn," we asked, "What does that mean?" Brad pointed us to this post by Joanne (*www.gothamgal .com/gotham_gal/2012/06/life-is-all-about-decisions .html*), where she talks about the choices and sacrifices she made in her career. That cleared things up nicely.

Our relationship is on its fourth decade now and along the way each of us has taken turns in the driver's seat and the passenger seat. When we met in college, Joanne knew exactly what she wanted in life and her career and Fred didn't have a clue. So we moved to NYC, where Joanne got a job at Macy's and quickly moved up the ranks to become a buyer. And then she left the big-company world and joined a series of apparel companies, one of which she ran. All during this time, she was the breadwinner in the family and the one with the big career demands. Fred was on cruise control.

Then, in her mid-30s, with two kids in tow and a third on the way, Joanne gave it all up to become a stay-at-home mom. Fred left his job and started Flatiron Partners and then Union Square Ventures. For the next 15 years, Fred was the breadwinner and the one with the big career demands. Joanne was in the supporting role.

Recently, things have begun to change again. Our kids are adults now and are starting to build their own lives. Joanne has taken her Gotham Gal blog and turned it into a one-person media/investment company. She writes, she produces events, she does angel investing, mentoring, coaching, and advising. It's her turn again.

This "game of give and take" goes well beyond business and careers in our relationship. Joanne cooks, Fred does the dishes. Joanne manages our big projects. Fred keeps the books. And so on and so forth.

Allowing each person to have his/her time in the driver's seat is key to a healthy relationship. When one person has all the fun, gets all the attention, and makes all the money, it creates unhealthy imbalances and leads to tension and resentment. A "her turn, his turn" approach requires both partners to take a backseat from time to time. And being in the backseat isn't all bad. Unless Fred is driving the car. That's the one place we don't do her turn, his turn in our relationship. Joanne does all the driving, thankfully for everyone on the road.

Fred Wilson, Union Square Ventures, *www.avc.com*
Joanne Wilson, @gothamgal, *www.gothamgal.com*

CHAPTER SIX

VALUES

As you can see from Chapter 5, you can be different from each other in almost every way. However, you need to share a set of common values to have a successful relationship. These values include how you communicate, the commitment you have to each other, and your shared definition of concepts such as responsibility, trust, and honesty.

We believe that the notion of what your best self is necessarily evolves over time. Some of us, like Amy, are children of divorce, who are uncertain of our relationship skills, but certain we want to have happier, stronger, more successful relationships than our parents did. Others, like Brad, grew up in households with parents who stayed married through the ups and downs and therefore have more confidence that marriages can survive the occasional crisis.

In this chapter we explore some of the core values that we share and believe are important to get alignment on early in your relationship. Our path, like many successful relationships, has had its share of ups and downs. These shared values keep us grounded in our common definition of what is important and good.

WORDS VERSUS ACTIONS

Communication, as we've said before and will say again, is the primary factor in having a happy relationship. Entrepreneurs are action oriented—they are constantly doing things, solving problems, continuously making decisions, and then acting on them. Great entrepreneurs are deliberate about the words they use, as they know they can have wide-ranging implications on their company.

This is equally true in a relationship. The specific words you use, how you use them, and linking your actions to words is incredibly important. This applies to special secret words to signal specific actions or requests, as well as hot-button words to avoid in all situations. For example, Brad hates to be called a moron, and Amy hates the c-word. We don't use these words when we talk to each other.

It's powerful to have words for specific situations to get your partner's attention. We've adopted the word *sweetie* as a soothing word when the other person is agitated, upset, or melting down. We use the word *lover* as a greeting to the other when we are feeling amorous.

You can talk good talk, and words do matter; but actions can become just as important, especially if you've developed patterns in which promises are not kept or good intentions are not translated into concrete behavior. When one of us says "sweetie," the other knows we are available to help. Even if the meltdown accelerates, the action of support continues and the partner not having the meltdown stays calm and engaged. This gives even more value to the use of the specific word, as action over time reinforces it and it's critically important to have congruency between what you say and what you do.

The other side of saying what you mean and meaning what you say is that you don't want to be anxious about having to be careful with every word you use. One of the beauties of being in a trusting relationship is feeling like you can be your real self, even if that self can be direct, random, irrational, emotional, or a pain in the ass. When the word *moron* snuck into Amy's vocabulary many years ago, as in "Brad, stop being a moron," Brad was bothered by it for a while. Eventually, he realized it was a word he hated given the emotion it created. Rather than saying, "Amy, please don't ever criticize me," Brad instead said, "Amy, I hate the word *moron*; please don't use it. It's fine to criticize me—just don't call me a moron." Amy proceeded to eliminate the word from her vocabulary, but continued to be direct with criticism when she was unhappy with something Brad did.

ALIGNMENT

In a rosy imaginary world of companies and relationships, there would be no strife, conflict, bad moods, irritations, annoyances, or failures. Although it's a nice fantasy, the reality is very different. While you can't have all the specific pieces perfect, you certainly can strive for deep alignment in your values.

Start with your individual philosophy of life. When we started going out, we spent many hours talking about our individual goals, aspirations, ideas, hopes, and dreams. As a young couple, our experiences played into these and we together began to develop a set of shared values. Early on in our relationship, we had plenty of conflict mixed in with the joy, and in the aftermath of the conflict, we tried to always learn something from what had just happened.

Over time, we developed a shared philosophy of life. This wasn't merely the intersection of our individual philosophies as our shared experiences modified them, but the result of many of the shared experiences that we had along with our reflections and conversations about them. Whenever we found ourselves with a fundamentally different perspective on something, rather than accept it as "well, we just disagree," we'd go deeper on what was going on as we searched for a common set of principles driving our thoughts.

Ultimately, our goal was to have our values be aligned. Each of us has modified our individual belief systems over time as a response to being in a relationship for 20 years. These aren't necessarily compromises; instead, they are an evolutionary development of our value systems to reflect the experiences—both good and bad—that we've had together.

We've worked hard to get our actions in alignment with our values. We make plenty of mistakes individually and together, but one of our values is to own our mistakes, so when we make them, we don't hide from them. We are careful not to compare our relationship to others, especially since we realize that we would only be comparing our actual experience to our perspective of someone else's relationship. Instead, we try to learn from what we observe from others, but focus on alignment between the two of us, rather than external factors or other relationships.

CHILDREN OR CHILD-FREE

One of the biggest decisions an individual or a couple will make is whether to have children. We decided early in our relationship not to have children, revisited this decision once a year for several years after we made the decision, and then declared it decided and final in our early 30s. The decision not to have children has remained unchanged for over two decades, despite all manner of external pressures, especially familial and cultural.

You don't necessarily notice how strong the current is for young married folk to have children until you step outside that current. We remember all kinds of condescending "you'll change your mind" comments from peers who apparently needed us to validate their decisions or from people in other generations. We had pressure from our families, who both "wanted grandchildren" and "didn't want us to waste our genes." As our friends had children, another cycle of "when are you planning to have kids?" began anew.

Fortunately, we were aligned on our decision, since neither of us wanted to have children. This made it easy; we expect it's equally easy when both partners do want to have children. But it's really difficult, especially in the context of an entrepreneurial relationship, when one partner wants children and the other doesn't.

Christine Overall wrote a powerful essay in the *New York Times* recently titled "Think Before You Breed," where she makes the important point that "people are still expected to provide reasons not to have children, but no reasons are required to have them" (*http://opinionator.blogs.nytimes .com/2012/06/17/think-before-you-breed/*). We encourage all entrepreneurial couples to be deliberate about their choice to have children, and in Christine's words, "think before you breed."

This is a hot topic, especially as more young women become successful and visible entrepreneurs. We spend Chapter 11 on this later in the book, primarily with contributions from friends of ours who have chosen to have children as they explain how they integrate and manage this into their entrepreneurial relationship.

HUMOR

We laugh a lot. Recently, someone told Brad that one of the noticeable things about his public speaking was that he smiled constantly as he talked. While we have deep, dark moments and plenty of stress and disappointment in our life, we have a healthy dose of happiness and humor woven throughout. As a couple, we believe you can never hug each other enough, say you love each other too much, or laugh too often.

Our friends Howard and Ellen Lindzon have an amazing marriage that has humor at its core. Howard can be a total pain in the ass, but he's also one of the funniest people on the planet. He literally has no governor—whatever he thinks spurts out of his mouth. Ellen balances this nicely, but at the core is a shared sense of humor. Here's how Howard thinks about it.

My wife, Ellen, and I are both 46. We have been married 17 years. If she did not laugh at me, she would have killed me by now. Somehow, someway, she thinks most of the things I do are funny. I am a lucky man.

Humor is a gift. I think we both share the same silly sense of humor. Though Ellen wraps her humor behind a more serious wall, with me it is what you see is what you get. Most people meet Ellen for the first time after spending time with me, and the first thing they tell her is … SORRY! The joke is that she knows.

Ellen has been my sounding board for business ideas and the decisions I have to make as an entrepreneur every day. My schedule as an entrepreneur has almost always taken precedence, and Ellen has been able to work with that schedule to help us create balance for the rest of our lives. Of course, there are periods where we get off track. We focus on the perspective of our mistakes when they happen to help us move on with our lives, as moving forward is healthier than constantly looking back.

Today, we live on Coronado, where the kids can walk to school, I can walk to work, we own just one car, and have the weekends mostly back to ourselves. We take the balance part of the life equation seriously, though, like any family, it is a big struggle to monitor and stay focused on it. As Ellen helps me diffuse work-life issues, I like to use humor to return the favor on family-life issues. With a Bar Mitzvah coming up, we both have insanely busy lives at the moment but are managing to enjoy the process because of the decisions we have made together leading up to the event.

Howard Lindzon, StockTwits, *www.stocktwits.com*
Ellen Lindzon, Mom and Advisor/Partner to Howard

We each enter a relationship with a history and baggage, sometimes cargo containers full of the stuff. A great, long-term relationship, whether it is a business relationship or personal relationship, is built on trust. Behaving with integrity in your business and personal relationships is one of the highest values you can have, and critically important to maintain if you want to survive an entrepreneurial relationship.

Early in a relationship, you are in trust "building" mode. You will each make mistakes; how you respond to them will help define whether or not you build trust. Having transparency with each other, but controlling the release of information into the world, is an important part of this. As a couple, we share everything with each other—we literally have zero secrets. However, there are many things that we keep private and don't share with anyone else. Knowing these boundaries is an important part of trust.

Recently, Amy shared something with a mutual friend that Brad had expected was told to her in confidence. When Brad heard about it, he realized he hadn't been explicit that it wasn't to be shared and made the point that it shouldn't be shared going forward, but also was forgiving when Amy apologized for misunderstanding the level of confidentiality and sharing it. Brad talked to the person who now had the information, whom he also trusted, and asked that the information be kept confidential. We were able to handle this situation quickly and without stress or drama because of the long history of trust that we have with each other.

It's not necessarily a fatal flaw if one person likes to share more with friends than the other, but the less revealing person may want to consider withholding closely held items if the partner just can't bear to keep secrets or feels awkward or uncomfortable with different people having different levels of access. This is part of developing shared values early in the relationship. We often have situations where people ask Amy about something they've told Brad, with the expectation that we share everything. While we have no secrets, there are many things that happen on a day-to-day basis that Brad doesn't share because he simply forgets about them in the endless wave of information coming his way. By trusting that we won't keep secrets from each other, Amy doesn't react negatively to this when Brad doesn't tell her something.

It's inevitable that as a couple you will breach one another's trust, especially since trust is subjective. For example, you can say you've been on time for 99 percent of your appointments, but if your partner doesn't feel like you're trustworthy, the 1 percent you are late for is all she sees. Rather than arguing about who is right or wrong, it's much more powerful to understand what is actually going on. For example, does your being late conjure images of car crashes and catastrophe, not that you only had four more emails to get to Inbox zero? Concentrate on rebuilding trust when it's breached and learning what is at the root cause of the feelings around trust and the breach, rather than reacting simply to the specific situation.

THE UNFORGIVABLE

There may come a time in your relationship when your partner does something that's entirely unforgivable, that you can't come back from. This is an awful experience that we hope you never have with your partner.

Brad had this experience in his first marriage. In year two of a young marriage between two people in their early 20s, Brad's ex-wife had an affair that went on for about a year before it became known to Brad. At the time, Brad was working 100+ hours a week running a company, trying to complete a PhD and experience young married life in Boston in the 1980s. In hindsight, Brad clearly failed in his marital relationship, and one manifestation of this was the affair his ex-wife had. But their relationship was too fragile to begin with, and it couldn't survive this infidelity.

In order to avoid this place, you have to work at communicating clearly. In Brad's first marriage, while infidelity was implicitly not acceptable, it was never explicitly communicated. Early in our relationship, we discussed infidelity and agreed that it was an "unforgivable"—we each committed to each other that we would never have any type of sexual relationship, or even emotional infidelity, with another person.

It is vital that partners agree on what those unforgivable actions are, especially in an entrepreneurial relationship. The entrepreneur is already spending an enormous amount of time and energy with her business; her partner will already feel lonely and neglected at times. Time and distance apart exacerbate this and bring up even more fears and anxieties if the unforgivable isn't explicitly defined. Having open communication and feeling free to bring up any and all concerns about the unforgiveable is fundamental.

There can be other unforgivable behaviors beyond infidelity. In our relationship, other "point of no return" issues include violence, alcohol abuse, and drug abuse. Neither of us have ever had any difficulties with violence or drugs, but there have been periods where Amy has been concerned with the amount that Brad drinks. When we realize we are in one of these periods, Amy brings it up and Brad explicitly acknowledges it and makes a concerted effort both to drink less and to be open about his change in behavior.

We aren't drawing moral boundaries here. We have friends who have open marriages. We have other friends who smoke marijuana or are frequent drinkers. We have friends who are deeply religious and others who are atheists. We have friends who are Republicans and others who are Democrats.

We have friends who tell everyone everything, and others who are very private. Different people have different ideas about these issues and about what is unforgivable. Our point is that you need to define these explicitly as a couple and give each other room to express what the boundaries are. And if one of you commits something that is unforgivable, you should have a way to deal with it or recognize that it will be the end of the relationship.

YOU CAN HAVE IT ALL, JUST NOT AT THE SAME TIME

The old cliché "you can have it all" makes the rounds every now and then, especially in romantic comedies. As a couple, we believe deeply that you can have it all, just not at the same time.

The entrepreneurial life has a distinct cadence to it. There are periods of intense activity, followed by stretches of disorientation, combined with

You may have lived in the Mountain Time Zone or Eastern Standard Time Zone, but when you date (or marry) an entrepreneur, chances are you have also lived in the Entrepreneurial Time Zone. Beginning with our first blind date on a nice, warm summer evening, my soon-to-be entrepreneurial boyfriend was over 30 minutes late to dinner. As I sat waiting for him in a trendy restaurant that he had selected for our first date, I figured he had either stood me up last minute or was in a bad accident. However, I was interested in meeting him and I patiently occupied myself by imagining what he looked like and what he did for a living. Being in the medical field, I'm used to doctors being late for appointments, but being late to a first date seemed, well, rude. However, things quickly changed as he frantically showed up and profusely apologized for being so late. With one handshake and a nice smile, he managed to win me over. He explained that his sister had been visiting from London and that he had offered to drive her to the airport. I remember thinking how nice it was that he wanted to help his sister; however, this marked my first experience with the ETZ. In other words, one year later, I have learned that entrepreneurs like to overbook. They are talented, driven, and hardworking individuals. They will be late, most likely on numerous occasions, and I believe that they don't intend or want to be rude. It's one of their character traits. They have a lot to accomplish in a short amount of time, and well, they sometimes set their own time zone.

Alexandra Antonioli

moments of emptiness. Basically, it's often a mess. So the notion that you can have it all is an elusive one.

Rather than trying to have it all every day, we encourage you to focus on setting priorities depending on which phase of the entrepreneurial cycle, and stage of your life, you are in as a couple. Recognize that you have to make choices about how you spend your time—together and apart—and what you do when you are together. Alexandra Antonioli describes this as the *Entrepreneurial Time Zone*.

At any moment in time, it is as important to decide what not to do as it is to decide what to do. Rather than thinking of it with regret, as potential roads not taken, approach it positively as doors opening and closing. When you let a door close, the door, and what's behind it, may still be there for you at some point in the future. Remember the choice to let the door close and revisit it at another point in time.

Entrepreneurs often have clear transitional periods—sometimes within the context of an existing company, but often between companies. When your company fails or is acquired, you often end up at the tail end of the intense/disoriented/empty cycle described earlier. In this moment, we encourage the entrepreneur and her partner to press pause. Take a break. Breathe deep. Recognize that you don't have to immediately go to the next thing. Be deliberate during the transition, and make sure you are opening the doors you want to before going through them.

CHAPTER SEVEN

SKILLS, TACTICS, AND TOOLS

Relationships are a marathon and not a sprint. In this chapter, you'll learn some of the skills, tactics, and tools we've discovered for running this marathon. We cover things to do before you are in trouble, as well as after you get into trouble in your relationship.

We hope our suggestions will stimulate other thoughts of things you can do. Take our ideas, modify and evolve them, and make them your own.

COMMUNICATION 101

An entrepreneur spends an enormous amount of time communicating. Endless meetings, presentations, email, customer situations, and random interactions consume much of an entrepreneur's time. At the same time, great communication is the foundation of a great relationship. This is true in all contexts; it's especially true with your partner.

At the end of a long day when Brad gets home, he's often mute. It's not that he's unable to speak, it's that he is simply all talked out. Amy, however, has often been talking to our dogs for the past few hours and is ready for some human interaction.

Early in our relationship, when Brad would walk through the door, the conversation would begin. "How was your day?" "What did you do?" "Who did you see?" "Did that thing you were working on go well?" "I fixed the blah." "I talked to your mom and we discussed blah blah blah." "Mary and blah blah blah were blah blah blah about blah blah blah." Amy had a busy life, and while we worked together for the first few years of our relationship, we often came home at different times. The first few moments of getting together at the end of the day were often a flurry of one-directional words.

Amy was using the conversation not to exchange information, but for connection. And Brad was unable to respond, not because he didn't want to connect, but because he was worn out from connecting.

We eventually learned that the simple solution was a hug. Upon seeing each other, we hug for 10 seconds. Just a hug. No talking. Just a hug. Something magical happens, the connection is made, and the need for talking for connection goes away.

That doesn't let Brad off the hook for talking. If he goes from the hug to his computer, that doesn't work. But the next minute or so after the hug can be the simple coordination of what happens next. "I need to take a shower and then let's sit and have a bite to eat." "I'm starving—I want to grab some food and let's sit outside and catch up." "I need a quiet night—can we snuggle together in front of the TV and watch a movie?" "I'd love to sit and talk for a little while, but then I need to go spend an hour in front of my computer." By having the marker of the hug to start things off, along with a clear articulation of what the plan is going to be, we end up connecting at the right time for both of us, rather than as a default activity when we first see each other.

TALK IN A WAY THAT CAN BE HEARD

"Brad, use your words." We've been together for 20 years, and Amy still says this at least once a week. Brad spends a lot of time in his head—when he's running, writing, reading, sending email, or just thinking. At some point in our relationship, we realized that Brad would often think a thought, believe he said it out loud, and assume Amy heard it. For a while, this was a source of conflict as Brad would believe he'd communicated something, Amy was certain he hadn't, and rather than connect on the issue, an argument about what was or wasn't said would ensue.

Rather than force Brad to change his behavior, we accepted this as the way Brad's brain worked. He needed a code phrase to prompt him to say out loud what was almost certainly in his head. "Brad, use your words" became that code phrase.

When Amy gets angry or upset, she stops talking. The thoughts race through her mind, but she explicitly doesn't say them out loud. If you aren't looking at her, you can't tell that she's furiously thinking about whatever is going on. But if you look at her, you see it in her eyes. The code phrase for these situations became "talk to me." When Brad first started saying this, it often generated more anger or upset, and often resulted in tears. But over time, it became a safe phrase meaning "just say what's on your mind—I won't judge, I won't react, I will just listen." When the words start tumbling out, Brad just listens. And listens. And listens. And when the words are out, he doesn't try to solve the problem; instead, whatever he says is a clear reflection that he heard the words.

Both of these examples are situations that could easily turn into conflict. While it's classical advice that applies to any relationship, it's especially pertinent to an entrepreneurial couple. In the first case, the entrepreneur is grinding on whatever is in his mind. His partner is using a safe code phrase to prompt him to let it out. This grinding is a normal mode for most entrepreneurs as they work through a problem; it's often uncomfortable to share the thoughts while they are being processed, but it's almost always better when your partner wants to hear them. In the second case, the entrepreneur can quickly go into problem-solving mode with his partner. But this is rarely the right move; empathy is usually what's needed, and just listening, hearing, and responding that you've heard is the first step.

COSMO QUIZ

Many years ago, early in our relationship, we took a version of the famous Cosmo quiz (*www.cosmopolitan.com/quizzes-games/*). We had been together long enough where we had shifted past the initial daily euphoria of being together and having endless sex, had moved in together, and were trying to figure out how to get along in the close quarters that was our apartment, which at the time was a loft near Fort Point Channel in Boston. We liked to joke that it was 24,000 cubic feet (since it was $30 \times 40 \times 20$), but if you've ever been in a single 1,200-square-foot loft with no walls except for the bathroom, you know there is no place to hide.

On a Friday evening, Amy presented Brad with a printed-out copy of the Cosmo quiz. By this point we had learned not to have heavy conversations on a Friday night, so it was merely the assignment for the weekend. We agreed we'd go out to lunch on Saturday, fill out our surveys independently, exchange them, and then discuss them.

We remember this as an awesome lunch. While there were plenty of things in the survey that were obvious and each of us knew, there were plenty of others that were confusing or perplexing. We quickly eliminated the obvious ones but then started conversations about the less obvious ones.

We continued the conversation over dinner, now narrowing the discussion to a few specific items that clearly were vexing the other person in relating and dealing with daily activities in the relationship. Some of these were classic gender/personality things, but others were quirks that were specific to one of us. By having the tool to guide the discussion, we learned a lot about the other person without ending up in a difficult discussion or starting from a position of conflict.

Over the years we've continued to do surveys and personality tests. While they don't change much, and we could probably answer for the other person at this point, it's always good reinforcement to see the answers on paper and to be able to ask, "Why do you think you feel that way about things?" without the other person feeling like they are being judged.

HOW TO RENEGOTIATE

It's 11:00 P.M. and the entrepreneur is still at the office. His partner is frustrated, expecting him to have been home for dinner like he promised. Sure, there was a short email around 6:30 P.M. that said, "I've got to stay at the office. We've got a crisis with customer X and I need to keep working for a while." But that was the last communication. You sort of feel like calling, but you sort of don't. You think to yourself, "The hell with him, I'm just going to go to bed and he better not bother me when he gets home."

Bad move. There's no question that the entrepreneur's actions aren't considerate and don't meet your expectations, but you knew what you were getting into. Being angry doesn't help, shutting down communication doesn't help, and turning a cold shoulder when he finally gets home doesn't help.

He probably feels guilty, knowing he disappointed you. He'd probably rather be with you. He's certainly tired, stressed, and possibly still wrestling with the issue that kept him late.

We had this happen in our relationship many times in the first decade of being together. In an era before cell phones, email, and text messages, Amy would often be stranded at a fancy restaurant waiting for Brad to show up. Brad believed he could travel across any geography the way Jack Bauer travels around LA—he can get anywhere in 10 minutes regardless of distance or time of day. We have many stories of Brad's inconsiderate behavior on this front, almost always justified by something that came up, but ultimately signaling that Amy was a lower priority than the other things going on.

We eventually renegotiated the terms of our agreement in the same way an entrepreneur renegotiates a deal. We both wanted a successful outcome and needed to find a balance that worked for us. In our case, it came to a head in Newport in the story in the preface of this book where Amy declared, "I'm done."

Brad's engineering brain simply needed new rules. At first, Amy resisted this for two reasons: (1) she was skeptical that the rules would hold up, and (2) setting a bunch of rules didn't seem terribly romantic. However, once we discussed the idea of the rules a little bit, Amy understood that the rules would be the contract Brad would uphold. The mere fact that he was willing to commit to a set of rules was actually romantic in and of itself, and it clearly prioritized Amy.

Following are some of the rules that we've implemented and continued to use over the past decade.

LIFE DINNER

We eat out a lot, both when we're at home in Boulder and when we travel together. We like to eat with other couples as well as alone, and our dinners together are often casual, social affairs. But we reserve one day a month, for a special dinner we call "Life Dinner."

On the first day of every month, we go out to dinner. It's not "date night" (we have plenty of those). Instead, it's a special celebration of being alive. It's a chance to reflect on the past month and talk about what's coming up in the next month, an opportunity to give each other a "non-Hallmark-promoted holiday" gift, which we manage to do most months.

Recommendation for all entrepreneurs: if you have a significant other, declare tonight Life Dinner. Here's how. Make a reservation right now at one of your favorite restaurants. Go out—just the two of you. Buy your significant other a gift. If you are male, buy her flowers in addition to the gift. If you are female, buy him flowers also (guys like flowers, too.) Or chocolate—chocolate is always good. Turn off your cell phones and hand them to the other person. Spend a long slow dinner enjoying each other's company. Talk about what happened last month—the good and the bad. Don't argue or justify, just talk about what happened, and more importantly, how you felt about it. Remember, positive feedback is more effective than negative feedback. But don't forget to talk about difficult things or ongoing challenges. Just don't try to solve the problems in real time; focus on empathy. And keep talking. If tears flow, that's okay; it happens. Use it to get to a deeper level about what's going on. But stay calm. Focus on empathy. Make sure you shift to talk about what's going on in the upcoming month. And remember the tears—and try to propose some changes to the tempo so the next month goes better. Being in a relationship with an entrepreneur is hard, possibly harder than being an entrepreneur. Recognize that and keep talking. If you drink, get a nice bottle of wine. Don't be afraid to get a second one. Order dessert, even if you are on a diet; it's life dinner, after all. Take your time. Don't ask for the bill before the table is completely clear and you are done talking. By this point you won't feel like checking in to Foursquare or checking your email—nothing that can't wait until tomorrow is going on, so enjoy the rest of the evening and night together. And don't give each other back your phones until the morning.

We have been doing this for 12 years. We miss one or two a year. That's okay as it's part of our fail 12.5 percent of the time rule (Brad gets to blow it one out of eight times). Occasionally we'll invite another couple, but usually it's just the two of us. Every now and then it's a total disaster. We can remember at least two times where the tears were so intense that the waiters stayed away for a while. But we hung in there and kept talking. And the tears eventually stopped and we got to a deeper place. And it was good, full of truthiness, and worth it.

Our gifts have ranged greatly over the years. Amy gets lot of art and jewelry. Brad gets Tom's shoes with skulls and crossbones, remote-control fart machines, and a Range Rover. It evens out over time, but it always brings a special smile to each of our faces when we see the other person enjoying their Life Dinner gift.

Try it. Tonight.

QX VACATION

It took us many years to really understand the importance of vacation. Early in Brad's entrepreneurial arc, he felt too busy to take a real vacation. It was uncomfortable to disconnect and go away, there were too many important things that needed his attention, and there was always an overwhelming amount of work to do, which expanded to fill all available time.

As part of our renegotiation, Brad committed to a week of vacation quarterly. But this was a special week—it would be "off the grid." No phone, no email, no computer. We decided that if the world couldn't live without Brad for a week a quarter, something was wrong with the world. And we knew that the notion that the world couldn't live without Brad for a week was a classic fabrication of self-importance that every entrepreneur makes at one point or another in his business.

We call our quarterly week off the grid a Qx Vacation. We leave on Saturday. Brad puts an out-of-office message on his email. He leaves his computer at home and hands his cell phone to Amy at the airport. He gets it back on Saturday when we return home from wherever we go. By having a Sunday at home to catch up, reentry is a little easier.

Sometimes we go to a fancy vacation place; other times we just go somewhere. The destination isn't important; getting away, being together, and doing things we like 24 hours a day is what matters. We sleep late, play tennis, exercise, read books, take naps, have adult entertainment, eat fun meals, and talk about whatever is on our mind. We prefer an unscripted vacation so we have very few previous commitments other than a couple of massages, if we are staying at a resort, or a daily tennis lesson.

We've tried to do Qx vacations at home, either in Boulder or at our mountain house in Keystone. These have been total failures. We've determined that a different environment is important. When the office, with the computer, is upstairs, it's like a siren call to the entrepreneur. "Just come check me a little—I promise I won't consume you" is the beacon the computer sends out. Once Brad sits down at it, it's all over, and when he emerges a few hours later, whatever disconnect was going on is now gone.

We've tried to have a little computer time available, justifying it with "just to pay attention to what is going on." Recently, we went to Scottsdale for a week of tennis, running, food, movies, and naps. "I've just got a few things I've got to finish up," said Brad. On Day 2, the computer was still out. On Day 3, two hours disappeared worshiping the gods of email. On Day 4, a gigantic fight ensued, which devolved into a conversation about "where are we going with our relationship." Now, after 18 years of being together, we know where were we are going with our relationship, so this was Amy's code for "I'm pissed off at you for not doing a real Qx vacation." The computer got put away. By Day 6, we were back in a happy place, but the Qx vacation was a bust.

We often do Qx vacations alone, but once a year hang out with other friends. These are special times; we end up having an amazing intimate week with another couple or a group of friends who get to see us in our most relaxed state. The friends are almost always other entrepreneurial couples, and we learn from each other how to relax and enjoy life without having to negotiate the endless demands on an entrepreneur's time.

Every now and then something comes up at work that needs Brad's attention while we're on vacation. This routes through Brad's amazing assistant, Kelly, who is very good at deciding what rates as important. It's a good goal to have people and systems in place at your startup company who can shield you from your always-on tendencies while you really need to be taking a restorative break.

MINI-BREAK/LONG WEEKEND/ONE DAY

We regularly hear our friends say, "There's no way I could take week off the grid." The excuses vary—work, commitments, kids, lack of vacation time. This is especially acute with entrepreneurs, who theoretically have control over their time but often don't exercise it, or feel a need to always be available.

Just try it. If you can't do a week off the grid, do a weekend. If you can't do a weekend, do a day. We love the concept of Shabbat, not because we are religious, but because the idea of no phone, no email, no computer, and no work from sundown on Friday to sundown on Saturday sounds delightful.

The first few times you do this it will be very uncomfortable. That's why going cold turkey is so important. Don't mess around with half measures like carrying your phone but promising not to check it or grabbing your iPad to read a book with the intention of not checking email, only to do it a little. Turn off all the electric things around you and be in the moment for 24 hours.

During this mini-break, do things that you and your partner have put off doing. Stay away from chores, but go to the museum you keep meaning to go to, try that new bike trail, go to a movie in the middle of the day, or just take a nap and enjoy whatever happens afterward.

THE PHONE

It's Friday night after a long week in 1991. We are in our mid-20s and lying in bed at around 10:00 P.M. Boston time after a delicious lovemaking session. We are mid-cuddle, starting to mobilize toward round two when Brad's phone rings. He instinctively picks it up. It's a cordless phone without caller ID, so he answers it "Brad Feld" as he always does. It's a Feld Technologies client on the West Coast who is having some kind of issue and decided to call Brad at home. Brad patiently works through whatever issue has compelled this person to call at 10:00 P.M. on a Friday night. It turns out not to be urgent, but the call lasts 15 minutes anyway as the person figures "well, I've got him on the phone, we may as well solve the problem." Upon his return to bed, Brad encounters significant warmth, but the prior amorous feelings have been replaced by seething anger. There will be no second round tonight.

The phone is simultaneously incredibly helpful and extraordinarily destructive to a relationship. Many entrepreneurs have a Pavlovian response to answer the phone: it rings, they answer, regardless of who is calling. An investor—I must talk to an investor. An employee—there must be an issue. A co-founder—my co-founder only calls when she needs to talk. A customer—I love customers and if they are unhappy, I'll fix it. A competitor? Maybe they are finally ready to talk about me buying their company. Ring, ring. It never ends.

However, the phone is also a lifeline between an entrepreneur and his partner. We talk every day, often multiple times a day. We start off each day with a quick call and say goodnight via phone every night. When we can, we make it a video call, using Skype, Google Hangouts, or Facetime. Ring, ring. This time I'll smile.

As an entrepreneur, use ringtones to your advantage. Brad has the "Imperial March" set up for Amy, "We Are Family" for direct family members, "Money" for his partners, and "Comfortably Numb" for CEOs. Everyone else gets a generic ring tone. When the Dark Lord of the Sith calls, Brad answers with a smile. When it's someone else and Brad is in the middle of something, it goes to voicemail to be dealt with later.

We used to have a separate business line from our personal line; this isn't the case anymore. Be aware of this. Since you likely have one phone number, anyone who wants to reach you will call your cell phone. As a result, the cell phone becomes a nonstop interruption device when you are home with your beloved. Solve this by leaving your phone in your home office, tethered to your computer. Don't carry it around the house. And never, ever bring it into the bedroom.

Finally, always answer when your partner calls you. As an entrepreneur, it doesn't matter if you are alone, giving a talk to 1,000 people, or in a meeting with an important prospect. Politely excuse yourself; say, "It's my partner calling and I always answer whenever she calls"; answer the phone; say, "Hi honey, I'm in the middle of something, can I call you back?"; and as long as it's not urgent, keep it very short. Then, when you finish whatever you are doing, call your partner back. We've been doing this for a decade. It's a powerful way to remind each other that you are the mutually highest priority and is reinforced every time you answer in front of a room full of people. For special bonus points, ask them to say hello to your beloved, hold the phone up, and listen to the delightful chorus of "Hello, Amy" followed by the smile that you know is on the other end of the phone.

THE COMPUTER

In today's always connected world, the computer has become as much of an extension of ourselves as the phone. As Brad sits in an Italian cafe in Gorizia at the end of a bike trip cranking out these words, he finds himself mildly annoyed that he doesn't have Wi-Fi access because it means he has to listen to "Call Me Maybe" for the 400th time today on the radio playing in the restaurant. But if there were Wi-Fi, he probably wouldn't be writing; instead, he'd be checking his email or looking at the latest "Call Me Maybe" meme-dubs.

Approach the computer as though it's your friend, not your enemy. Start your day off with a Skype or a Google Hangout. End your day the same way. When you are both online, keep a chat window open and whisper sweet nothings back and forth throughout the day. Dash off a quick "hi, I love you" message. Share a website link that one of you has discovered during work, even if it's an Lolcat.

When you are together, make sure you agree on the rules of engagement around the computer. When we are watching TV, it's perfectly acceptable for Brad to have his computer in his lap and pound away on email. He seems to be able to absorb whatever part of a French romance movie he's being subjected to that he doesn't care about while doing email. In contrast, it's not okay for Brad to open up his laptop while sitting at the kitchen bar watching Amy cook dinner. In these moments, a little golden retriever eyes and some conversation go a long way.

We've always had a separate office wherever we live, even when it was a 1,200-square-foot loft. In this case, it was the northwest corner of the loft. A computer lives in the office, and early in our relationship Brad would suddenly vanish and then reappear in front of the computer. As our houses got bigger, this became more obvious and correspondingly annoying. When the office was on a different level of the house, Brad could disappear and not be noticed for a while, which was an entirely different issue, but signaled the same problem.

Today, when one of us wants to go sit in front of the computer for a while, we ask. Often, the other will also join us at their desk, quietly typing away with our favorite music in the background. Or other times it'll generate a conversation around doing something different—going for a walk, heading out to a movie, or even taking a nap. By being deliberate about sitting down in front of the computer, we change our entire tempo.

THE TV

If you have a TV in your bedroom, stop reading this book, go into your bedroom, disconnect the TV, and take it out of there right now. We'll wait.

TV manufacturers, cable companies, and content providers have done an extraordinary job of convincing us that we need a TV in every room in the house. The bedroom is not one of them. In our universe, the bedroom is used for only two things: sleeping and sex. Okay, 2.5 things—occasionally reading in bed.

Think about it. As an entrepreneurial couple, you already have precious little time together. Why let this time be invaded by a TV, even if it's just background noise? Be together, in the moment, and let whatever happens happen whenever you are in bed.

We recommend that entrepreneurial couples have only one TV in the house. Put it in a place where TV watching—whether it be a movie, sports, or just mindless junk—is an intentional activity. This is not a moral judgment on television watching or on TVs as an object; rather, it's a way to make sure you are focused on each other, rather than on an inanimate object that shows bright, color pictures that change a lot. When you aren't in the room with the TV, turn it off.

SILENCE

Amy once went on a 10-day silent meditation retreat. It was the longest time we had been physically disconnected during our relationship up to that point. While we've traveled separately for much longer stretches of time, we were always able to at least talk on the phone on a regular basis. In this case, "silent meditation retreat" meant "silent": no contact, no interaction of any sort.

When Amy got home after 10 days, there were lots of hugs and tears. We then sat down and she proceeded to spend the next five hours telling Brad every little detail of the trip. "On day 3, I got an itch on the left side of my nose and tried to use my breathing and meditation to make it go away." We laughed a lot, especially about all of the little details rattling around in Amy's brain that permeated the silence. She has done a few more retreats whenever she "needs to scrape off a whole lot of crazy."

We got comfortable with silence early in our relationship. Rather than let it be an awkward time where we had nothing to talk about, we just enjoyed being in the same physical space working on our own separate things. We are both readers and writers and spend long stretches of time in deep thought about whatever we are working on. We've learned how to turn several hours on the couch near each other reading books into a very intimate time.

For most entrepreneurs, there simply isn't enough silence. Otherwise, empty moments are taken up with a quick email check on the iPhone, a scan of recent tweets, or a quick phone call. The bulk of the day is full of endless conversations and interactions. Sometimes the only silence is at home. Starting your day with either some formal meditation or just being outside with a cup of coffee to enjoy the sunrise and be aware of the immensity of the morning sky can set a less frantic tone for your entire day.

For the partner of an entrepreneur, there can be long stretches of silence throughout the day. In Amy's case, her daily companions are dogs, which, while being amazing friends who are incredibly attentive, have weak conversation skills. When Brad shows up, everyone appears at the door, trumpets blaring and ready to play. And talk. And often silence, at least for a little while, is the transition that is needed.

To learn more about sharing this quiet time together, take a look at the great book *Five Good Minutes with the One You Love: 100 Mindful Practices to Deepen and Renew Your Love Every Day* by Jeffrey Brantley and Wendy Millstine.

WALKS

We have a four-mile walk near our house that we call "going to the reservoir." It's both descriptive and metaphorical—it's a round trip walk to the Moffat Tunnel, a project from the 1920s that created a small reservoir near our house. The walk is on a private road so there usually aren't any other humans anywhere to be seen. We put on our running shoes and sunscreen, fill up our water bottles, and head out the door with our dogs.

The walk takes about an hour and ends up having four 15-minute segments. The first is typically chitchat, just catching up on whatever is going on. Sometimes one of us is in a talkative mood; other times it's just warm up, mental and physical.

Once we get going, we tend to spend one or two segments talking about something heavy. This doesn't always happen, but usually something pops out of one of us that generates a response in the other. Sometimes these are calm, thoughtful conversations; other times they are emotional ones that quickly get at an issue that is bothering one of us about something in our life. Because we've gone to the reservoir so many times, it's not uncomfortable when tears flow or anger flares if emotions come to the surface. We've been here before; we know that by the time we turn around and head back we'll be at some meaty stuff, and by the time we are halfway back home things will have calmed down.

The last segment of these walks is usually cathartic. We often walk in silence, just listening to our breath. We are a little physically tired from the exercise and emotionally tired from sharing our thoughts. But we feel safe in a comfortable environment with each other.

We don't purposely set out on these walks to solve a specific problem. But one of us often prompts the walk because we know something is going on that should be discussed. It's a subtle, but important, signal for us.

THE DAILY HUG, KISS, "I LOVE YOU"

It's one of the simplest, easiest things to practice, but so easy to forget or neglect. Make sure you don't head out to work without a morning hug, kiss, and saying "I love you." It's easy to do this before or after (or both!) if you're practicing "Four Minutes in the Morning." It's also the best way to end your day. Studies have shown that a solid eight-second hug releases all kinds of happy oxytocin chemicals in the brain and makes you feel good. And it's just a nice thing to do with your partner.

APOLOGY AND FORGIVENESS

Being in a partnership is one of the very best paths for practicing forgiveness. You and your partner may have a lifetime together of making mistakes and apologizing and asking for forgiveness. Practice apologizing when you hurt your partner's feelings. Offer forgiveness when your partner has been careless with your feelings. Know that you will try to be your best self but that you will often fail and will need to hone your apology skills.

IF YOU ARE ALREADY IN TROUBLE

Our relationship started in a period of emotional distress for Brad. He had recently separated from his first wife after she'd had an affair for about a year. He was depressed and was expending almost all of his energy as CEO of his startup company, which was up to about 20 people at the time. The days were long, and while our relationship had lots of the highs of a new love, it also had lots of dark moments from Brad's depression and fatigue from work.

During this time Amy was amazingly supportive. Neither of us perceived it as a "fix Brad" dynamic; rather, one of Amy's great strengths is to be extraordinary in a crisis. Amy fully supported Brad's work while encouraging him to take better care of himself, was patient with his dark days, and open about her own feelings when the range of Brad's emotional highs and lows started to wear her out.

What Amy couldn't, and wouldn't, deal with was any sort of fatalistic thinking. She was clear early on that if things trended in that direction, immediate professional help was needed. Rather than skirt the issue, we talked about what would happen if Brad had any type of suicidal ideation, no matter how small or random. We made ground rules so that it was safe for it to come up, but also clear what to do if it did.

On one of our early vacations together through Sedona, Arizona, Brad was in a particularly dark place. He had recently sold his company and was going through what in hindsight is the entrepreneur's equivalent of postpartum depression. Sedona is a stunningly beautiful place of vibrant red mountains; all Brad saw was gray rocks. The food is a delicious southwestern contemporary fusion; all Brad tasted was Tex-Mex stuff. We woke up each morning to a glorious sunrise over the desert; all Brad wanted to do was cover his head with the sheet and stay in bed.

One day while driving, Brad said, "I just had the thought of yanking the steering wheel to the left and putting the car into oncoming traffic." This triggered a predetermined rule that Brad was required to speak the action and then do something that immediately created a safe environment for us. Brad carefully slowed down the car, pulled over to the side of the road, and got out of the driver's seat. We switched sides and Amy drove from that point forward for the rest of the vacation.

We didn't talk about it again until dinner. By that point the crisis, and the danger, had passed and we were able to have a rational conversation about it. The rocks were still gray, but the food tasted a little better. The momentary thought was clearly an emotional nadir, but the preexisting rule created a context for a simple and safe reaction.

WHEN TO SEEK HELP

If you are having anxiety or depression that interferes with your ability to live a whole life, please seek professional help. While we never did couples counseling during this period, we considered it and talked openly about it. Instead, Brad's psychiatrist was willing to meet with us both as long as he felt like he was primarily supporting Brad. We did this several times, and each of these sessions was powerful as both of us were incredibly open about what was going on in the moment. Brad's therapist, who was extremely experienced with couples, was able to quickly integrate Amy into the sessions without either undermining his relationship with Brad or ending up taking sides. This is difficult, but it can be done.

If Brad hadn't had such a skilled and experienced psychiatrist, we would have done couples counseling, as we are both believers in the power of therapy as a couple. In our case, we didn't need it, but we augmented the dynamic by talking with friends of ours who had done couples counseling. We made sure we weren't alone in our struggle as a couple, especially with the backdrop of Brad's entrepreneurial activities, and actively searched out other entrepreneurial friends who were struggling with their own issues as couples.

Early in our relationship we became a couple you could talk to about whatever you wanted. We greatly prefer intimate dinners with friends to big-group events, and would often find ourselves out to dinner with another entrepreneurial couple where the partners were struggling to balance the conflicting demands of a startup with a healthy life. We were young, so while many of these discussions didn't include the pressure of children, several of our friends were already young parents and we quickly were exposed to the additional layer of challenge that children create in a startup life.

For the first decade of our relationship, Brad was a member of the Young Entrepreneurs Organization and participated in many local and international events. We made friends with many other couples who were members, went on some amazing trips together, including a long cruise in the Caribbean that was remarkably fun and generated some lifelong friend-ships, and found a peer group with whom we could talk openly about our relationship and work-life balance challenges.

There is no magic formula to getting the help just right. Instead, we encourage you to try different things, like we did. But do try things; don't avoid the conflict and hope it will go away. If you need professional help, don't hesitate. While some people may have negative biases, as in "you don't need to go to a shrink!," try it and experiment. Early on, Brad rationalized it as "spending an hour a week on Planet Brad—hanging out with someone whose job was to help Brad figure out himself." Looking back 20 years later, this had a profound positive impact on each of our lives.

FUN

Remember that no matter how dark things get, you are in this together as partners. When you are struggling, it often doesn't take much to change the momentum other than going back to the beginning of your relationship and doing something that is simply fun. We have a number of these things, whether it's watching a silly movie together on the couch while eating pop-corn, wandering around Pearl Street in Boulder while holding hands, or just sitting across from each other while eating sushi. The fun doesn't have to be extravagant; rather, it should be a grounding experience that brings the two of you back to a center point in your relationship.

CHAPTER EIGHT

COMMON ISSUES AND CONFLICTS

Although every relationship is unique, there are several common issues and conflicts that are particularly prone to developing in a relationship with an entrepreneur. These are the qualities that attracted you to your entrepreneur, but now they've gone too far or gone on too long. Of course, not all entrepreneurs have these issues, but big swaths of the entrepreneurial ecosystem are populated by people who are goal-oriented, ambitious, driven, creative, optimistic, autonomous, forward-looking, independent thinkers, and leaders. That's the good side. The dark side is that entrepreneurs are prone to a series of personality extremes that can be an ongoing challenge to a happy relationship.

Power dynamics in a relationship are complicated. It's important to acknowledge that they exist, and that even the most egalitarian couples still have issues around who makes a particular final decision. The entrepreneurial partner may be used to making all the decisions at work, and indeed that may be an important part of the leadership role she plays at her company. The partner at home, who may not be working outside the house, still needs to be acknowledged as making a vital contribution to the financial life of the couple and be empowered to make decisions.

WORKAHOLIC

Workaholism is the first and most obvious tendency of the entrepreneur that interferes with having a happy life for herself and her partner. Always on, never satisfied, stressed out from being in a constant state of emergency,

moving from one task, project, or company to another without ceasing—
these are common signs of workaholism. You can work extremely hard
and intensively without being a workaholic. The core issue is the inability
to turn off work and be focused on something—anything—else. Working
obsessively at the expense of everything else isn't good for an entrepreneur.
A state of exhaustion is hardly the ideal condition for efficient, effective
work or for being in a relationship, or taking care of your physical health,
or much of anything else for that matter. Being able to work intensely for
a certain amount of time, and then taking a break to restore yourself and
your mind, body, and relationship is a much better path than working
until you break.

There are several aspects to workaholism. Being an adrenaline junkie
and loving the high that comes from fighting metaphorical fires at work, or
feeding the ego by being in constant crisis mode, can both give an entrepreneur an inflated sense of self-worth and the idea that they're indispensible
to the success of their company. It can be thrilling to solve big problems
all day, and sitting quietly with your partner and a book can feel boring in
comparison. Shifting gears on a daily basis can be hard enough, let alone trying to take a week off with your family for vacation. These are habits worth
developing: decompress at night, take one weekend day off, start your day
in a calm way, show your partner and your family that you care, make time
for yourself. Listen to your partner, family, or friends if they express concern
not just about how much you're working, but whether you're able to enjoy
life away from your company.

TIME MANAGEMENT AND SCHEDULING

The crux of many significant conflicts in an entrepreneurial partnership is
time. As an entrepreneur, you may feel that there just aren't enough hours
in a day to honor your commitments to your company, your partner, your
health, and your self. Many people in the twenty-first century feel that way.
Our culture is in the midst of a phase where "busyness" is often perceived
as meaningful and important, rather than valuing people who choose to
do meaningful things. Creating an amazing startup company is valuable
and meaningful, but it is only one aspect of a whole life. Having time to
do what you really love, whether that's inventing a device that will warn of
impending heart attacks (that one must be coming soon, right?) or playing Ultimate Frisbee, or reading the latest Zadie Smith novel, or all of the

above, means you need to create systems that make time your friend and not your master.

We've all heard the modern parable of first putting the big rocks into your jar of time and then pouring in the sands of tasks after you schedule what really matters to you—another deceptively simple but true idea. The real challenge is that you need to know your goals first and then do your time allocation. What is most important to you right now? Today? This week? This year? You can only prioritize your commitments if you're very clear on what they are. This takes work and, as always, communication with your partner so that you're aligned on your individual ideas as well as what you want to do together. You may not always come to agreement on how to spend Saturday mornings (cleaning house or sleeping in?), but you can take turns and keep monitoring whether each of you feels like you're aiming for fairness.

After these rich, fascinating, and regularly ongoing conversations with yourself and your partner, you can use technology to help you schedule. Amy has access to Brad's Google calendar and can set appointments well in advance for together time, as well as see what he is doing. Looking at his calendar helps Amy set her expectations of how much energy Brad will have at the end of the week and/or whether it's time for him to reconsider his time commitments. Brad's terrific assistant, Kelly, schedules Brad's time and helps him calibrate what's reasonable or possible.

But technology is not always your friend. Setting limits on technology is an important part of time management for an entrepreneur. You do not need to do just one more email right before bedtime. You really don't. You need to sleep well and restore yourself and reset your brain chemistry during a nice night of rest. Stepping away from the computer at least an hour before bedtime helps make this happen. Taking one weekend day to be away from your electronic devices may seem to be a radical and revolutionary act. If this seems nearly impossible or outlandish, it means you really need to try to make it happen so that you can connect with the physical world and your physical friends and partner. Those who need to take breaks from technology are often the least likely to do it. Ask your partner what he thinks is a fun amount of time to turn off your email, phone, iPad, and computer. And then ask what a minimum acceptable amount of time looks like and whether it's the same as the fun amount of time. These conversations can be difficult if your ideas about fun and reasonable diverge widely; but these are exactly the important conversations to have so that you understand each other's expectations.

Again, the important questions are around values and what you want your life story to be. It's lovely to have things to look forward to together. Having them scheduled on the calendar and committed to in writing does make them more likely to happen than just having good intentions. Play Dates for just the two of you, or with close friends, or Adult Time Play Dates (Saturday mornings?), dinner and a movie, quarterly Big Escape vacations— all of these are nice to see on the calendar among trips to Toledo or industry conferences in Orlando.

While you're scheduling things, we think it's particularly important for men to have their own friendship networks, in addition to the social time you spend as a couple with your partner. Whether you golf or play poker or perform in an AC/DC cover band, it's worth allocating social fun time apart from your partner. It may not seem like you need yet another commitment to find time for, but having broad social networks of their own has been shown to be an important element of men's happiness and mental health. More women tend to schedule girlfriend lunches or hikes to blow off steam, and spread their emotional connections across a web of relationships. Men tend to have fewer social connections, which can leave them vulnerable to emotional isolation if their intimate partnership ends or is in distress. If you're a man, make time for social time without your partner. This also prevents a common dynamic where the woman ends up carrying the bulk of the emotional connection work.

When you're thinking about how you want to spend your time, or you're assessing how you have been spending it, a pie chart is a useful tool. Can you divide your chart into thirds of work/play/sleep? Our friend and executive life coach, Jerry Colonna (*http://themonsteri nyourhead.com*) recommends divisions of "One third of your time for the external you. One third of your time for the internal you. And one third of your time for the Other," which can also be described as "One third taking care of business. One third taking care of the inner you and the physical you. One third for family, friends, community, and the world at large." Having thirds is a more dynamic construct than having a duality of work versus life, which isn't a very revealing construct anyway. Ask your partner whether he thinks you're approaching this kind of pie chart. You can track your time along these broad categories if you're having big conflict about how much time you're actually spending in each category. The data might be surprising and will certainly be useful.

Time management should be about constructing a whole life that satisfies you. During the beginnings of your company, you can establish good habits of valuing your friendships, community, health, and family as well as your startup. It's actually easier to establish boundaries and limits on your time as an initial condition of the complex system that is your life.

One of the real challenges facing entrepreneurs is that they will be bombarded with all kinds of new, exciting, shiny invitations to travel or speak at conferences or join boards of directors or evangelize their amazing company or product. These are hard to resist. There are also customers, who are obviously vital to the success of the company, and they always need more of an entrepreneur's time, too. Learning to say no is so hard. Learning to say no really means learning to say yes to more of what you want to do with your life. "I'd really love to do X, where X is be a keynote speaker at TED; but I'm already committed to Y, where Y is spending time working on your vegetable garden," can create ambivalence, anxiety, and uncertainty for an entrepreneur. How do you turn down "opportunities" that would help your company grow and be successful in order to be at your daughter's chess tournament? Clarifying what you truly value helps you say no to time commitments that are actually bad for you, your health, your partnership, and your stress levels. Entrepreneurs don't want to disappoint anyone. Not all of you are people-pleasing approval seekers, but a fair share certainly are.

Learning how to say no and setting limits on other people's expectations as well as your own expectations of yourself takes courage and discipline. As hard as it is to accept, you're going to disappoint some people. What you do get to choose is who to care most about disappointing, which should include yourself, your partner, your family, and your closest friends. Your team of employees and your customers are on the list also, but not at the top. People will also realize that when you say yes, you really mean it because you do know how to say no.

The issue of travel nicely, or unfortunately, brings together a plethora of other issues and conflicts into one arena. Travel is perhaps the single most challenging aspect of the startup company life for an entrepreneur and his partner. It involves time management, commitments to others, commitments to self and health, exhaustion, being unavailable to your partner, and flying. Under our definition of *work* as time that Brad is not available to play with Amy, travel is a large component of our conversations about how to spend our time when we are together. One of the many hard things that being apart for many nights in a row does is create dissonance or different modes upon reuniting.

We often have awkward or uncomfortable moments when Brad returns home after being on the road from Monday through Friday. After the initial happy reunion moment, Amy can feel as though her territory is being invaded, which takes the form of her telling Brad, "Don't touch that pillow on the couch," or "I was saving that last banana for me." This isn't particularly welcoming or gracious behavior, but develops as a response to having alone time where Amy is in complete control of her environment and then has to adjust to Brad's presence. We call this "reentry adjustment disorder," which can happen on a daily basis for people who have kids. The primary caregiver has spent the day doing his best work, but maybe hasn't had a lot of adult conversation or opportunities to speak in complete paragraphs and is longing for this with his partner. The entrepreneur can come in the door after a day spent talking and listening and just want some quiet time without any words at all. We know from experience that the irritability and disconnection will pass with time, so we usually do a neutral activity like watching a movie at home. You and your partner may be able to take turns, or assess during a phone call during the commute home whose need for connection or whose need for quiet takes precedence. Again, try for a sense of evenness and fairness while taking turns with reentry adjustment disorder, whether it's on a daily basis or after a long travel week.

You and your partner should have conversations about how to make up for time away or whether that is even possible. Brad and Amy try to give welcome home gifts and "look what I found in the Toledo airport that made me think of you" gifts, but there's no pressure or expectation that these are super special. It's just another positive habit that says we care about each other and think about each other even when we're apart.

All of these issues are compounded when an entrepreneurial couple has children. Many entrepreneurial couples have kids and the traveling continues. Following are Jil Cohen's thoughts on how she and her husband, David, the CEO of TechStars, approach this. Jil and David use several different tactics to manage the challenges of a heavy travel schedule and children.

David runs TechStars, which operates in five cities, and he also runs several venture funds. Because of this, he has to travel very frequently. We both love being in Boulder and being together, so this has been a difficult dynamic for us both. Over the years, we've figured out some great compromises that make it work for us.

Sometimes David's travel gets really crazy. There are some months when he's in Boulder only two or three working days. We can usually see this coming a few months in advance, and we've learned to plan ahead for times like those. For example, if we know that September through November are unusually heavy travel months for David, we'll plan for a "no-travel month" immediately following it. That gives me something to look forward to and I know there is a light at the end of the tunnel. When he comes home from these high travel periods, I try to help him shake it off and relax a little. I might schedule him a surprise massage, or just be aware that this might not be the best time to ask him to clean out the garage or spend a full day chasing our toddler. It's harder on me, but I want him to know that I understand it's hard on him, too.

David is great at minimizing time on the road, but sometimes I worry about that. He used to take a redeye to start his trip or on the way home just so he wasn't gone longer than he needed to be. But that burned him out, and when he finally got home, he was less rested and couldn't focus on our family. As a result, we have agreed that he shouldn't do redeye flights very often any more. When David is on the road, he is working 15-hour days, and it makes sense for him to at least get a good night's rest in a hotel instead of being forced to try to sleep on a plane.

We have a rule together that any trip over three nights is something we talk about in advance and we try to plan ahead. We try to minimize these, but of course they happen with some regularity. One solution we've come up with for when the trip is more than three nights is to think about having some or all of the family join him. For example, each year TechStars holds a founders conference for their alumni companies. We generally like to bring the family and spend a week someplace fun and different. It also keeps me more connected to David's work. I love seeing how the companies that he's working with have advanced and grown. It gives me more insight into the positive things he's doing and the impact TechStars is having on others, and it makes some of the sacrifice of his travel schedule a little bit easier.

The last trick we've learned to help during David's heavy travel periods is for me to get in a visit with my extended family. Sometimes I'll take our son to visit my sister and her family in Dallas, or drive up to the mountains to spend time with my parents. Squeezing in a quick trip that might not otherwise happen frequently enough is great. It also relieves David of a little bit of stress or guilt about having to leave us yet again. He knows we are keeping busy and having fun experiences and that I'm getting help with child care.

When David is home, he carves out time to focus on the family. He very rarely works on weekends anymore except for sneaking in some email once in a while, usually late at night. He's learned to be more "present" with the family when he is home. This quality makes up for what is sometimes lacking in quantity. For us, it works. We feel in balance.

Jil Cohen, Mom
David Cohen, TechStars, *www.techstars.com*

GENDER DIFFERENCES

Boys and girls are different. Maybe. Or boys and girls are really different. Maybe. Or boys and girls aren't different at all except for how society creates gender. Maybe.

Clearly, gender differences are a complex and murky topic. You and your partner can have lots of lively conversations about what is true for you. We have found that there are differences in communication styles along some continuum of gender and a spectrum of emotional intelligence and empathy. There are all kinds of academic research about how boys play to win and care about rules, and girls play to include everyone and care about taking turns. Some of these behaviors continue into adulthood and into your partnership. There are big ongoing debates about whether women's brains have more mirror neurons and therefore women are better at empathy. You can enter dangerous territory in the "biology is destiny" conversation, but it may be the case that some conflicts that never seem to get resolved with your partner are simply because you're from different genders, or different points on the gender spectrum, even if your biological genders are the same.

It's an area rich for exploration within your partnership about how much of how you see the world and communicate is due to your gender.

BEING ON TIME

Amy used to say that there were only two things she really wanted to change about Brad: that he didn't care one tiny whit about fashion or clothes or appearance, and that he was always late. (Note the broad and inaccurate use of "always" language.) One evening in San Francisco in the mid-1990s, before cell phones, just after passenger pigeons delivered messages, Brad and Amy had a dinner date at Postrio, which was then a lovely restaurant with enormous James Rosenquist paintings on the walls. Brad was late. Very late. And then later still. Amy waited so long that the maître d' felt sorry for her and brought her a complimentary flute of champagne. By the time Brad arrived, Amy was livid and hardly in the mood for a romantic dinner. This scenario happened frequently for the first decade of our relationship. It took Brad that long to understand the message his lateness sent—his time is more important than Amy's time. And Amy would worry that Brad was hurt, as well as being angry at the inconsiderate treatment.

Now that we have cell phones, this dynamic is slightly different. You can call to say that you're running late but you're on your way and haven't been killed in a car accident. It makes it easier to apologize and ask forgiveness. However, the underlying message of inconsideration remains the same. It also creates a lot of unnecessary stress to be rushing around in a high-adrenaline state. When you're scheduling appointments, give yourself some breathing room. It's called breathing room for a reason. If you have a few moments between calls or meetings, you can take two or three minutes and enjoy some deep breaths that bring extra oxygen to the brain and calm your heart rate. Close your eyes and focus only on the sensation of your breath entering and leaving your body. You'll be able to be more present in the moment for your next meeting, and able to be more considerate of that person and yourself.

Be realistic. Brad still optimistically thinks that the travel time between our house and his office is 0 minutes, when empirically it's closer to 30. If you're counting on teleportation to be on time for things, you're going to be late. Trying to cram in just one more thing probably means that you're not doing your best work, which misses the point. Brad has vastly improved his on-time arrival rating, which eases stress in his partnership with Amy, as well as with businesspeople with whom he was chronically late for meetings. However, he still doesn't care one iota about fashion.

GETTING READY TO GO

This is a more mysterious source of conflict, but likely all about control. We know many couples for whom getting out of the house is a huge struggle and cause of irritation and annoyance. We see this dynamic at our ski house

when various friends come to visit. The repeated returning to the guest bedroom for gloves or helmets or goggles by one person while the exasperation
level builds in the other partner is readily apparent. In a typical case for us,
Brad gets ready in about 20 minutes as long as he doesn't have to shave. Amy
isn't particularly slow, taking 30 minutes from shower to out the door, but
often squeezes it too close, so that when she comes racing out and Brad is
doing just one more email she is impatient and short-tempered with him.
The conversation goes something like this:

> *Amy:*   Why aren't you waiting for me to go when you know we're run-
>   ning late?
> *Brad:* I'm ready. I'm just doing some email while I wait for you.
> *Amy:*   Why can't you wait by the door instead in front of your computer?
> *Brad:* Because I'm not a golden retriever?!?—which makes Amy laugh
>   and defuses the situation.

Often, Amy's tardiness is due to a touch of social phobia and preferring
to stay at home rather than enter any social setting. Brad knows this and
tries not to escalate her anxiety about getting out the door. This is another
example of knowing your partner's particular foibles and trying to lighten
the situation with humor.

BEING RIGHT OR BEING HAPPY

Do you want to "be right" or "be happy"? In our relationship, Amy cares a
lot about being right, and for her, being right can bring about being happy.
Brad cares a lot about being happy. As a result, our arguments are generally very short.

This doesn't mean Brad is passive. Quite the opposite—he clearly
expresses his opinion about things and engages in a debate whenever
there is something being discussed that he disagrees with. However, tem-
pers almost never flare up, because it's not important to Brad to win the
argument.

Early in our relationship we discovered this difference in personality style. Amy is often, but not always, right. Rather than escalate the
argument, when Brad really feels that Amy isn't right, he goes and col-
lects data. Google made this a lot easier, and then Wikipedia took it up
another level.

Amy has also learned how to be graceful about being wrong. Rather than sulk or get cranky, the phrase "wrong again!" or "consistent, but wrong!" sung with joy emerges from her lips in the situations where Brad's data suffices. And then we both smile.

Small differences in style and speed can accumulate into big chasms in your decision-making harmony as a couple. If you're in a new relationship, it can cause friction to feel like your autonomy is constrained by having to check with your partner about every little thing. But she may feel excluded or diminished by not being included in decisions that impact you as a couple. Each of you will need authority and autonomy over some decision-making arenas where you don't need to involve your partner; but it will be important to establish some decision-making methodologies for joint decisions. Some of the areas that we have assigned decision-making authority to Amy include household furniture purchases, vacation locations, and Brad's wardrobe and hairstyle.

As an entrepreneur, you're likely to be a fast decider and not spend a lot of time revisiting decisions that have already been made. Your partner may need more time to process the underlying reasons for a decision, and will mostly likely want to be involved in more decisions than you're used to seeking input on in your startup company. Patience with each other's styles will be useful, as well as figuring out what areas you can share decision making in and what areas belong to one of you individually. We have been lucky that we have similar styles, which is to make decisions quite quickly and move on to the next one. We make plenty of mistakes and wrong decisions, but we have the same speed in deciding how to correct errors. Try not to do a lot of fault assigning or blaming your partner for errors that have already been made. The error is in the past; let it go and focus on remedying the present situation.

Money decisions can be especially thorny, where one partner can feel that the other is trying to control everything or hoard power. We do have a financial threshold above which the other needs to get involved. When Brad is making an investment decision with our own money, he has free reign up to an amount where Amy would be uncomfortable not having some input in where the money is going. The threshold amount has increased over time, but there will likely always be an amount that Amy wants to have a say in when it's their personal dollars. This is true for philanthropic decisions as well. Amy makes the vast majority of decisions about which nonprofits to support, but for large grants, Brad wants to know what the rationale behind the decision is. He also supports organizations with sums that Amy likes to know about. We very rarely veto or vote down a suggested investment or grant, but it's always worth at least a quick conversation to include each other.

WHAT COMPATIBILITY REALLY MEANS

When you're trying to live with someone who is different than you, it can be the little daily things that wear on you over time. Are you a night owl or an early bird? Do you listen to music throughout the day, or do you need silence when you work? Vegetarian or paleo-carnivore? Morning news on television or NPR or no news at all? Coffee or tea? Smoker or non? (Egads.) Cats or dogs? The list of differences is extensive, and you and your partner will need to figure out what things matter to you and what you can either let go of or take turns having what you want. It can be hard to compromise when the choice is between listening to Mozart or listening to N.W.A. and the Posse. (Try headphones.)

Compatibility doesn't mean you need to be identical twins to live happily together. Compatibility really means respect: respecting your partner's differences, acknowledging that she might have different ideas about a morning routine, or how important cloth napkins are when entertaining, or how many shoes are enough. We believe that striving for an environment of fairness and taking turns can smooth out some of these differences; but some of the minor irritants of daily life can become precipitating events for big fights or serve as stand-ins for deeper, unaddressed conflicts. Try to communicate clearly about when you think it's your turn to choose the music or whether you have a deeper values conflict about money and shoe budgets. Try different modalities and talk about what works and what doesn't. Keep the air clear and don't let irritation become the dominant pattern in your daily routines.

The cliché "opposites attract" is one that you often see played out in real life between partners in an entrepreneurial couple. Here's an example from two newlyweds, Sarah and Bart Lorang, CEO of FullContact.

Bart

Sarah and I met during graduate school in the fall of 2009. I sat behind Sarah during class. Unbeknownst to me, Sarah couldn't stand my presence. I can be loud, opinionated, obnoxious, persuasive, and overly confident. Eventually, Sarah switched seats to get away from me.

Oblivious, I didn't really notice.

It turns out Sarah and I are complete opposites. We're also perfect for each other.

She's warm, generous, kind, courteous, patient, and thoughtful. I'm none of these things. I'm a hard-driving entrepreneur. From the time I wake up in the morning to the time I fall asleep, I'm totally obsessed with my company, Full-Contact. It never truly leaves my mind.

But when it does, it has everything to do with Sarah. She has a way of grounding me in reality and soothing me when it's needed most.

Sarah's been there from the beginning. I started FullContact about three weeks after Sarah and I started dating. In fact, she likes to claim that she was the inspiration for FullContact. Sarah is obsessed and anal-retentive about her address book—it's always perfect. I am lazy and don't want to spend time updating my address book. So there might be more than a little truth to that.

Sarah lets me talk endlessly about the ups and downs that are inherent to growing a startup. She is always supportive and infinitely patient.

On more than one occasion during FullContact's existence I privately talked with Sarah about giving up and calling it quits (see *www.fullcontact .com/2012/07/12/from-basements-to-brad-feld-a-startup-story/*). But Sarah kept pushing me forward. She urged me to continue. She scolded me for considering quitting. Without her urging, we wouldn't have gone to TechStars, wouldn't have raised investment capital, and FullContact wouldn't exist.

For the past three years, Sarah has watched this "thing" called FullContact grow from an idea into a company and as our relationship has grown, so has the company. In many ways, it's not just my baby, but her baby, too.

Sarah

They say opposites attract, but I never really believed that was the case for me. I suppose this is largely because I always thought the mythical "they" was referring to outward-facing characteristics—you know, the good girl and the bad boy. I would very much describe myself as the good girl. I was the kid with perfect attendance, always on the honor roll, and doing extra class assignments for fun. As an adult, I'm not much different. I worked full time and went to school full time while earning both my undergraduate and graduate degrees. I have been blessed with a successful and challenging career. I co-founded and am a board member of a local nonprofit that helps families with developmentally challenged children, am on a second board for another nonprofit helping treatment of special needs children, and even maintain a blog about my path to domesticity. Long story short, I am an overachieving nerd who generally comes across a bit too proper and prudish upon first meeting.

If you had asked me what my opposite would look like a few years ago, I would have said that person would be an underachiever, have little respect for education and learning, and would completely disregard rules, laws, and any other societal norms. Well, I was wrong. My partner, Bart, is my complete opposite and is none of those things—except maybe the last point to some degree. We have taken multiple personality-profiling tests, strength-finding tests, and other measurements for compatibility and are polar opposites on every single one of them.

So what does that mean? In short, Bart and I just process information differently. He is nothing like the "bad boy" image I had in my head for my opposite. When planning a vacation, I have a four-page to-do list, with sublists for things like packing built in. Bart, on the other hand, might have a mental list of three bullet points: book a flight, find a hotel, and throw some things in a suitcase. I'll put a heavy emphasis on might, because he doesn't even always put that much thought into a trip. At work, if someone is presenting something to me, I need it given to me in advance, and in writing, so I can process the pitch, think through all sorts of scenarios, mentally process all of the details and minutia, then write down my comments, next steps, and so on. I want to be presented with a lot of detail so I understand every element of what we're talking about. In the same situation, Bart would want a quick, verbal meeting presented in bullet points. He would immediately scoff at any detail one might try to give him and keep making the presenter go back to a 30,000-foot overview approach. He makes decision quickly and almost impulsively, whereas I take a while, and definitely overthink things.

If Bart and I didn't have the tools to communicate, I could easily see how our relationship would have failed from the very beginning. I'm the girl who keeps things in and lets them build up until I just blow up one day. Bart always says what is on his mind and doesn't mince words. I avoid confrontation like the plague; Bart welcomes it and sees it as a sport. I have to admit that Bart is the much better adaptor in our relationship—he is amazing at checking in with me to see how I'm doing, forces me to talk, and tries his best to give me the time and detail I need to make decisions. I'm still working on summarizing, well, everything, better for him.

But more than just coping, communicating better, and understanding how the other processes information, I think we work so well as a couple because I absolutely love all the parts of Bart that I just don't understand or could even begin to emulate. He is always pushing me outside of my comfort zone (and my comfort zone is where I love to live), makes me very conscious of looking at life through a different lens, and just generally makes me feel like the most important person in the room. Bart is one of the most passionate people I know, is more dedicated to his work that I could ever be, and is bolder and more courageous than I could even dream of being. Bart makes me a better person by just my watching him. And almost as important as my undying respect for him, I know how much Bart respects me and always asks my opinion so he can see the full picture. Simply put, I think our two halves really do make a whole.

Bart Lorang, FullContact, *www.fullcontact.com*
Sarah Lorang, Professional Service Snob, Pseudo-Blogger, *www.domesticdilettante.com*

CHEERLEADER VERSUS CRITIC

An entrepreneur's partner plays a dual role when giving the entrepreneur feedback. There are days where Amy is Brad's biggest cheerleader, spurring him on to greater heights, defending him against criticism, and encouraging him in moments of self-doubt. There are other days where Amy is Brad's biggest critic, openly challenging his ideas, asserting a different opinion and perspective, and actively debating a decision or course of action.

We encourage this in our relationship. However, it's Brad's responsibility to be clear about what mode he needs at any given time, especially if Amy is in a mode that is not being helpful. We start from a perspective of trust. Brad trusts Amy to be both his biggest fan and most honest critic. But Amy knows that if she's being a critic when Brad needs a cheerleader, or being a cheerleader all the time and not being critical of things she observes and disagrees with, she's not necessarily helping. And rather than fight Brad when he expresses that she's in the wrong mode, she immediately switches.

This needs to feel like a safe discussion. It can be as simple as "Sweetie, I need you to be a cheerleader right now" or "Sweetie, I need your perspective on this issue." Note the specific language: Brad uses the word *sweetie* to signify that he's making a specific type of request and then, rather than make a fuzzy demand, he's clear about which mode he needs Amy to be in.

TOGETHER AND SEPARATE

An area where you may have different needs that baffle your partner is alone time separate from him even during the finite amount of time you have together. It may feel selfish to ask for time just to be with yourself and your own thoughts and not always be connected to your partner, but it is, as always, important to ask for what you need. If there is a lot of friction around carving out alone time, try getting up earlier in the morning so that you have time for quiet and contemplation before the rest of your household stirs. If you're a night owl, take 30 minutes before you go to bed to turn off your email and do what you need for your solitary self. Exercise can be another time to be alone with your thoughts so that you're doing something good for your mind at the same time that you're taking care of your body and health. Ideally, your partner will support your needs for alone time, but you may need to express that it's not a form of rejection of her or your relationship and that you're different from her in this way. Susan Cain's book *Quiet: The Power of Introverts in a World that Can't Stop Talking* explores the richness and value of solitude and the creative restoration that can come from having time without external stimuli, even the presence of your partner.

HIS SHIT, HER SHIT, YOUR SHIT TOGETHER

Each of you comes to your partnership with a particular history and personality, full of wonderfulness and some delicate hints of eccentricity with top notes of anxiety and need for control over rich base notes of generosity and humor. We are all fine wines. The complexities of your partnership can be enhanced or exacerbated by each of your quirky histories. If someone with a high need for control is in a relationship with someone with a high need for autonomy and freedom, that's going to cause ongoing conflicts unless you can each compromise some and take responsibility for your particular brand of crazy. If one of you has an anxiety disorder, he will likely need to get professional help outside of your relationship and work very hard to segment his issues from conflicts that involve the two of you together. If one of you was raised in a household with alcoholism, he will likely need to be extra alert to his use of alcohol as a coping mechanism, as well as a cluster of behaviors that served him well in that childhood environment but are not adaptive in an adult relationship. Try to take responsibility for your own issues and work to repair your own self in addition to working to build a healthy relationship with your partner.

SHIT HAPPENS—NOW WHAT?

Into each life some rain must fall, to quote Henry Wadsworth Longfellow, or if you prefer a more current pop culture source, The Ink Spots with Ella Fitzgerald. How you deal with the hard times both as individuals and as partners can be one of the hardest tests of your relationship. It can also bind you together in ways that can't be measured. Startup companies often fail. Even if they survive, they often have brutal down cycles and teeter on the brink of failure. Bad things will happen to you as individuals, including sickness, car accidents, and death of beloved pets. Different people have different coping styles, which can cause dissonance and disconnection between you at times when you need support the most. Andrew Zolli and Ann Marie Healy's book *Resilience: Why Things Bounce Back* is full of useful information about how to deal with and learn from adversity. Knowing that your partner is committed to supporting you through good times and bad can really help mitigate the inevitable slings and arrows of outrageous fortune.

TO GET MARRIED OR NOT

Of course, the decision about whether to marry and when can be a very hot and emotionally spiky topic. The "get married or break up" juncture is a common one in partnerships. There are no simple answers here. You both (obviously) need to be really ready for legal marriage before you take that step. By the time you're having the marriage conversation, we hope you've developed excellent habits of taking turns sharing your honest feelings as well as really listening to your partner. It's hard to find a middle ground if you're not in the same position at the same time. If you're the one who wants to get married and you come to the slow realization that your partner just isn't going to get there, you have some tough decisions about how much you want to share a life with her as opposed to how much you want to be married. This kind of emotionally loaded topic is one that you may agree to discuss on a schedule, like once a quarter, or that you'll revisit it in six months to see whether either of you is moving closer to the other's position. And then leave the topic alone for that period of time. We're not big fans of ultimatums of basically any kind in your partnership; but it may make sense to set an outer boundary time limit, like three years, to come to a final decision on what is likely to be the single biggest decision of your life.

ANXIETY AND DEPRESSION

There are several actual psychological disorders that entrepreneurs are prone to, especially the twins of anxiety and depression and spiraling up and up into mania and bipolar disorder. It can be hard to distinguish focusing on your company and worrying about success and failure from genuine anxiety. If you're an entrepreneur who really cannot turn off, to the extent that you're not sleeping at night and your partner is really annoyed or concerned about you, even though you want to relax and let your mind rest, you may have an anxiety disorder.

Symptoms of an anxiety disorder include:

- Feelings of panic, fear, and uneasiness.
- Uncontrollable, obsessive thoughts.
- Repeated thoughts or flashbacks of traumatic experiences.
- Nightmares.
- Ritualistic behaviors, such as repeated hand washing.
- Problems sleeping.
- Cold or sweaty hands and/or feet.
- Shortness of breath.
- Palpitations.
- An inability to be still and calm.
- Dry mouth.

- Numbness or tingling in the hands or feet.
- Nausea.
- Muscle tension.
- Dizziness.

If you're experiencing these symptoms, please seek professional help. Being an entrepreneur is frequently a high-stress path, but if you're suffering from anxiety, there is help available.

If you stop enjoying work at all, have feelings of dread, or trouble sleeping, you may have depression. If you think you may have depression, please seek professional treatment. Symptoms of depression include:

- Difficulty concentrating, remembering details, and making decisions.
- Fatigue and decreased energy.
- Feelings of guilt, worthlessness, and/or helplessness.
- Feelings of hopelessness and/or pessimism.
- Insomnia, early-morning wakefulness, or excessive sleeping.
- Irritability, restlessness.
- Loss of interest in activities or hobbies once pleasurable, including sex.
- Overeating or appetite loss.
- Persistent aches or pains, headaches, cramps, or digestive problems that do not ease even with treatment.
- Persistent sad, anxious, or "empty" feelings.
- Thoughts of suicide, suicide attempts.

Depression carries a high risk of suicide. According to WebMD, more than 1 out of 10 people suffering from depression commits suicide (*www.webmd.com/depression/default.htm*). Anyone who expresses suicidal thoughts or intentions should be taken very, very seriously. Do not hesitate to call your local suicide hotline immediately. Call 1-800-SUICIDE (1-800-784-2433) or 1-800-273-TALK (1-800-273-8255)

Warning signs of suicide with depression include:

- A sudden switch from being very sad to being very calm or appearing to be happy.
- Always talking or thinking about death.
- Clinical depression (deep sadness, loss of interest, trouble sleeping and eating) that gets worse.

- Having a "death wish," tempting fate by taking risks that could lead to death, such as driving through red lights.
- Losing interest in things one used to care about.
- Making comments about being hopeless, helpless, or worthless.
- Putting affairs in order, tying up loose ends, changing a will.
- Saying things like "It would be better if I weren't here" or "I want out."
- Talking about suicide (killing one's self).
- Visiting or calling people one cares about.

If you or your partner is exhibiting symptoms of anxiety, depression, suicide, or other mental illness, please seek professional help.

CHAPTER NINE

BIG ISSUES: ILLNESS, RELATIONSHIP FAILURE, AND DIVORCE

While the common conflicts and issues discussed in Chapter 8 can be challenging, there are several categories of challenges we call "big issues." These are the ones that create enormous amounts of stress in a relationship and often lead to the breakdown of the relationship. Some of these, like a serious illness or accident, can happen suddenly and unexpectedly. Others, like the failure of a relationship, or a divorce, can build over time. Regardless of whether it's unexpected or something that's anticipated, the moment of stress often sneaks up on you and appears suddenly out of nowhere. But these mechanisms for either surviving the issue, or the seeds of failure, are generally planted much earlier.

Each of us watched the other struggle through the breakup of a previous serious relationship before we got together as a couple. The impact on how we each approached our relationship, what we were sensitive to, and how we dealt with conflict was influenced by our previous failed relationships. Fortunately, we knew each other and our former partners and were able to talk openly about the challenges. Regardless, many of our reactions to our previous relationship created challenges for our new relationship.

We've also had to deal with illness and death as a couple. As a colleague of Brad's likes to say, "Life is a fatal disease." There is no denying that death ultimately comes and when you are confronted with it, or a serious illness, either in your relationship or with close friends, your own relationship can be tested.

SERIOUS ILLNESS OR ACCIDENT

There are times when your company simply cannot be the highest priority in your life, and that is when you, your partner, your child, or someone for whom you are responsible becomes seriously ill. It's such a cliché to say that without your health you have nothing, but it's absolutely true.

In the spring of 2012, Amy slipped on some ice outside our house, fell, and badly broke her wrist. Brad was in San Antonio at the time on his way to SXSW, where he had four intense days of meetings, presentations, and parties. Following is a blog post Brad wrote at the end of the day after Amy fell and hurt herself.

This morning I was taking a break between meetings in San Antonio at TechStars Cloud to check my email when I saw a note from my wife, Amy, with the header "I just broke my wrist." The email said, "Fell on stairs. At urgent care. Got x-ray. Have "dinner fork"–type fracture. Pam and Ryan will get me home. Not hurting too bad. Right wrist so also lucky."

I called Amy immediately and got her voice mail. There isn't anything more disorienting to me than hearing that my beloved is in distress and not being able to jump into action to help her. I sent her a note that said, "I just tried to call. Call when you have a chance," and then tried to get my mind back into my next meeting. She called about 30 minutes later and we had a short, tearful conversation, but then she went into some room at urgent care where she couldn't talk on the phone. I didn't hear back for two hours but in that period of time decided that I was heading home first thing tomorrow morning to be with her.

My awesome magical assistant, Kelly, dealt with the 20-ish SXSW meetings and panels I had set for Thursday through Sunday. The notes back from people were very supportive of my choosing to go home to Amy, even though I'm sure I've inconvenienced or disappointed a few of them. By the time Amy and I finally connected, she was doing okay but glad I was going home. By about 1:00 P.M. I settled down and wasn't thinking about her every two minutes and feeling helpless as I went through my meetings.

I had a super day at TechStars Cloud. The gang down here is doing great stuff; there are some really neat companies that are developing nicely (and quickly), and the vibe is dynamite. While part of me was excited about SXSW, the introvert in me was dreading it. This was the first leg of the trip, and I was gaining energy from the focused interaction with the TechStars Cloud folks, which I hoped would sustain me through four days of SXSW extrovertness.

Life got in the way. Being with Amy is infinitely more important to me than four days of nerd craziness. As I sit here in my hotel room wound up and unable to sleep I long for a teleportation machine that would get me home in 30 seconds. I'll be home in 12 hours, but that feels like a long time. I know Amy is fine, but the magnetic pull of what matters to me overwhelms my patience right now.

Yesterday at TechStars for a Day in Boulder, I gave a short talk about obsession. As part of it, I focused on the importance of taking a long-term view and being obsessive about what you do in a way that you can sustain over a lifetime. I made the comment that unexpected things will happen continually throughout life and you have to be flexible enough to react to them, especially when they are difficult, painful, or tragic in a nonwork dimension. I had to live with those words today and it was easy. So while I'll miss a bunch of friends at SXSW, I'll be spending those four days with the person who matters the most to me on this planet. And that feels good.

We were lucky; Amy's accident, while serious, healed quickly. After six months she was 95 percent back to normal. In contrast, our longtime friends Paul and Renée Berberian had a much more serious accident, and it profoundly changed the way they look at, and live, their life.

We were spending a month at our house in Alaska when Brad got an email from Paul's business partner, Todd Vernon, that said simply, "Paul and Renée had a major accident. They are in the hospital in critical condition. Call me." At the time, Brad was on the board of Paul and Todd's company, Raindance Communications, which was a public company. So, in addition to worrying about their friends, Brad and Todd also had responsibilities as a director and an officer of a public company. Brad remembers this time clearly, and Paul and Renée's story also deeply influenced how we live our lives. It follows.

My mom knows what death looks like. She has been caring for people her whole life as an ER, neonatal, and geriatric nurse on top of being by the bedsides of my father, my grandparents, her brother, and two of my aunts at the time of their passing. So when she showed up at my ICU bedside two days after my family was involved in a horrific head-on collision in Kauai, I knew things were bad.

My wife's injuries were severe, and she was airlifted to the top trauma hospital on Oahu—separating her from me and our daughter. Most of the family went to her bedside; my mom came to Kauai to be with our daughter, who thankfully was spared from major injury. When I saw her, the first thing I asked was, "How's Renée?" She looked at me like she never has in her life and said, "It's not good, Paul. She may not make it—I don't know. You must pray."

It was eight days before I was able to get to her bedside. My mom was with me the entire time. As I recovered, we talked and she updated me on Renée's progress. On the last day of my stay in the hospital my mom said something that has altered my life view. She said, "You'll heal. Renée, if she makes it, will have a long recovery, and she may not be the same. The mental stress of this trauma can destroy your marriage—you have to be there for Renée if you want your marriage to survive. The odds are not in your favor." Not really the pep talk I was looking for, especially in my pain. But I knew deep down she was right, and I resolved to recommit everything to our marriage and family.

Nine years later, we are doing fine physically, and we are still happily married. So what has changed—did I really "recommit"?

The most important change was internal: my idea of success and happiness changed. Before the accident, I aspired to run a bigger company, with more power, money, and responsibilities. After the accident, I resigned as CEO of a public company, put our house on the market, and set in motion a plan to take a year off and travel the world with my family once we all recovered (which we did in 2006). In the past, I wanted more things. Now I want fewer but higher-quality things. In the past, I dreaded vacation. Now I long for it. I simply want less.

Occasionally, I slip and my materialistic side kicks in pretty hard, but something else also kicks in—my memory of my mom talking to me. And also what an old Armenian priest once told me in broken English, "Marriage is not 50/50. It is 100/100—even when she is not 100, you must be because you will not be 100 all the time." It's the same message: I must make my marriage work single-handedly and trust that Renée will do the same.

At times I can get frustrated with something in our relationship and I imagine creating a big fight over it or pointing out flaws, but I generally have learned to pause and turn it around. I try to take my frustration and shower her with love—buy flowers when I'm pissed, super clean the house or run errands when she isn't as attentive to me, come home from work early when she's in a bad mood. And so far it works. It's not a trick—it's focusing energy on an issue. A fight or an argument is really a way to express feelings and resolve an issue. You can do that with acts of kindness as well, even when you don't feel the kindness reflected back.

This wasn't a conscious change of my behavior. Renée went through years of rehab and surgeries after our accident. Many days, weeks, and months she simply was not able to be her fun, outgoing self. She wasn't able to be a mom or a wife; sometimes her pain became anger or despair. She worked so hard to just be happy and present for us—a Herculean effort, especially with so many chronic injuries. How could I be mad or selfish? I tried to be selfish, but it didn't help. Only kindness and love can help lift her spirits and ultimately help our relationship.

So the accident made me see the beauty of our relationship and realize that the only thing that can keep us together is giving 100 percent as often as possible. And when I fail to give 100 percent—which is often, I know—she has my back and is there cranking away at 100 percent herself.

Renée Berberian

A horrific collision on Kauai has forever changed our family and the way we view life. This experience has influenced and changed us all, each the same and each differently. People who drink irresponsibly and or use drugs and drive really upset me. Lucky to be alive, the words "you can always make more money, but you can't make more time," an expression my late father-in-law coined, took special meaning and forever solidified in my brain.

Ten family members dropped everything, purchased one-way tickets to Hawaii and split forces between Kauai and Oahu, providing great comfort to Paul, our seven-year-old daughter, Marlo, and I on the different islands, where we were hospitalized.

We dealt with multiple surgeries, drug complications, potential loss of limb and life during extended OR time, ICU time, and orthopedic floor time, followed by occupational and physical therapy. Word reached locals and the mainland bringing an outpouring of love from strangers and friends alike, boosting our well-being with encouragement by way of cards, emails, phone calls, gifts, and flowers.

Once home, Paul and I, both wheelchair bound, were in extreme pain, on a radical medication schedule, and required physical therapy four hours a day, five days a week. Family and friends rallied with meals and service, shuttling Paul and me to doctors and physical therapy while additional drivers managed our daughter's schedule for school, piano lessons, play dates, and soccer.

I had truly felt that as a society, we'd become so busy, we had forgotten to check in, to care, to feel, and to empathize. It was humbling to know that I was wrong. People genuinely inspired me.

Healing physically took nearly three years from 2003 to 2006. Recovery was bittersweet as we endured the ups and downs of missing our daughter's life, enjoying a normal food diet, fear of being far from a hospital, suffering pain in short car transfers, eating in restaurants, hiking, outdoor sports and activities, and finding courage for additional surgeries. I especially missed travel and the moments of magic it brought to our family.

I was grateful for life but felt guilty because I was bitter regarding having to think about and acknowledge how I felt. I missed feeling good, and while it's productive to admit "everything isn't perfect," one must step away from that bitterness to gain hold or drown.

Embracing the new normal is absolutely necessary. The accident robbed us of so much, yet here we still are. Nine years later, we continue to heal, still deal with complications, and face additional surgeries. We have accepted this new normal, and on many days we do embrace it. For the most part, life feels conventional without feeling ordinary.

We attend events our daughter participates or performs in. We eat out, we travel, we enjoy a variety of foods, we hike and participate in outdoor activities, and our friends don't worry that we'll break like a fine porcelain doll.

The relationship I share with Paul is one of love, trust, and friendship. Neither of us is completely selfless. Perceived need, pain, and medication can cause an individual to become self-absorbed and selfish. Through our love, trust, and friendship, we are able to step back and accept. We are able to step back and forgive.

Paul and I celebrate 19 years of marriage this November and wouldn't trade our lives for any others. Paul has made me laugh since I met him; he's made me smile in spite of tremendous bouts of pain, and he continues to find the humor in the everyday. I love him.

We are all who we are, and while we can view things differently, many things remain the same. We get used to our new normal and cannot change the idiosyncrasies of our past.

I still want things done a certain way. I expect people to do their job to the best of their ability. I still want family vacations, even though our teenager wants to spend time with friends. I still primp for my husband and want him to think I'm pretty in spite of all the scars. I still have bad hair days, and I still, no matter how hard I try, want things to be as right as they can be.

Fortunately, 80 percent of my time is spent doing things I want to do. When faced with the 20 percent, I give my all. There are always going to be things that must be done, regardless of one's desire to do them. No matter what I'm doing, I give 100 percent. I've accepted my scars and fight my pain.

We don't know when someone is having a really bad day or when he or she has put on a smile just to make others feel more comfortable. People are really brave in times of insufferable pain, and it is often to bring joy to someone else.

I'm more grateful for Paul and the husband that he is. I recognize the love Paul shows me on a higher, more conscious level. I appreciate kindness more. I recognize kindness more often. I do stop to smell the roses. I give people a break. I give people the benefit of the doubt. I ask more questions. I forgive more. I am more open to ideas. I have more faith in mankind. I am more tolerant. I make an effort to understand a situation or what someone is trying to tell me. I am more sensitive to others who are in pain. I want less responsibility. I want less materialistically. I enjoy purging and freeing our lives of stuff.

Paul Berberian, Orbotix, *www.orbotix.com*
Renée Berberian, Zuzingo, @zuzingo

FAILURE—THE MINIMUM VIABLE RELATIONSHIP

Brad's first marriage ended in a divorce. He married his high school girlfriend and their marriage lasted three years. It was a tumultuous one, not because either of them was a particular emotional person, but because they were young and didn't really understand the dynamics and priorities of their relationship.

Brad was working 100 hours a week on his first company while working toward a PhD at MIT. He traveled a lot, but even when he was home his mind was often at work. His first wife worked a 40-hour-a-week job, and the disparity between entrepreneur and entrepreneurial spouse was profound. While Brad didn't consciously realize he was neglecting his relationship, his ex-wife felt it every day. At some point, the relationship simply failed.

Keith Smith is the founder and CEO of BigDoor, a young startup in Seattle. Keith is divorced with children and recently broke up with a girlfriend of several years. Following is Keith's story of how he struggles to think about and understand how to be an effective partner in a relationship.

I fell in love for the first time when I was seven years old. Every Thursday my parents would host a Rook game night, and I would place myself there at the table, quietly watching and observing. My folks thought I liked cards, but I was there for the stories. Our family's closest friends ran a startup, and as the night progressed, they would invariably start recounting their stories from the trenches of the startup world. You wouldn't think a seven-year-old would be much interested in business, but to me their stories were thrilling and exciting. It was around that table that the dream of being an entrepreneur became my first love and my enduring passion.

Fast-forward three decades and I'm currently deeply in love with my fourth startup, and also winding down my latest failed romantic relationship. My startup is the now three-year-old BigDoor, and we've developed a platform that creates user loyalty in the digital world. My latest relationship lasted five years, and we just parted ways because we never figured out how to make loyalty work in the real world. Ironic, but not entirely surprising given that nothing in the life of most entrepreneurs seems to be able to compete with the all-consuming passion we have for our work.

As with any failure, the early and unexpected shutdown of my relationship is forcing me into my *build, measure, learn* iteration loop. Like any self-respecting entrepreneur, I've done a root cause analysis (RCA) in an attempt to discover some validated learnings about myself to ensure that my next loop through the cycle goes better. The remnants of moving boxes and packing tape are still littered throughout my house, so this breakup is still extremely raw for me. I'm quite sure I'll be processing it for a while, but it probably doesn't take a licensed psychologist to figure out a few of the obvious things.

For starters, anyone who uses words like *love* and *passion* to describe their work, and words like *validated learnings* and *iteration loop* to describe their relationship, may have a difficult time developing a successful romantic relationship with a real person. Therein lies much of the challenge for those in a relationship with an all-consumed entrepreneur: we often possess a warped set of priorities. I wanted this relationship to work almost as much as I've wanted anything in this world. In other words, just a little bit less than how much I want BigDoor to work. This wasn't just a subconscious prioritization, driven by night after late night of urgent work. This prioritization was a conscious choice, discussed and recognized by both of us. How many women do you know that would be excited about the deep romance inspired by a conversation like that?

Adding to the challenge is the fact that many of the skills that entrepreneurs develop to help us survive and ultimately succeed in a startup are in direct opposition to the skills we need to build a long, happy, and stable relationship. Embrace risk. Fail fast. Move even faster. Solve problems quickly, and without waiting for every fact to reveal itself. Multitask well. Shape the world around you to match *your* vision. These are things that will generally serve you well in a startup. But I've come to discover that most girlfriends don't appreciate having their relationships run on weekly sprints and being held accountable to innovation metrics.

One day last week I started my morning absolutely euphoric: we'd just landed a big new client. Later that same day we lost a different client, introduced a bug into our production code, and then had a server outage. I left the office around midnight feeling like I had just been run over by a bus. That was not an unusual day. Life in a startup almost always comes with an emotional roller coaster. I've worked hard to develop a set of skills that help me deal with those ups and downs, and those skills often present themselves to the outside world as a thick skin. Given that these skills are required for my company's very survival, I find it difficult to turn them off. The result is that my loved ones are often left scratching their heads as to why I seem intent on dissecting, understanding, controlling, and fixing everything around me, and why I often seem emotionally impenetrable by outside forces.

So my failed relationship RCA tells me I've got screwed-up priorities, a well-developed set of exactly the wrong skills, and I come off as being emotionally unavailable. An emotional pivot is required, so I'll work on improving in each of those areas. But the reality is that I'll likely continue to spend more time and energy on building and iterating within my startup. So maybe I just need to find someone who can appreciate the minimum viable relationship that I can provide.

Keith Smith, BigDoor, *www.bigdoor.com*

BEFORE YOU GET MARRIED

Brad and his first wife got married shortly after they graduated from college. Neither of them brought significant financial assets into the relationship and, as most young married couples, expected "to have and to hold, from this day forward, for better, for worse, for richer, for poorer, in sickness or in health, to love and to cherish till death do us part."

Your partnership may begin before either of you have any assets to fight about. However, like numerous friends of ours whose relationships haven't survived the stresses of the entrepreneurial life, when there are meaningful assets involved, there is an entirely new set of conflicts when a relationship fails.

But it isn't as simple as agreeing to and negotiating a prenuptial agreement. The first conversation around a prenuptial agreement is often an important one about whether this agreement dooms you to failure or indicates a lack of trust before you formalize your relationship. Furthermore, given that money is often at the core of a prenuptial agreement, the hot topic of your own attitudes toward money, and how this plays into your relationship, gets tangled up at the beginning of the discussion.

It's hard to balance the optimism and warmth of a young relationship that is about to embark on the formalization of marriage while at the same time categorizing who owns what and how things are titled in the downside case of the marriage failing. Power and control are often a central part of this discussion, which is made even more awkward when the entrepreneur in the couple switches into negotiation mode, even if she doesn't realize it.

We don't have a prenuptial agreement. Brad is quick to say that if our relationship ever fails, Amy gets everything and he'll start over from scratch. While this isn't balanced, the mere fact that we can have a serious conversation about this helps diffuse the tension around it. We've decided to trust each other completely and take the chance that if things don't work out for some reason, we'll figure it out.

DIVORCE

Occasionally, a marriage will reach a point where you hit bottom and there is no recovery. While this is never easy, it is part of life. It's made more complex in an entrepreneurial relationship, especially if the couple entered the marriage with nothing but now has substantial assets that were created during the marriage. Any failed marriage with children has ensuing custody and child support issues, which again can be made more complex by the unpredictability of an entrepreneur's income.

If you legally formalize your relationship, undoing your relationship also becomes a legal matter. At the moment that a relationship is failing, it's often easier to be in denial about it and throw all of your energy into your company. As Brad discovered, this just makes things worse, as the ultimately day of reckoning will come and, if you avoid it, you are simply delaying the inevitable. While unromantic, this is no different than avoiding dealing with serious challenges in your business—that passage of time with inaction often simply makes the ultimate outcome that much more painful.

A close friend of ours, Jenny Lawton, bravely shares her struggle of a failed marriage that unfolded over a long period of time. As you'll see from her story, she didn't simply deal with the failure of her marriage, but instead has to deal with how it impacted her business and her own sense of self as she worked through it.

The ups and downs, highs and lows, of an entrepreneurial business taught me a lot about believing in myself, learning how to adapt, and trusting that everything would ultimately work out in the end. In all my years in my entrepreneurial endeavors— high tech, bookstore, and coffee shop—I never lost sight of the impact that I had on other people's lives. I literally held the financial future of my employees in my hands. As a result, I realized that there was no easy way out when the going got tough and that the only way out was through whatever was in front of me.

There are a lot of things in life that have taught me the benefit of resilience and tenacity. There have been those days where all that I could see in front of, above, and beyond me was black skies, bleak outlooks, and options with no upsides. By sticking it out, pushing through, thinking outside the box, and knowing that quitting was just not an option, I found that the black days didn't last long and the ensuing results were often different and interesting but not bleak and bad. There were a lot of concepts and takeaways that I relied on, and still rely on, to push through. Some of my favorites are keeping within my zone of control. When things start to spin wildly or results aren't what I am expecting, I've found that taking a few minutes to center myself, draw a circle around my two feet, and staying within that zone will keep me present and in the moment versus focused on coulda, shoulda, woulda–type thinking.

I'm a big believer in the Newtonian concept that there is an equal and opposite reaction to every action, so I try to rely on this concept to both keep me grounded when things are really great and energize me when things are not so great. So when I was in the midst of a divorce, unable to touch any funds or take out loans or change any control in my bookstore and coffee shop, I just pinched myself every day and reminded myself that I was healthy, alive, and doing something that I loved. In the deepest, darkest days of my bookstore's succumbing to the world of online discounted books and big-box competition, I chose lessons to learn from the situation that I was in. With payables out of control and revenue nowhere near what

I needed it to be, I learned how to communicate and work with vendors. Books are returnable at nearly what you bought them for, so I learned how to manage inventory. Customers were key to my business and their loyalty was critical, so I learned how to make sure that they were always delighted with their experiences.

Just the concept of why my marriage fell apart—and how many times it fell apart before it finally ended—is a great study in entrepreneurial living. Entrepreneurs can be a tough bunch. We are passionately engaged with the life of the company that we founded and are growing and taking places. And this passion and energy and love can be misunderstood and compete with the other parts of life. With my first business, my company grew so fast that it simply required more and more of my time. I needed to network, be engaged in the greater business world, learn and grow from other entrepreneurs, engage with my customers, travel to all of our locations, and keep current with the business world.

My husband ended up staying at home with the kids because his salary was only paying for child care and it was a lot easier to have someone home full time. Only I didn't count on the cost of the resentment, the anger, and the jealousy—the inability for him to see that all the time and love and commitment that I put into the company so that it would succeed was benefiting all of us. It paid for the multiple computers, the great vacation houses, the housekeeper, the lawn person, the groceries from Whole Foods, the cars, and the private school for our kids. It kept us warm and safe and fed. It gave my children an opportunity to see that you can have a dream and make it happen. That you can make a difference in the world and that you can follow your passions. Unfortunately, my partner spent as much energy working against me as for me, so that anger and resentment, doubt, and frustration were overlaid on the intensity of running a high-tech, entrepreneurial company.

I think the first rule of being in a relationship as an entrepreneur is making sure that the business really isn't allowed to become an affair. It isn't an affair. It is what feeds the heart and head of the entrepreneur and what makes them a full person. I never missed my kids' events; I took them on fantastic vacations and was able to spend long vacation hours with them. I wasn't there every morning, and I wasn't always home for dinner, but they were loved and cared for. They could call me whenever they wanted without question, and they loved to visit and engage and feel a part of my entrepreneurial world. As soon as the company becomes "the other person," it's all over.

An interesting lesson that I've learned along the way is that a business is truly like a child—once they are born, they don't shut down or go away. Once you open a business, it has a life. It ebbs and flows, has growth spurts and temper tantrums, and there is just simply no option like walking out the door. I think that I came to this conclusion partly as a result of a very startling awareness I had a few weeks after I had my first child. I remember being at home with him and realizing that I couldn't just walk out the door and do something without him. I couldn't just take a walk; couldn't go on a drive; heck, I couldn't just lie down and take a nap. I had a baby and that baby was fully dependent on me for everything. It was a very big aha moment.

When I decided to buy my bookstore, it was a big move—really big move. I was going from having worked in the high-tech world, having successfully sold my company and ridden the public company wave way, way up and then way, way, way (way) down. I was working as an entrepreneur in residence with Mobius Venture Capital and totally loving my life. I had insanely smart and creative and interesting people to work and interact with, and there were cool opportunities in front of me to do "the next thing." If only it were so simple . . . I was also married, with two young children and a stay-at-home husband, and had just moved from Massachusetts to Greenwich, Connecticut, to be closer to the headquarters of Interliant, the company that had acquired mine and that I had been working for.

Once I had moved on from Interliant, I went to my husband and announced that it was now time to move to Boulder to work with Brad and find the "right next thing." He said, "You can go, but the boys and I will be staying here." There was a lot of teeth gnashing and stomping about it, but he was resolute—moving again was not an option for this family. Did it matter that I was the breadwinner and had made it so that we could comfortably live in Greenwich? That my ability to continue to support us was based on working within my networks? That staying in Greenwich, cut off from my networks and mentors and connections, was going to impact all of us? That I'd have to start all over again and re-create myself? Or that, maybe, my husband should start working instead of staying home?

Cut to the present—I mean it's a whole book of what went right and wrong and a very jagged path full of switchbacks and crevices and ravines that I am still trying to navigate and climb fully out of. Anyway, cut to the present. I didn't move to Boulder—my kids meant too much to me. My husband refused to work again because his stay-at-home status was payback for all the long, hard hours I had put into working to support our family in whatever unbalanced way I accomplished that success. And, so, to keep the peace and keep my sanity, I bought a bookstore. And I remember, very clearly, asking for advice from Brad on whether it was a wise move. He said, "You can always just close it down and reenter the technology world if it doesn't work out."

Brad was ultimately right. Because I ended up, after 10 years, successfully doing both of those things. But shutting down my bookstore and reentering the workforce after having run a vibrant, crazy, wonderful retail store for

10 years was quite possibly one of the hardest things I've done. Shutting down a business that the entire town is in love with, pays the salaries of a handful of people, has taught countless kids the love of books, and brought a lot of fun into my life was hard. Even as it was losing me money, fantastically underwater, and painfully failing.

Jenny Lawton, MakerBot, *www.makerbot.com*

CHAPTER TEN

MONEY

M oney is one of the greatest sources of conflict and marital discord in any relationship, but it can be especially difficult in a relationship with an entrepreneur. You come from different backgrounds, you enter the relationship with different amounts of money, your families have different financial situations, and you have different values about what the money is for. This changes over time, as at any point in time you may have too much, or too little, and during a startup company's lifetime, it can change rapidly and dramatically. You may have very different tolerances for risk in your personal finances, independent of the potential turmoil of your startup's finances.

DEVELOPING A SHARED FRAME OF REFERENCE

When we first started living together, Feld Technologies (Brad's first business) was a healthy, growing company. Both of us worked together at Feld Technologies and at the time we got together as a couple, Brad's total compensation (salary and share of profits) was about $300,000 per year while Amy's was $30,000.

Prior to moving in together, we each had a frame of reference. Amy was living in a small apartment, sent money to her mom each month, and saved whatever she could. Brad had a housekeeper, went out to nice dinners regularly, and while he never spent anywhere close to what he made, he always had plenty of extra money, which he saved.

After moving in together, Amy suggested that we create a weekly chore schedule for cleaning the apartment. We'd alternate weeks, have a checklist, and hold the other person responsible. Brad responded that while that was a nice idea, he was going to have a person named Linda (his current house-keeper) handle his weeks, and he'd be totally comfortable if Amy wanted Linda to handle her weeks also.

Amy also suggested that they share "going out expenses" 50/50. Brad countered that they should share them proportionally based on their income (which was about 90/10), with Amy paying occasionally when she felt like it. Over time, we dropped this as we merged our finances.

Developing a shared frame of reference was difficult for us. We were each proud of contributing to the economics of our shared life together. Since the relationship was new, it was also a way for us each to maintain some semblance of control. And it was often the source of tension, as we struggled to figure out how to make joint decisions around money.

WHAT'S THE MONEY FOR?

Early on, we had a number of philosophical conversations about what the money was for. We were each in our mid-20s and were still figuring out what mattered to us. Amy grew up without much money, although her parents were very generous in investing virtually all the money they had in education and experiences for Amy and her sisters. Brad grew up in a family with more money, but it was all self-made as his father was a doctor and his mother was an artist. We had some context from our childhood, but quickly ended up in a situation where we had to figure it out for ourselves since the amount of money we had quickly accelerated with Brad's success as an entrepreneur.

The question of what the money is for is fundamental to establishing your value systems around money. Money can buy you many things, both tangible (cars, houses, trips, shoes) and intangible (security, freedom, autonomy, choice), and at its core is a fuel you use to fund your experience on this planet.

Recognize that in most relationships you are combining two different backgrounds around money. However, these different backgrounds don't have to result in different value systems. Instead, put effort into defining a shared value system. One great example for us has to do with one of our shared loves: collecting contemporary art.

We both loved art but were nervous early on about buying it. On a beautiful Saturday wandering around galleries in Boston, we ran across a piece of art that we loved. It was from an artist named Gerry Bergstein and immediately captured each of us. But it was $5,000—more than we had ever paid for a piece of art up to that point. We agonized as we walked around the block and decided not to buy it. We talked about it more over dinner—was a $5,000 art purchase outside of our value system? We thought we could afford it; we were spending $5,000 on vacations at this time, but we just weren't able to pull the trigger. But the result of our conversation was that we decided we would collect art, at a level we could afford, but it would be a shared experience for us that we would use some of our money for.

Several years later we were actively collecting art from a number of artists we loved. A $5,000 purchase was still meaningful, but we made a few of them a year. We were at the Massachusetts Institute of Contemporary Art one Saturday as we wandered around Back Bay together and saw a Gerry Bergstein installation. We flashed back to that day a few years earlier when we passed up buying one of Gerry's pieces. We realized how much progress we had made in developing a shared frame of reference for what the money is for. We decided to find Gerry (which we did) and buy some of his art. Today, we count his art as some of the most important art we collected early on in our relationship, and every piece brings back fantastic memories for us while reinforcing our value system of what the money is for.

EARLY ON: NOT HAVING ENOUGH

At the beginning of your entrepreneurial journey, it's likely that you will be in the position of not having enough money. Whether you are young and have no savings, or are older and are now draining your savings on a monthly basis as you fund either your company or your existing expenses while not drawing a salary, you will feel pressure from not having enough.

Once again, communication is a powerful tool that should be at the forefront. As a couple, talk openly about both the situation and the pressure you are feeling. Make sure as a couple you know where you stand, how much money you actually have, what your monthly burn rate is, and how long you can go before you are out of money. Ambiguity around this when one partner thinks one thing and the other has a different perspective is the worst situation to be in.

If you start from an open perspective, the stress of not having enough doesn't end up on one partner's shoulders. While one of you may handle the day-to-day money stuff, each of you is taking responsibility for how much money you have and are spending, and the decisions you are making around it. Develop good habits around it. There are thousands of books around managing your finances that say essentially two things: (1) have a budget and spend at or below it, and (2) know what your personal balance sheet looks like.

Agree early on how you will work with money. Do you have separate accounts and budgets, or do you pool everything? We think it's a good idea at least initially to have joint accounts for household expenses and savings that you both contribute to on an agreed-upon basis whether it's the same percentage of income or same dollar amount, as well as having separate accounts that you control so that each of you has control over your own discretionary spending. And you can use your own accounts for gifts and nice surprises for your partner! Figuring out comfortable budget limits can take some time, but it's worth having those conversations about how much you can afford, or want to spend, on housing, dinner and a movie, and shoes. As we discovered, pooling everything is hard to figure out early on in a relationship, but once you get to that point all of the discussion and pressure shifts dramatically, as you are now in a joint relationship.

Most important, try to feel wealthy now. Even though you may not be financially secure, you are pursuing your dream to create your own business. As a couple, you can both go all in on this dream and participate in your own individual ways. While you may not feel like you have much discretionary money, if you have clean drinking water, a functional electric grid, and your health, you are wealthier than many other people on this planet. Try not to lose perspective on this as you feel the daily financial pressures of your startup.

HAVING ENOUGH TO BE COMFORTABLE

Your new company is having some success. You are paying yourself a decent salary. Money, while modest, is coming in a little more than it is going out. The need for a financial austerity program has diminished.

Our culture has this schism between puritanical all-work and consumerism all-play values. The entrepreneur in the couple has likely been spending most of her time in the all-work category. Between the pressures of the startup and then managing the overhead of life, there's been no time, or money, to do anything other than work. And work. And work.

It's difficult to make the shift from the early stage of the startup, where there aren't any additional financial resources, to the middle stage, where suddenly there are some. Rather than stay in the puritanical all-work mode, it's healthy for you as a couple (and each of you individually) to dip your toes into the play pool. While the cliché "all work and no play makes Jack a dull boy" applies, buying things you don't need with money you don't have is a consistently bad idea, as many people found out in 2008 during the mortgage debt crisis. There is an important balance here.

It won't surprise you that once again communication is the most important tactic here. More and more research shows that people derive happiness from experiences rather than things, after a certain standard of material wealth. While you may still be early on this curve, check with your partner and make sure you are in the same place. It might surprise you that a new car is not on the list but a weeklong vacation off the grid, just with each other, is.

THE FIRST BIG EXIT

The magic day has come—you've closed on the sale of your company. After all the pressure of the previous years, and the intense pressure of the past six months as you went through the sale process, you are done. You check your bank account and there is more money there than you ever imagined. You have dreamed about this, but now it's real.

We recommend you do two things. First, take 90 days off from making any significant decisions about the money. People will come out of the woodwork to help you—financial advisers, friends, family, and other successful entrepreneurs who have already been through a big exit of their own. The advice will come fast and furiously, and you will feel pressure to figure out where to put the money, how to invest it, and whom to hire to help you.

Don't succumb to this pressure. Some people will be well intentioned, with a goal of helping you; others will be in it for themselves. Financial advisers view you as a newly minted mark that they might be able to land as a client; family members will view you as deep pockets that can help bail them out of their own financial challenges. By taking a deliberate break from making a decision, you can collect data dispassionately, seeing what the landscape looks like, and letting the dust settle before you start making commitments.

Our friends Tim Enwall and Hillary Hall echo this notion of taking a deliberate break from making a decision. Tim and Hillary have been a startup family for 15 years, since 1997, when they started their first startup, Solista, that grew from one person (Tim) to 50 over two and a half years and ultimately was successfully sold to Gartner in 2000. In 2004, they started their second—Tendril—which is going strong today. In between, they spun off a startup, Intellocity, and invested in about 10 others.

Here is Tim and Hillary's story of what they did after the sale of Tim's first company.

Fortunately, our belief in our startup carried with it a successful financial liquidation event that was sizeable but not so large we could retire for life and do whatever we wanted (not that we'd stop working anyway because we're both hardworking types). Money was never an object for us; the object was always to provide a fantastic benefit to society and, in so doing, that benefit would be rewarded by having highly satisfied customers who were willing to pay for that benefit. For most of the successful entrepreneurs we have known over the past decade, money has never been an object—it's only a scorecard. When we did receive that sizeable check, we were first tempted to spend it on many things. Once we caught our breath, though, we made one of the best money decisions we've ever made: we decided to wait for at least six months before spending anything more than a few thousand dollars. That gave us the time and space to figure out what was really important to us and what kind of portfolio we wanted to build.

Tim Enwall, Mobiplug, *www.mobiplug.co*
Hillary Hall, Boulder County Clerk and Recorder, @HillHall

We aren't suggesting that you leave the money in a checking account. But focus on two things: (1) capital preservation and (2) lack of commitment. Find a simple, low-yield place to park the money, spread it between several different institutions that are highly secure, and chill out as you let a little time pass. Don't worry that you are only getting 1 percent return on your money for these 90 days; it's better than finding yourself tangled up in a set of relationships you don't want, or with investments in financial instruments you don't understand.

Our other recommendation is to set aside 10 percent of your windfall, after taxes, to spend on a splurge. If you just sold your company and made $1 million after taxes, you could buy a new car. If you made $10 million after taxes, you can buy a new house. If you made $50 million, you can buy a really big house. Or, if you like art, you can buy a piece of art that is 10 times anything you've ever bought before. Or spend a week at the nicest room in the Four Seasons in your favorite city. Or fly first class to Paris together, stay in a hotel you've only dreamed of staying in, and eat out every night.

The splurge doesn't have to be tangible, nor does it have to be on only one thing. You've worked incredibly hard to get to this point; figure out shared things and experiences that will be special to you. While they don't have to be tangible, the memories can be long lasting. But do it in the first 90 days. Don't wait—it's a significant moment in the transition you are having as an entrepreneurial couple from "not enough money" to "enough money."

SLEEP-AT-NIGHT MONEY

With your first big exit, you can start having the conversation about "what is enough." We categorize this two ways: "sleep-at-night money" and "fuck you money."

Sleep-at-night money is the amount you should have in liquid instruments immediately available to you. At different points in your life, you can define this based on a variety of different factors, but ultimately it's a subjective judgment about how much you need to live unencumbered for a period of time.

After the sale of Feld Technologies, we thought hard about calling it quits and moving to Homer, Alaska, where Amy grew up. We realized that we could easily live in Homer for 25 years with the money we made from the sale of the company, even if we didn't make a dime of new income. We were each closing in on 30 at the time, so this felt like a long time.

That realization helped us define the amount of money that we needed for our sleep-at-night money. We also realized that neither of us were "done" and had no real desire to simply check out. But by defining this amount, we were clear about what we were willing to risk going forward.

We also realized that if we were to check out, we had our fuck you money. We felt free to check out, even though we didn't want to. This impacted our decision making going forward. Once we decided not to check out, we then had a conversation about what our real fuck you money number was. It turned out to be a lot higher than our sleep-at-night money number.

We weren't ready to have this conversation until after Brad's first exit. But once we had some money, it became valuable for us to clearly define these numbers. We exceeded the fuck you money number a long time ago, and it was liberating, but it didn't keep escalating as we had more success. Once we had passed it, we could shift our thinking toward using any incremental money that we made as a tool for what we wanted to do in life, rather than a measure of our success.

THE DISORIENTATION OF HAVING TOO MUCH

It sounds absurd that someone might have a struggle with having too much money. However, this often happens when an entrepreneur has an extraordinary success.

Brad has been through many highs and lows in his entrepreneurial career. As both an entrepreneur and investor, he's had many things work and many things fail. As a couple, we've been together through the entire arc of the experience.

When things fail, there is always a period of sadness that often corresponds with deep relief that the experience is over. However, whenever things succeed, there often is a similar period of sadness or even depression. We've come to call this the entrepreneur's equivalent of postpartum depression.

As an entrepreneurial couple, you expect some magical thing to happen the day after the big deal closes. A magical thing does happen: the sun comes up exactly like it did the day before. The world continues on, ignorant of your most recent victory. As you walk down the street, almost everything is the same. Your bank account may be flush, but you are still living your life.

This can be incredibly disorienting. The sale of Feld Technologies closed on a Friday. We had a wonderful weekend celebrating, which mostly consisted of sleeping late, wandering around Boston, and having a nice dinner Saturday night. And then Brad got up at 5:00 A.M. on Monday morning and went to work. Wait, what? It was Monday—that's what he did on Mondays. By the middle of the week we were in crisis. The 14-hour days were continuing, the pressure was unchanging, and nothing was really any different, except we had a bunch of money instead of our previously illiquid equity in Feld Technologies.

When one of the angel investments Brad made several years later went public and was worth on paper more money than we had at the time, it was once again disorienting. We had reinvested much of the money we'd made from the sale of Feld Technologies in new startups. Brad was a very prolific angel investor and had helped start a number of companies. We had our sleep-at-night money, but we no longer had our fuck you money, and this was the windfall that gave us our fuck you money again.

While we couldn't sell a share for six months since we had to wait for the initial public offering (IPO) lockup to come off, this was a time period of rapidly escalating public stock values. The number grew, along with several other exits, and we started having a different conversation about what to do with it. By now we were firmly ensconced in a house in Boulder. One night, while sitting under the stars in our hot tub, Brad brought up the idea of buying a plane. Amy's immediate response was, "What are you talking about? I want you to travel less, not more." The idea of a plane was quickly dismissed, but the irony of the disorientation around the money was not lost on either of us.

A decade later we were deep in the process of building a gigantic dream house to replace the house we had been living in. It was the summer of 2008 and we were at our house in Homer for the month of July. Every day, Brad got up and worked on his first book, *Do More Faster*. Amy got up and worked on the endless tasks associated with the design of the new house. When we returned to Boulder in August, we were completely stressed out by the house. The book was done, but now each of us was feeling immense pressure from the daily decisions around the house. And we hadn't even started. After a sleepless night, we decided to pull the plug. One month later, the global financial crisis began. While we could have afforded the house, the level of macro uncertainty would have created pressure that neither of us wants to contemplate. We dodged a bullet.

Money is a tool. Don't ever let having it distort your view of what a meaningful life is. Use it as a tool. Don't be disoriented by it.

REACTIONS FROM YOUR FAMILY

Your new wealth can be confusing to your family, especially if you are the first person in your family to become wealthy. It's often a huge source of tension between partners, especially if one of your families has more significant financial means than the other as you try to figure out how to respond to requests and use your money as a tool for helping your family.

There is no right answer. We've figured out an approach that works for us and has allowed us to be generous and supportive of many family members without feeling tension between us because of the specific allocations. We've also come to terms with the difference between a loan and a gift and at this stage in our lives almost never give loans, except in business situations, as we don't want the baggage associated with it. Instead, we delight in writing a check to a family member as an occasional gift, without expectation of anything other than a thank you.

For the past 15 years, we've often gone on an annual vacation with Warren and Ilana Katz. We met Warren and Ilana early in their relationship, when Ilana became the seventh employee at Feld Technologies. At the time Amy was working at Feld Technologies and, soon after Ilana joined the company, Warren started his company, MaK Technologies. We each became close friends, have experienced the past 20 years of our respective entrepreneurial and life arcs together, and have learned much from each other.

Warren sold his company five years ago, and suddenly Ilana and Warren found themselves in the position of being newly wealthy. Ilana talks about this eloquently, along with how she has come to terms with this in the context of her family.

"People are funny about money" is an old adage that often rings true, especially when one family member's net worth escalates. I speak from experience.

Our financial success triggered a bombardment of financial demands from my family. You name it, they asked for it: private school tuition, bailouts of foreclosed properties, health insurance money, and fancy parties are a few examples. I was browbeaten with thick ladles of guilt and informed about my responsibility for bailing a family member out of deep IRS debt.

When I didn't succumb to pressure, I was called "chintzy and cheap" and solipsistic, among other things. One family member said I was "dead" to them when I rebuffed a financial solicitation. I was hurt, devastated, and confused. As the youngest of four children, I hated that they tried to use me as a financial net. I always lived within my means, even when I didn't earn a lot of money. Why couldn't they do the same? On top of that, I saw myself and my husband as generous, always picking up the tab for dinners, and buying thoughtful gifts at appropriate times.

The only thing that seemed to matter was that I didn't give in to their requests for money. While I didn't regret my decisions, I felt guilty and resentful each time they held their hands out for us to pay.

One day, after receiving yet *another* request, I couldn't take it anymore. I sent a succinct note to my entire family officially declaring "I am a daughter and a sister, not a bank." It didn't entirely arrest the funding inquiries, but setting a clear, necessary boundary helped clarify my stance while also relieving pent-up frustration.

Sadly, it took me 20 years to write that note! During that time, I pondered why people are funny about money. This list isn't exhaustive, by any means, but it encompasses a lot of my experience.

Jealousy: Why can't I have that, too? I deserve it! I want it! Jealousy doesn't serve any of us well, but like all emotions, we can't always control our feelings.

Entitlement: Hard work entitles a person to a desired level of financial success. Nobody is entitled to anything in this world. Sometimes you work hard and are financially rewarded. Sometimes you get other rewards and accolades from hard work such as recognition for discoveries or talents. Sometimes you just keep trying and trying and reap no rewards beyond life lessons that you may or may not see. Life isn't always fair.

Misperception: Once you are rich you will always be rich, there is plenty of money, and no money worries. Easy come, easy go. If you make a lot of money, you could just as easily lose it if you aren't mindful of how you spend and manage it. We see news stories all the time of people losing their fortunes. Curt Schilling is a recent example.

Differing value systems: You should always write a check to someone else for a good reason. People can't fathom that a good reason for *them* might not be categorized as a good reason for you.

Wealth implies responsibility: If you have more money than someone else, you should take care of other people's desires and perceived needs. People make choices and need to be responsible for the consequences and rewards those choices may bring. Someone is not always going to be there to bail you out.

With regard to dealing with financial appeals from family members, my lessons learned include:

People are likely to criticize when you don't give in to their financial demands. Don't be surprised. Stay true to your beliefs. Faltering from your ideals by falling prey to pushiness will make you feel resentful and uncomfortable.

Finances are a private matter. As long as you and your partner are in sync with spending, that is most important. You don't have to explain or share this information or your reasoning with anyone.

Don't throw good money after bad. If you find yourself shelling out money to save someone time and again, chances are a deeper problem exists. I'm not saying money can't help certain situations, but writing emotional checks will wear on you. Be honest with yourself about the reality of giving, lending, or helping someone with money. Remember that it's always okay to step away from an emotional situation, even for an hour, to be alone so you are not in someone else's pressure cooker. Sound decisions aren't made under pressure.

Ilana Katz, Novelist and Boston Subway Fiddler, *www.ilanakatz.com*
Warren Katz, Mak Technologies, *www.mak.com*

INVESTING

Once you've had an exit and have some money you will find yourselves with a lot of new friends. You will meet every private banker who works with "high-net-worth individuals." You will be invited to events to talk about the macro economy from people you've never heard of. You will be on email lists about wealth management. You will be invited to invest in an endless number of random funds, by friends, friends of friends, and relatives of friends. And all of your entrepreneurial friends will start referring new entrepreneurs to you who are raising a seed round for their company.

While some people find this exciting, much of it is mind numbing, oppressive, and time wasting. After the exit of Brad's first company, we explored each of the different things we were confronted with. While this was in the 1990s and there was more friction around both the communication and the discovery of us as a couple with some fresh bucks, we still encountered numerous dead ends, charlatans, and time wasters who were just trying to peddle whatever they were selling, without any real concern for the financial return.

At first, we didn't have a strategy for what to do with our money. We heard about asset allocation strategies, read a few books about managing our money, and talked to a few people who had a lot more money than we did. We quickly discovered that there was no magic answer and that many of the perspectives were conflicting. As a result, we came up with a deliberate strategy that we've used for the past 20 years.

Safe money. We have put away a certain amount of safe money where we have no concern about the capital appreciation of this money. Instead, we are 100 percent focused on capital preservation and liquidity. This is money that we can have access to immediately. We keep it in a combination of U.S. Treasury bills and AAA-rated bonds and make sure there are no "yield-improving features," such as auction-rate securities, which blew up unexpectedly in 2008. This amount of safe money grew as we got older and is now a stable amount as we've reached the sleep-at-night comfort limit.

Public company investments. We decided many years ago not to spend time trading public equity or debt. The only public equities we directly own are ones from companies we have been involved in that went public, or ones we received as a distribution from a venture capital fund we are investors in. We have a very clear strategy for liquidating these public holdings over time. We do determine a specific strategy when we end up with meaningful amounts of public company stock on a company-by-company basis, but once we decide what our strategy is, we stick with it. And we generally liquidate our position within a year.

Private company investments. We have a large number of private company investments, through Brad's venture capital firm, our angel investments, and the venture capital funds we have invested in over the years. We view these investments as a core part of Brad's work, and while we are very conscious of the amount of our net worth that is tied up in these private investments, we never count them as liquid until we can use the money to buy beer or shoes.

Real estate. We own several houses and significant land with a long-term hold strategy. Every time we've bought a new piece of real estate, we expect that we will hold on to it until we die. As a result, we've bought real estate as part of our life, not as a core investment strategy. Since we plan to hold the real estate forever, it is a good asset for us to borrow against to generate short-term cash, and we have been comfortable using this real estate as collateral for financing our own cash flow. The real estate is the only asset we have that we are comfortable borrowing against.

Managers. We are very careful choosing managers for our money. We have several managers we trust with different assets. One is responsible for our safe money, one is responsible for equity and retirement funds, one is responsible for public company investments, and our family office coordinates and reports on all of the managers. We do have many individual investments in different venture capital funds, and a few private equity, real estate, and hedge funds, and we interact with these managers directly.

Cash flow. We live within our means. We enjoy life and spend plenty of money, but we are very clear about what our limit is. We pay attention to our cash flow with the goal of steadily increasing our liquid net worth on an annual basis. In order to do this, you need to know how much money you actually have and where it is located. Our family office tracks all of our financial data, and we receive consolidated net worth statements on a monthly basis. Both partners need to understand what your actual financial situation is on a regular basis.

Filters. We have developed a crisp set of filters about how we engage with anyone who approaches us about investing. In general, we have no interest in exploring anything other than investments in private companies unless either (a) it's someone we already know and trust, or (b) we explicitly discover something we are interested in.

While there are lots of nuances in our strategy, this is our broad approach. We aren't pretending to be your financial advisers, but we wanted to give a clear example of how we think about it after working at it for over 20 years. Our fundamental belief is that you should have a strategy; talk specifically about it with each other on a periodic basis (at least once a year); have a clear set of ground rules for how to engage on a daily, weekly, and monthly basis; and revisit your strategy, especially when something happens that surprises you either on the upside or the downside.

ANGEL INVESTING

After Brad sold Feld Technologies in 1993, we decided we would take much of the money we had and reinvest it as angel investors. Brad started a company called Intensity Ventures and between 1994 and 1996 made about 40 investments in early-stage startups. Brad helped co-found some of these companies, was a board member for others, and was simply an investor in the balance of them. Today, the idea of a successful entrepreneur's becoming an angel investor, often known as a super-angel, is widespread; in the mid-1990s it happened, but it wasn't very common and we didn't have a road map for it.

Fortunately, Brad's angel-investing career was very successful. He had a clear strategy, which included investing either $25,000 or $50,000 in each company. While Brad had plenty of zeros, he had two investments that returned over 100 times his investment. After making another 30 or so angel investments in 2007, Brad started seeing many more angel investors emerge as the super-angel dynamic became visible. He codified his strategy in a blog post in 2010. Following is a summary of the strategy.

Be promiscuous. To be a successful angel investor, you have to make a lot of investments. Brad generally made about one investment a month when he was active as an angel. While this pace may not be right for everyone, if you are doing less than four investments a year, we don't think you are making enough. Play the field—it increases your chance of hitting a monster and it's a lot more fun.

Have a long-term financial strategy. Early on, Brad decided that he was going to write the same size initial check in every angel investment. In the first phase (1994–1996) this was $25,000. In the 2006–2007 phase this was $50,000 (although he broke this rule by occasionally doing $25,000 or $100,000 and, in several cases, even more). Brad always assumed he'd double down on each investment before the company either raised a venture capital (VC) round or was acquired, so when he put $25,000 in, he was really allocating $50,000 to the company. Then, Brad decided how much he was going to invest over a particular time period. In the 1994–1996 time period we decided to invest $1 million in angel investments. So that gave Brad capacity for 20 investments (he did more—oops). In 2006–2007 he allocated more (and did more). However, since he had a time frame and an amount per company, he had a baseline pace that he could go at before we got uncomfortable with how much he was investing.

Understand the difference between 0X and 100X. Brad had two angel investments return over 100X each. Since he had a strategy of investing the same amount in each company, all he needed was one 100X to allow him to have 99 companies completely flame out and return 0 and he'd still break even. With two investments at over 100X, he now had a built-in gain of significantly over 3X across all of his investments and was playing with house money on the rest of the investments.

Choose people over ideas. Brad has never regretted making new friends through an angel investment that failed. He has always hated working with people he didn't like or didn't think were A+. It's an easy filter—use it.

Decide quickly. Brad's best investments as an angel were made after one meeting, and he's often committed in the meeting. Sometimes it has taken him longer, usually a second meeting or a long meal. But there's no reason for an angel investor, especially an individual one, to drag the entrepreneur through a long, protracted due diligence process.

Don't torture entrepreneurs. Remember, you are supposed to be an "angel investor," not a "devil investor." If you really want to be a great angel investor, decide quickly and then help the entrepreneur get their financing done! Be a force for good in the universe.

Run in a pack. The best angels run in packs. They share deals. They love to work together. They don't feel obligated to invest in each other's stuff, but they often do. And they communicate with each other. If you run in a pack, different people will take the lead role in different cases. Sometimes Brad would be the lead investor in an angel deal and with a $25,000 check pull together a $500,000 round. Other times he'd just be one of the $25,000 checks in the $500,000 round and pawn off the work on one of his friends. Either way, he had a lot more fun playing with others—especially when the companies win!

Not all successful entrepreneurs find their stride, or enjoy the experience of being an angel investor. Here are Tim Enwall and Hillary Hall's thoughts.

It turns out we're very lousy investors. We invested in about 10 different startups as angel investors. Some had minor outcomes; many had very bad outcomes. In retrospect, and without talking with seasoned entrepreneurs who had gone through a couple of successful outcomes, it seems quite clear that we would be lousy investors. Entrepreneurs are, by their nature, optimists and dreamers. We see the opportunity in everything and are prone to dismiss the risks. When we drive forward, the sheer energy and belief often propels our own effort to success, but when we apply that same optimism to someone else's optimism, well. … Everything seems like a great idea! When that happens, you have a lousy investor.

Tim Enwall, Mobiplug, *www.mobiplug.co*
Hillary Hall, Boulder County Clerk and Recorder, @HillHall

Angel investing is not for everyone. But if you do it, have a strategy.

RETIREMENT

Do you have a magic number for defining success? "If I only had $2 million, I'd be fine." Then you have $3 million and suddenly, "If I only had $10 million, I'd be successful." Years later, when you have $10 million, you suddenly redefine success as having $20 million. We encourage you to wipe your mind of the construct of the magic number that defines success, as most people who have this find it keeps sliding up and away from the present.

One area where it is actually a good idea to have a magic number is retirement. You may be a young person and retirement either feels very far away or isn't something that you plan to do anyway. However, starting to save now for the future is very clever, and understanding your retirement number is important.

After Brad sold his first company, we realized we had enough money to move to Homer, Alaska, near where Amy had grown up, and live the rest of our life on our savings and a modest annual income, which Brad was comfortable he could make simply by being a technology consultant and adviser to startup companies, and Amy could make by teaching at the community college. We contemplated this for a little while, but realized that at 28 years old, neither of us was ready to retire. But at that moment we knew we had our retirement number, understood what it meant, and were ready to reinvest what we'd made in the next cycle of our work experience, rather than choose retirement.

But retirement isn't only about a number. It's about how you spend your time as an entrepreneurial couple. Our friends Will and Sandra Herman have had an amazing marriage throughout the time Will was on his entrepreneurial journey. In his early 40s, after several large successes, Will decided to retire. Here's Will and Sandra's story about adjusting to entrepreneurial retirement.

After spending a couple of decades starting five companies, cleaning up the wreckage of a couple of those that failed, running both private and public incarnations of a few that succeeded, and spending up to half of every year on the road and away from home doing all that, Will sold what turned out to be his last company about 10 years ago. At the time, his plan was to take a short break and start something new. Events and the recognition that his kids only really knew him as that guy who showed up to hang around now and again changed things. Will decided to "retire" to spend more time with his family.

Sure, Will had attended all the dance recitals, rarely missed a game, and did everything possible to attend all school events, but now he would actually get involved. Coach, volunteer, chauffeur, be a homework partner, and maybe even help around the house. Perhaps he would even start doing some consulting work from home.

This scared the crap out of Sandra, who had left work to build a home for her family and to raise their two children. Sandra had made everything work. The kids had their safe, nurturing, and educational environment, and Will, when he was around, was well managed. She was the glue, the bridge between everyone and the balance. At home, she had her own space, her own structure, and pretty much all her own schedule and rules. Will's decision was going to, potentially ... actually, ruin all that.

Once a CEO always a CEO? Let's just say that Will isn't a go-with-the-flow kind of guy—as an entrepreneur or as a husband and father. He wasn't about to fit into an existing environment. He had to meddle, change, and criticize. Table manners, bedtime, and car pools all needed changing, according to Will. Everything worked fine without him—it was just going to work better with him, damn it! Sandra knew it was coming and, like the Little Dutch Boy, tried to plug all the holes Will was creating in the dike. She warned, cajoled, and hoisted flags, but Will continued to run roughshod over Sandra's domain.

Eventually, Will decided that this "retirement" thing really might not be his gig. Rather than starting something new and giving up his new quality (in his mind) time with the family, he decided to get involved with startups, venture capitalists, and small companies in a nonoperational fashion. He would advise, sit on boards, invest, and help with merger-and-acquisition (M&A) deals. The goal was to stay involved without impinging on family time. He decided to work from the house, which, as everyone knows, requires quiet, open phone lines, and privacy. None of which are available in a house with two kids in their early teens. More stress? For sure, at least initially.

Ever so slowly and with Sandra's subtle hand guiding everyone, the family started to get used to having Will around, and Will, in turn, started to get with the program. Okay, the program had to change a little. What entrepreneur concedes everything? It probably helped that Will threw himself at the ventures he became involved in. They occupied time and brain cells that had been left to their own devices for too long. At times, the companies became, as a group, a full-time job, causing several people to refer to Will as the busiest retired guy on the planet. After a while, he stopped thinking of himself as retired, although it's not clear that there is a name for what he does.

Are there any retired entrepreneurs? It's hard to imagine. The classic definition including spending days puttering in the garden or playing 18 holes 6 days a week certainly doesn't hold—unless, of course, that involves genetically engineering a new type of flower or working out to join the PGA Tour. Life is rarely binary, though, and there is a spectrum of nonretirement choices that can offer many people exactly what they need or want. Discovering what that mix is takes some trial, error, and discovery, though.

Will and Sandra's not-retirement journey held many lessons.

It's hard. Take it too lightly and you'll find yourself in serious hot water. Unless one or both of you are saints, there is going to be a lot of stress.

If you can, avoid not-retiring from your home office. Physical separation for at least a few hours every day makes everyone happier.

Try to figure out what you're going to do in not-retirement. Figure this out before actually wading into the deep end.

Have hobbies, sports, or pastimes. If you don't have fun, intellectually or physically challenging activities that you enjoy, the days can get long for anyone entrepreneurial.

Find the key to your work/retirement balance. After some time, Will found that he could work with a relatively large group of companies and vary the amount of operational involvement he had with each. It satisfied his need for day-to-day action while allowing him to avoid getting too tied down.

Talk. Sandra observed what was going on much better than Will. She consistently drove the discussion and, most often, the solutions.

It's a tremendously rewarding and life-changing experience if you can figure it out. Creating a new and better life balance alongside a new career is hugely satisfying.

Would we do it again? Yes, in a heartbeat. We are closer than ever and have had opportunities to share lives that most people never get. Will's schedule varies from 40-hour workweeks to virtually zero and is mostly under his control. This schedule is incredibly balanced and rewarding. On one hand, it satisfies the intellectual and entrepreneurial needs that Will has; on the other hand, it leaves as much time and energy as we want to dedicate to our personal interests and to each other. It wasn't always an easy path, but the destinations are great.

Will Herman, Retired Entrepreneur
Sandra Herman, Mom

PHILANTHROPY

When Amy was in college, she decided that she would always give some of her money to philanthropic causes. When she had very little money, she would still write a $25 check each year to Planned Parenthood, National Public Radio, and the Nature Conservancy, organizations and causes that were very important to her.

About a year after we started living together, we decided to be deliberate about our philanthropy. We had more money now in the form of current income given the success of Brad's company. While we didn't have a significant amount of savings, we decided to give away 10 percent of our adjusted gross income from the previous year.

We've used this approach as our budget since. We've developed a systematic approach to our annual giving and usually exceed our 10 percent target. While we aren't big enough fishes to join the Giving Pledge, where billionaires commit to giving away the majority of their wealth, we're on that path anyway since we've derived so much satisfaction from having an impact while we are alive, rather than defer it until after we are dead.

Lots of entrepreneurs we know don't feel like they have money to give, especially early in their entrepreneurial career. However, all of us can afford to give something right away, including time, talent, and treasure, which could include equity in your new startup. Following is an example by Tim Enwall of doing this via the Entrepreneurs Foundation of Colorado.

Many entrepreneurs aren't very good at philanthropy because we are wired to deploy capital to profitable ends. Hillary and I learned that philanthropy is very important to us because it supports the community that supports us. In our second startup we went one step further, which was to have our startup support the community through the Entrepreneur's Foundation of Colorado (which is part of a national affiliation of Entrepreneur Foundations).

EFCO takes 1 percent of the founding capital of a business and benefits if that stock is ever liquidated—the money goes to the community. It can go into a community benefit fund or specific nonprofit target categories. EFCO is a great way to connect a startup to philanthropy because the nonprofit thrives if the company thrives. Instead of individuals getting credit for the giving, the entire corporation gets the credit.

Everyone associated with the company shares a sense of pride in both the initial grant and the eventual contribution to the community. And the company name is on the donor list, so the community understands the connection with our startup.

Tim Enwall, Mobiplug, *www.mobiplug.co*
Hillary Hall, Boulder County Clerk and Recorder, @HillHall

While we don't pass judgment on what anyone decides to do around philanthropy, it has been an incredibly powerful shared experience for us to talk about what we can do together with the wealth we are generating.

CHAPTER ELEVEN

CHILDREN

We don't have children. When we talk about work-life balance, we are often told "it's different if you don't have children." We completely agree; in our case, not having children was a deliberate choice. Neither of us has a rare genetic disease that prevents pregnancy; rather, we decided early in our relationship (in our 20s) that we didn't want to have children. We agreed to revisit this decision once a year, and did so, until deciding in our early 30s to definitively not have children, and we haven't regretted that decision at all.

We believe that each individual has the power to make choices about their lives, and that your attitude can be a self-fulfilling prophecy. If you think you have time for something, or you think you don't, you're right. If you think you can just press pause on your relationship for a decade or more while you both focus on raising children and having careers, it's likely that you won't have a relationship to pay attention to when you're finally ready.

We get a lot of "it's easy for you because you didn't have children," which completely overlooks the fact that our choice not to have children was just that—a conscious, deliberate, thoughtful decision that we didn't believe we could figure out a way to have the work life, relationship, and the individual lives we wanted and have children, too. We don't believe you can have it all, and that there are trade-offs to any decision. The decision not to have children did make things easier for us, and we still almost didn't make it through. If you decide to have children, you decide a whole lot of other things about your lives at that juncture.

When approaching this topic, we know that we have no experience or credibility to talk about the dynamics around an entrepreneurial life in the context of children. So we've asked a number our entrepreneurial couples with whom we are friends to write about their experiences.

START WITH A COMMITMENT TO EACH OTHER'S DREAMS

Our friends Tim Enwall and Hillary Hall share their reflections on startups, family, and money—as told by Tim with heavy edits by Hillary.

Hillary and I decided to start our first company at the worst possible family moment—at the beginning. I say "we" because the decision to have one member of the family devote the time, passion, and energy to a startup is really a decision to have all of the members of the family pursue the same path. In our case, we had adopted two special-needs girls, biological sisters, two months before we put our shingle out. Two months. Girls who required a little more tender love and care early on than in a normal situation. Seems like perfect timing, yes? Tim's first week on the job was on Mother's Day. Away from home in another state. Typical startup fare.

In many ways, though, this represents the essence of how we have (somewhat) successfully navigated our way as a family—with a deep commitment to each other's dreams and souls, a profound recognition of the sacrifices all members of the family make, and careful time management.

We have seen many dreamers never start their own company or pursue their dreams because their partners are not deeply committed to the others' dream and soul. Those couples we know who have been through many startups together have this in common—they know at an energetic level that their partner has a calling, that they have a burning need to pursue a dream. This is beyond the casual "sure honey, do whatever you want" level. This is a recognition that when one's partner is pursuing their dream, they are satisfied down to their soul and, in so being satisfied, are that much more alive. That level of aliveness is a gift few partners can ever give, and successful couples recognize this.

Conversely, the partner pursuing their startup dream can travel one of two paths: the path that recognizes the slight piece of insanity that comes with the level of commitment one makes to a startup and, therefore, the burden and stress their partner experiences; or the path that is wholly unable to empathize with their partner's experience of loss of companionship, extra work at home, explanations to friends and family of why their partner can't be with them at a weekend social gathering, explanations to kids of why their partner isn't home tonight (or last night, or the night before, or …), and the stress that comes with making many of the non-startup decisions every family must make. Again, we've seen many couples split in the first year or two of a startup because of this lack of recognition, and we've seen many single entrepreneurs never be able to have a family because of the lack of empathy for what their dates go through.

In our case, it took coming almost to the brink of splitting our marriage up before we (meaning Tim) recognized this. I realized (with a heavy dose of, uhhhh, "help" from Hillary) that I was overweighted to the startup side—spending too much mental time, even while at home, focused on issues far away from home and even less time on Hillary because of the children. This period was when we developed our picture of sine and cosine—the arc of two partners' lives that ebb and flow, realizing that when they are at their farthest from each other, they must come back together or infinity happens. Essentially, it hit me like a ton of bricks the kind of impact I was having on Hillary. It's almost like an addict who has no concept of the impact they have on other people's lives until some forcing event causes them to face the brutal reality that their addiction is not just for themselves.

At every company event or gathering—whether it's the company Halloween trick or treat, the holiday party, or even casual gatherings—I try very hard to this day to first acknowledge the partners of all of our employees because I know at the core the difference in sacrifice each partner makes between a startup and a "regular company."

Which brings us to time management. As the entrepreneur, especially if you have children, get used to the idea that you have zero personal time. You have two calendars: the startup calendar and the family calendar. That's it. There's no time for the gym, no time for golf, no time for reading. Either that or get used to not sleeping much. Why? Because you've recognized the level of pain your addiction is causing your family and the amount of time devoted to your startup such that every waking moment not spent on the addiction needs to be spent 100 percent focused on family. Not kind of focused, 100 percent focused. In our case, 6:00 to 8:00 P.M. was walled off as family time—more specifically, "dad is going to read to the kids, put them to bed, and handle other kid chores so mom can catch a breath" time. There was really no other choice. If I had concentrated on my addiction (startups) and my personal well-being, then I would have had to give up sleep—something I knew was more important to my well-being than anything else.

In our case, we were fortunate to navigate through the early family trials and tribulations and even more fortunate to experience the monetary gain that is one of the scorecards for a successful startup.

Money is no easy topic for startup families. It can (and frequently does) swing from one extreme to another. If you are like most entrepreneurs, starting your company is often done on a shoestring, with limited financial reserves, feeding your addiction, your passion, and your calling. Frequently, this means either you are funneling your savings, funneling your second mortgage, or funneling every ounce of everything you have into the endeavor. We found that another key to family harmony was to accept that we might be destitute. At one point we looked at each other and said, "What's the worst thing that can happen?" I said, "We could have no money." Hillary said, "Well ... we've done that before, so we can do it again." This is serious business, and we were making a serious investment. Like all serious investors, we had to be prepared to lose it all before making the commitment to invest. This was essential. We have, again, seen so many dreamers who themselves or whose partners cannot stomach the idea of losing their nest egg, their second mortgage, their home, their belongings. It's very tough to create the proper level of devotion to your startup's success unless you can be "all in"—but you have to be. We were.

Tim Enwall, Mobiplug, *www.mobiplug.co*
Hillary Hall, Boulder County Clerk and Recorder, @HillHall

RAISING THE BABY

Brad is not good with babies; he simply doesn't understand them or know what to do with them. Offer a six-week-old to Brad to hold and he will cross his arms and politely decline. Ask him if he wants to babysit your three-year-old and he'll patiently suggest that it's a really bad idea and you don't really want him to do it.

Raising a baby is hard enough; raising it when you are trying to get your startup company off the ground is much more than double the challenge. Following are Todd Vernon's thoughts on trying to combine these two.

Starting a company is like having a new baby. Sometimes, to make things even more complicated, you actually also have a new baby. In both cases, you are literally going into battle, saying goodbye to your life for a while. You are going on a tour-of-duty that, if things go well, will result in a sassy but moderately self-sufficient three-year-old—Going Concern.

But you are concerned. Raising the baby is about keeping the faith, keeping the team happy and energized. You know this is the most difficult thing you have ever done, but you are excited because you know it's a higher calling. You are building something that will change the world. You can do this!

The plan is never what you thought it would be. Your friends were that couple who hiked everywhere with their baby. GigaOM, TechCrunch, they went everywhere. But you feel trapped—your baby (and you) just isn't ready for all that yet. But, as they say, when you're going through hell, just keep on going.

Thankfully, I had/have a copilot in this journey. Raising the baby is much easier with two. Having a partner is essential to the stability, perspective, and the balance to the journey you have embarked on.

In my life, that partner is my wife, Lura. She is a bona fide rocket scientist. Lura was an aerospace engineer at NASA and wrote technical papers I can't hope to ever understand. But to me, she is simply my copilot.

The baby "Baby" was generally Lura's domain. As a true mother, she generally knew the direction and instinct of what was the next move. She valued my input, but she was the pilot of that journey. If there was a baby issue that needed to be addressed, she provided the accelerant to get it done.

The baby "Going Concern" was generally my domain. With her support and nonobjective opinion, I always seemed to know what to do tomorrow. As the CEO of Baby Going Concern, like Lura, my first instinct was to correct the issue with a flame thrower. But in her infinite wisdom, she would counsel, "See what you think tomorrow."

Doing something that has never been done by you is a noble and difficult task. Starting a new company is literally a task that will keep you up at night and is a mission that is 24/7. Much has been written about work-life balance, but the fact of the matter is that to some degree your work has to be your life. You must construct that life with the people who understand the mission, love the mission, and have the perspective that can help you see it to the end.

Lura Vernon, Mom, @luraellen
Todd Vernon, Lijit, *www.lijit.com*

DEFINE YOUR ROLES AND RESPONSIBILITIES CLEARLY

Jud and April Valeski have been married for 15 years and have two children, a 10-year-old boy and a 7-year-old girl. Jud is CEO of Gnip, a company he co-founded five years ago. Jud's story is one of discovery, as he learned that you get to define your own rules now, and society can't bring much to bear with respect to what makes you a good parent. While others may judge you, what you decide to do as a parent, with your partner, is up to the two of you. How you define *balance* is all up to you.

My wife is the primary caregiver for our family and always has been. I like to think I could've done her job, but in reality, I probably couldn't have. Regardless, our roles are well suited/tailored for each other. I win bread, and she nurtures our souls and builds great humans; she keeps us alive in a very literal sense of the word.

I was fat and happy in a great job at a large media/technology company when we had our first child. It was nice to have that cushion when going through that initial birth; lots of flexibility (financial and time) to try and bring this kid into the world "right." However, as he started to grow and become more person-like, I found myself telling him things about life. "Take risk!" I'd encourage him to push through boundaries (ride a bike). I'd encourage him to push through pain. I'd shown him beautiful moments. But then, when I looked at my life, I wasn't walking the talk. I was a big company executive with as lazy a lifestyle as you could imagine. I imagined my child growing older and ultimately asking me what I did for work. I vividly painted that picture, that moment, and the exchange. I realized that my response was going to be anything but great. "Son, I'm 35. I work a few hours a week, bike ride a lot, fly around the world sometimes, and make a lot of money." Effectively, "I'm retired."

So, out of one side of my mouth I'd be telling him how perseverance is a crucial quality and how hard we all need to work to become smart so we can do great things, while out of the other I'd be planning my next bike ride with friends. As a new parent, I realized this was not the example I wanted to set. Do as I say, not as I do, is not how I wanted my child to see me or the world.

My wife and I talked for a bit about this dichotomy, and my passion for software and Boulder, Colorado, and we realized jumping out of a cushy situation into the unknown was the right thing to do. In 2006 I left BigCo, and joined a startup.

I took a massive cut in pay, though I didn't have to travel anymore, which I calculated was about $40,000/year in salary trade. One thing we, wisely, never did was spend all the money I'd been earning. We lived way below our paycheck while it was large, so taking a cut didn't impact lifestyle; that's general advice I recommend that everyone follow.

Workloads shifted significantly, and we had to redefine how we engaged with each other and our kids. I traded things like extra time with family for new, fresh experiences that my kid would have a front row seat for.

Startups are hard no matter how you slice it. Blend in partner and parent responsibilities, and things can get dicey. I often talk about discretionary energy. Just like discretionary income, it's something you control the use of. We all have it. From a simple choice around whether or not to fix coffee in the morning, to choosing to write a book. There's a big difference between punching a clock as an employee at a startup, and spending some or all of your discretionary energy on one. With children, this allocation gets trickier.

Startup One didn't go well, and I left it after 18 months. I learned an inordinate amount from the experience, but it was time to do another one. Through a fortuitous set of events, I wound up co-founding a new company where I still am today, five years later. By this time my daughter had been born.

In the vein of wanting to set a good example for my kids, my wife and I agreed to keep pushing down this startup path. We kept coming back to the value we as individuals, as well as our kids, would get from the experience, and it was exceedingly high. We believe the old model of "go to school, go to college, go get a great job" is broken, and that we needed to exemplify, as best we could, new alternative ways of doing. We want our kids to see innovation firsthand. We want them to see challenges stared down and beaten with bare hands (not abstracted away by the more traditional career path system). We want them to see problem solving in the real world. We want them to see their parents cope through the ups and the downs. These things drive us, as a couple, to participate directly in the startup ecosystem.

Indirectly, our kids are part of the ecosystem, too. When we engage with "work" events as a family, everyone engages with an extremely diverse set of people, ways of thinking, ways of approaching challenges, ways of considering problem solving in the world around us. We are surrounded by people pushing social, technical, and behavioral boundaries. We are not surrounded by people who approach life as a clock to punch. I love this.

When one of my kids is face to face with some challenge and asks for help (or clearly needs it), I can draw on fresh real-world examples to teach them and empathize with them around. Startup life mimics childhood in so many ways, with its constant change, swings from up to down and back again, and new fresh things to do and learn about every single day. There is never a dull moment. I believe the result is a tighter bond with my children. I don't come home fretting about something my boss told me to do. Not because I'm the CEO, but because, regardless of your title or role in a startup, the startup firm itself relies on everyone's being the boss/CEO of their domain. As individuals we are responsible for what the startup does every day. I wanted my kids hearing my wife and I talk about the decision-making process and how I was going to propel the company forward in my own way. I did not want my kids hearing my wife and I talk about how I was a victim of some circumstance I didn't think I could control. Yuck!

I've been talking a lot about my motivations for doing a startup. The motivations are very important to me because without the right ones in place, things would fall apart. I otherwise wouldn't have the foundation to draw upon when things get particularly challenging. I'm not going to go into all the mechanical differences between a startup and "regular job," as those are well documented elsewhere. If you're interested in startup life at all, your motivations are fundamentally different than those if you want to work at BigCo. They could be as simple as equity desires, but for me they go way beyond that. This is a lot bigger than my personal economics.

Getting life balance right regardless of what you're doing is obviously imperative to living a fulfilling life. It's easier in some circumstances than in others, of course, but it all comes down to balance.

Doing a startup with kids requires that many more variables be balanced out in your world. There are simply that many more balls in the air to juggle. Your friends in the office are part of your family in a startup. Not only do you spend a lot of time with them day in and day out, but the intensity of that time is 100 times stronger than a typical "job" scenario. This means your family is essentially the folks at the office *and* your folks at "home." While one of those matters more than the other, when you're trying to do a great job at both, the lines get blurry. Judgment calls sometimes land on the wrong side of the line, more so than when you have only one family.

We would do it all again. The experience has been one of the most amazing in my life. I always think I can be a better father and spouse, but I do believe I'm always doing the absolute best I can on those fronts, and a significant portion of that is due to the feeling of "alive" I get by being involved in a startup. Just like a shark always needs to be moving to stay alive, startups give my brain the oxygen it needs in order to stay alive and thrive.

If you're considering joining/starting a startup and have children, or are planning on having children, make sure you either have the right motivations in place (not necessarily mine), or will be in a role at the firm that allows you to keep a sane schedule at home. The latter is generally just harder at a startup. Those roles exist, but they're rare. Startups, often by definition, require discretionary energy from everyone on the team in order to succeed. If you can't allocate it because you're putting it all into your true family, you should reconsider joining a startup.

April

As the spouse of a startup founder/CEO, life happens in the most spontaneous and energetic ways. It is full of all sorts of challenges, and my number one priority is to nurture and balance our family life. Our children have embraced the lifestyle and all of its "ooh and ahh" moments. They cry when their dad leaves town and cheer when he comes home. They share in the love and respect we have for one another as we manage the highs and lows. Their dad is a hero most days, and a tired grump on others. And, at the end of the day, when Jud can hardly handle another five-course restaurant meal, and I've stomached another box of mac and cheese with the kids, we are openly and wholeheartedly in it together—40 fingers and 40 toes cuddled up and dreaming.

Jud Valeksi, Gnip, *www.gnip.com*
April Valeski

MANAGING YOUR KIDS

Greeley Sachs is married to Seth Levine, one of Brad's partners at Foundry Group. Greeley had a promising career before deciding to have kids and made taking care of her children her primarily responsibility. Here, she makes some specific suggestions about how to manage your kids in the context of an entrepreneurial partner. Greeley and Seth have three children, which we've learned from them is a lot more than two.

A few years ago when I was lamenting to my father that my husband had been either traveling or working late more than he had been home, my father remarked, "At least he isn't serving in Afghanistan." Thanks, Dad! That kind of generous empathy has helped a lot!

Despite the lack of a willing ear, my father was correct in that whenever you feel that life is hard for you, there's always someone who has it harder. I have a husband who travels frequently, but he's not in harm's way and he loves what he does. It's helpful to keep this in mind when, for example, your child is expelled from preschool (for the second time) or the water heater has exploded or you're laid up with the flu and you have healthy, active kids who need dinner, and your spouse hasn't been home in days.

In the interest of transparency, I don't work outside the home. I do some volunteer work that takes about 10 to 20 hours a week, and I help at my kids' school on a regular basis, but I don't have to go to an office every day. This has helped maintain a calm, happy life for my family and me. I realize, though, that this is an easy life compared to that of friends of mine who have started their own companies, or have spouses who are deeply entrenched in the startup world, with both parents working full time. I decided to ask each of them how they make it work, and here are the common themes they shared with me.

Don't overschedule. From the outside, this seems incredibly easy, but three of the people I spoke with spend two to three hours most evenings driving their kids to after-school activities. One of the parents I polled takes her seven-year-old to two weekly soccer practices and one weekend game, not including ballet and tutoring on other nights. (Wow, that kid had better end up on the Olympic team for 2020 to justify that amount of schlepping.) Kidding aside, parents are led to believe that if their child isn't participating in multiple after-school activities that they are somehow failing them and they will grow up to be unathletic outcasts. One of the least frantic people I polled (who runs her own company) limits the activities to one night per week, per child; that way, they have at least one night a week to be home as a family without any obligations. That seems very sensible.

Don't try to do everything perfectly. If your child has to routinely choose outfits from the unfolded mountain of laundry piled on the family room sofa, it's okay. Scrambled eggs for dinner is still dinner, and your child does not need their lunch presented in a biodegradable bento box. If you think I'm joking, I'm not. I know multiple moms who craft James Beard Award–worthy bento boxes for each child every day for their elementary school lunches. Give yourself a break and do things well, but stop trying to be perfect.

Get help! Each family I spoke with had a different idea of what type of help they need. One friend of mine doesn't want help with her three kids, but wants to come home to a clean house and a prepared dinner. Another has a babysitter for after school to help with homework and taking kids to soccer. One couple I know has a sitter each Saturday morning, so they can go for a hike or bike ride together.

The suggestions above can benefit any parent, but the trick is in making it all work when your spouse has been traveling for days on end to raise money for his genius new company or your wife has been at work past midnight for a week preparing for the launch of the new technology she developed. Managing a family while your spouse is focused on his/her business can be isolating. When my husband was starting his company, I ran into a friend who politely asked if we were still married because she hadn't seen us together in over a year.

Many times at dinners with my husband's colleagues I have been greeted with the withering look that says, "Crap, I'm seated next to the mom who has nothing interesting to say." I've had to come to terms with the fact that I gave up a career for the life I have and that might not make me the most fascinating dinner companion, but for me, having my own thing that brings me happiness outside of my family is what keeps me sane in a world of isolation and children.

This is the single most important piece of advice I have: It's good to have an interest or hobby outside of your family and work. Even if you have the busiest week of your life scheduled, take an hour or two to do something that makes you happy. Go for a hike, paint a picture, see a foreign film, and give yourself permission to be more than a parent and your spouse's spouse. Conversely, give your spouse the time to do whatever it is that makes him/her happy.

This is where I get back to the comment from my father. It's important when you're married to someone who is trying to create something to be an optimist. Look at the long-term impact of his/her potential success and whether or not being creative and entrepreneurial makes them happy.

Greeley Sachs
Seth Levine, Foundry Group, *www.foundrygroup.com*

BE DELIBERATE ABOUT TRAVEL

Many entrepreneurs travel every week and even some weekends. While this can be hard on them, it can even be more challenging for the spouse who is left alone with the kids. Brad travels so much for his work that early in our relationship Amy would often say that one of the reasons we chose not to have kids is that she didn't want to be a single parent while in a marriage. See Jil Cohen's thoughts in Chapter 8 for more on this. Try to ease the stress before resentment builds in the primary caregiver. Commit to time together without your children so that you're still building your partnership even in the throes of childrearing. We believe that even partners with children can find four minutes in the morning to be together. It's good for children to see you making time for each other in the midst of busy mornings. Sometimes it's not their turn to be the center of attention.

THE STAY-AT-HOME DAD

The challenge of being a stay-at-home dad is one that is discussed in many relationship books. There's an interesting twist to being a stay-at-home dad when your spouse is an entrepreneur, and we asked Mark Florence, who is married to Nicole Glaros (TechStars Boulder managing director) to tell his story.

Being a stay-at-home dad married to an entrepreneurial woman is tough, but not any tougher than any other marital arrangement. From my perspective, we are a team; we have a goal in mind, which is to raise a happy, healthy family while staying happy and healthy ourselves. While it is true that this is no easy task, it is certainly more easily accomplished with a teammate. My wife and I try to be team players. We support each other whenever we can. The stronger of us at the time of need props the other one up. We try not to keep track of who's doing more or less, but instead look at the big picture to just make sure it all gets done, and to the highest standard we can manage. These days, the concept of role reversal in the home is not such a wild idea, but I still get surprised and otherwise interesting reactions from folks I'm just getting to know when I tell them that I am a stay-at-home dad. Women tend to light up and seem genuinely impressed, while men are confused for a moment, and then want to know what it is all about. It took me a while to accept this role completely without feeling strange in front of people I did not know. It's not that I feel threatened or otherwise uncomfortable with the fact that my wife has the role of financial support while I take care of the kids. For a while it was how I perceived how other people saw me in this role. I finally stopped worrying about it completely when I came to the realization of how important my role is to my family. I put everything I've got into teaching my children how to be loving, caring, intelligent, and respectful people. I realized that no one is better qualified to do this for my kids than I. Incidentally, my wife is infinitely more capable of bringing home the bacon than I, so as a team, we have taken the best positions we can to win the game!

While I try to give all that I can to my kids, I think that it is important to take a little time to do something for yourself. You cannot be the best parent or spouse that you can be if you are not happy yourself, or at least somewhat sane. A little time away from the kids each day or week can go a long way. I go to the gym most days, and for two hours I get some great physical exercise, and time without someone needing me constantly. I also take some time each week to pursue my favorite hobby, which is playing music. My wife, being a team player, does her best to make sure I have time to go down to my studio and practice, or record, or whatever. It's amazing, after being totally burned out from the kids, what a little time to yourself will do. Most times after just a couple of hours, I miss my kids and can't wait to get back to loving them.

It doesn't hurt that I have such an amazing wife. She really tries her best to give me all the support that I need, and in turn that encourages me to do the same for her. In general, I try not to be selfish. I try to realize how hard we both work to keep our family going. It's easy to feel sorry for yourself, to take a myopic view and to blame the other when you're overwhelmed. Whenever one of us starts to feel this way, we will talk about it. It's been said a lot but cannot be overstated: communication is key. We'll express our frustrations to each other in a nonoffensive way, talk about how we can rearrange things, or otherwise manage the issues at hand together.

Mark Florence, Full-Time Dad
Nicole Glaros, TechStars Boulder, *www.techstars.com*

CHAPTER TWELVE

FAMILY

While we don't have children, we do most definitely have family. Siblings, parents, and extended family play an important role in a startup life. In addition, many partners begin relationships when working at the same company, like we did, or end up working at the same company that has been founded by one of them. Figuring out how to approach this intricate relationship can be challenging as well as incredibly fulfilling.

BEING MARRIED TO THE CEO

Krista Marks and Brent Milne started their first two businesses simultaneously. One was a consumer Internet company, and the other did hardware consulting as a bootstrapping strategy. There were four founders with equal stakes; Krista and Brent were married, and Krista was the CEO. Following are their thoughts on how they managed this dynamic.

Credit: Erin Sage Photography

During the earliest days of our startup journey, we fortuitously stumbled across an idea. Perhaps there were other great ideas from those days, but this one stands out to us in hindsight—and it wasn't related to the business or a product, but rather to how we worked together. We made the decision to systematically avoid discussing work outside of the office. Our initial motivation for doing this was simple; we were hoping to keep a modicum of sanity in our lives, and this idea seemed like a possibly helpful device. It was already clear to us that a startup could quickly become an all-consuming proposition for us. Given any engaging project, we both have a tendency to become hyper-focused. In the context of a regular job, this was never a huge issue; we were very productive, and all the talk of "work-life balance" seemed to us overrated. We enjoyed our work; we enjoyed working; and we derived a lot of satisfaction, sense of purpose, and even enduring friendships from it.

Doing a startup, however, is a very different proposition from other sorts of work, and some of the differences are subtle. A heightened level of intensity struck us immediately. Every decision, every action, every observation took on deeper shades of meaning. We partially anticipated this before we jumped into doing a startup, but only partially. In imagining what a startup would be like, our expectation was that the financial stress and commitment would be the major causes of increased intensity and focus. In our experience, that turned out to be wrong. While they were a factor, the much bigger factor was our emotional investment and commitment to the startup. We quickly realized that founding the company had become a central part of our personal identities. There is a reason that the co-founders of companies often talk about the experience through metaphors of marriages and children—those are the only analogous settings that we can think of that create a similar sort of intense experience, often to a point of obsession.

Given that co-founding a company is similar to a new marriage, with similar sorts of intensity, stresses, and impacts on personal identity, it makes sense that combining that relationship with an existing, key relationship—doing a company with a spouse, a sibling, or even a good friend—involves more than a touch of high-risk alchemy. There is a very real possibility that the mix of old and new relationships could blow up in an ugly way. While, yes, the opposite might happen and both a richer relationship and a successful venture might emerge, we don't have any tips on how to assign probabilities to the possible outcomes, nor even in retrospect do we know exactly why we ended up on the good end of the spectrum. But we do think that the decision to separate work and home life was an extremely helpful tool and, in particular, that not talking about work outside of the office became an important firewall between our business relationship and personal relationship.

At first, the separation was artificial and forced. The company was pretty much all we were thinking about, day and night. However, we were at the office for long hours every day, running at a dead sprint, and when we left work it was pretty much only to go home and crash. It wasn't that hard not to talk about work as we were mostly bleary and only half coherent as we found our way home. After a month or so, we decided that we should institute a date night and leave work in time to have a nice romantic dinner and some quality time together. Our first such date quickly became a comedy, because we sat in silence and one of us would occasionally ask the other "what are you thinking about?" and the response was always "work." After three or four rounds we were laughing and it became a running joke, and eventually we found something else to talk about.

But we held firm to our rule, and gradually, a variety of benefits emerged, and the occasional awkward displays we put on in restaurants, like first dates short of conversational steam, seemed justified.

Founders typically wear a lot of hats in a startup, and after a while you get used to switching between roles and personas. In our case, Krista had the role of CEO in addition to founder and partner. As CEO she would often get information first. We had never mentioned to our co-founders that we had a rule about not talking work at home; they learned of it one day early on when Krista came into the office one morning with important information to share. She'd gotten it the night before, and our co-founders were surprised that we hadn't talked. When we told them about our rule, they were relieved. The fact that we didn't talk about work at home defused any risk of us being seen as some sort of alliance, and it helped to enforce that all of the founders' relationships were on the same level.

For our personal relationship, the rule had even more important benefits. Over time, we evolved distinct relationships in our home and work lives, even taking to always using our given names at work and our nicknames at home. Just as our partners had been relieved, we were pleased to learn that we could maintain two very distinct and separate, but healthy, relationships with each other. We each wore many hats in the context of our business; the fact that we only wore our married-couple hats at home and our work hats at work became a natural pattern. Many things call for creative solutions in a startup, not least of which are ways to maintain and nurture existing personal relationships.

Krista Marks, Kerpoof, *www.kerpoof.com*
Brent Milne, Kerpoof

Emily Huh works at Cheezburger, a company founded by her husband Ben, who is the CEO. Following is Emily's approach to managing working with her entrepreneurial husband.

People tell me all the time that they don't know how I can work with my husband and then ask how do we do it and manage to stay sane with seeing each other all the time. I think some might expect me to say that it's like a reality show where we scream and yell at each other and one of us throws a stapler at the other in anger. Fortunately, it's a lot tamer than that.

Of course, Ben and I have disagreements and frustrations when working with each other just like anyone has with a co-worker or boss. Working with your husband is extremely tough, and throughout the five years that we have worked with each other, we both have questioned at times if we can continue to do this. But we always come back to saying this is one of the most amazing experiences we can share with each other, and we know that the positives completely outweigh any of the challenges of working with each other.

Since Ben is the CEO, I am like any other employee. When I make a mistake, I'm called out on it. And because Ben expects more from me and wants me to do my best, he is even harder on me and pushes me more than other employees. It is sometimes difficult to understand that when it's 11:30 P.M., but being married to an entrepreneur and being a part of the business, I know this is a position I can never say "later" to or stop thinking about. It's in his blood, so it's in my blood.

Throughout the years, we have learned how to better balance our work life and personal life, so we can focus on being with each other versus working on the business. We've set guidelines of when we can talk about work outside of the office unless it is a priority issue. On our walk home, we take that time to discuss any issues or talk about the day, but when we get home, we make a conscious effort to wrap up any issues and will even send emails to each other instead of talking about it, so the other doesn't feel the pressure to respond right away.

The life of an entrepreneur and being married to an entrepreneur is not one that everyone can enjoy. I credit my parents with my ability to thrive from this way of life. My father was and is still an entrepreneur. Through the ups and downs of his business ventures and my mother trying to raise two children, we were used to a life where risk was okay and it was encouraged to try new things and deal with the unknown. My parents were able to provide for us throughout all those years and we had an amazing childhood, so seeing them take these risks and survive through them all makes me realize that Ben and I can endure all of these challenges and unknowns in the future.

One of the hardest things about being an entrepreneur is the emotional aspect. The fear of failure and the anxiety that you carry weighs on you, and you are not only worried about yourself, but you're concerned for your employees and their livelihood. This takes a toll on both of us, especially Ben. There are great days of excitement when everything has fallen into place, and then there are the low days when such chaos seems to ensue that it's hard to even get out of bed. You wonder if you'll be able to make this a success and question why you even decided to become an entrepreneur in the first place.

But I know I need to be that support system for Ben and push away any fears I have. Even though he is the head of the company, I'd like to say that I provide the emotional support for him. I know that it's not about the right thing to say, but it's the steady confidence that I have in him and his vision, and that I'm always standing next to him through every step of the day excited for the next adventure.

Emily Huh, Cheezburger, *www.cheezburger.com*
Ben Huh, Cheezburger

WORKING TOGETHER

Ben and Emily work together every day. We also worked together at Brad's first company. In our case, we worked together and were friends before we became a couple while we were still in separate previous relationships. After our respective relationships failed, we started going out but were very quiet about it for the first six months. While several close friends knew we were dating, and then living together, we struggled with how to be public about it in the context of our work relationship.

Matt and Mariquita Blumberg also worked together when they first started their relationship. Matt is the founder and CEO of Return Path. Prior to starting Return Path, Matt hired Mariquita to work for him at MovieFone. They worked together for a year before they started dating and then kept their relationship a secret for another year until they became engaged. They've been together for the entire time that Matt has been running Return Path and, even though they no longer work together at the same company, the work closely together on their family as well as physically together in the same home office when they aren't at work. Following is their experience.

When we think about this topic, we can break it down into three different kinds of Working Together. And each one is instructive in its own way toward building the perfect *Startup Marriage.*

We worked together professionally. Matt interviewed Mariquita when he was a grunt analyst and she was a senior at MIT in 1994. At least one of us thinks it was love at first sight. But then Matt quit his job at Mercer the week before Mariquita started, so it took another three years before we actually worked together, when Matt hired Mariquita to work on his team at MovieFone in 1997. The dating started in 1998, shrouded in secrecy. Engagement in 1999. Wedding in 2000. Working together while dating was a fantastic experience, though not without its challenges. What better way to spend a ton of time together and to learn all about how each other's brains were wired? The company clearly got the best of it, with the two of us working longer hours than anyone else so we could come in together and leave together without suspicion! If anything, we were "too" professional about it as a result of the secrecy factor, and excessive caution caused a bit of a strain on the personal. Had we been "out in the open," it might have been different. An interesting note is that, at another point in his career, Matt interviewed extensively for a job reporting to co-CEOs who were married (and not running a family business—running a venture-backed company), and it seemed like a really, really bad idea to work for a husband-and-wife team in that setting, no matter how great they were. One meeting Matt joined with the two of them featured a full-blown fight that included references to things said in the bedroom the prior night!

We work together on our family. A marriage is the ultimate form of a startup—building the type of shared environment, with shared values, shared resources, and working toward a shared common goal that successful companies also rely on. You are co-founders in the most important type of organization—a family—and a constantly changing one at that, with kids arriving, growing up, and having continuously new and different needs. A family needs to be led and run, consciously, thoughtfully, and with a clear division of roles and responsibilities. We work together to set goals for ourselves individually, our kids individually, and our family as a whole, just like you would in any organization. And we hold ourselves accountable to what we are trying to accomplish with regular check-ins. It isn't all work—the play part of the family is critical as well—but being intentional about what we are trying to build as a family takes time and has been an important commitment for us.

We work side-by-side in the same room. No matter what your job is, you work at it. And these days, even if it's not a "desk job," you work at a desk. On a computer. Online. With email and calendars. And if both of you are home together, you're working in parallel, if not together on something. We have developed a pretty good way of doing this over the years that works for us. We share an office with a giant desk where we can work face-to-face. We constantly, gently, interrupt each other as needed, and the interruptee is good about responding as quickly as possible, once he/she has finished processing the most immediate thought. Perhaps most important, we understand enough about what's going on in each of our lives to be immediately helpful on whatever issue comes up, regardless of what the issue is.

The bottom line of all three of these examples is that in 2012, there is no longer a distinction between the personal and the professional. We can't imagine sustaining a healthy marriage without both of us being in the details of both of our lives, 360 degrees around. Whatever the venue, the topic, or the time, each of us is there for the other, working together on it.

Matt Blumberg, Return Path, *www.returnpath.net*
Mariquita Blumberg

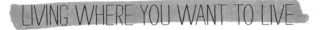

LIVING WHERE YOU WANT TO LIVE

We strongly believe that you should pick the place you want to live and then build your life around it. We moved from Boston to Boulder in 1995. Amy grew up in Alaska and Brad grew up in Texas, so Boston simply didn't feel like home for either of us. When Brad sold his first company in 1993, he promised that we'd be out of Boston by the time he was 30 years old. Two months before Brad turned 30, Amy said, "I'm moving to Boulder and you can come with me if you want." We didn't know if Boulder would end up being our home, but after six months we knew it was and have never looked back.

Mark Solon is a partner in a venture capital firm he started called Highway 12 Ventures. This was the second firm Mark created, after starting one in the 1990s in Boston, where he lived before he met Pam. After they had been together for several years, Pam and Mark Solon decided to move back to Pam's childhood home in Boise where Mark started Highway 12 Ventures. Following is their story.

So much has been written over the years encouraging young people to "do what you love" and to "follow your passions." Conversely, you don't see much devoted to making sure to give equal weight to "living where you want to live." It's our belief that where you live is equally as important to your happiness as what you do, and we lived that notion out when we moved from Boston to Boise in the spring of 2000.

Pam: I'll always remember when Mark woke me on April 11 that year and whispered, "Happy Birthday, let's move to Idaho." He shocked me, as we never had discussed it before—but as he described in Brad's earlier book, *Do More Faster*, he had dreamed for years about living in this beautiful place where I was born and raised. After the initial surprise wore off, I knew we were off for a huge life change, and I couldn't wait to get there. Within 24 hours, he resigned from the private equity firm he was a partner in and we put our house up for sale. Despite being very pregnant and having a one-year-old, I never worried about our careers or how we'd support ourselves. I trusted we would figure that part out. All I knew was that we'd be raising our children in a place that moved us both deeply and that everything else would be okay.

Mark: I realize that saying "where" is as important as "what" is a broad generalization. If your career ambitions are intricately tied to a certain locale, then this opinion doesn't have a lot of merit. However, if you're like the vast majority of us, it's never been easier to create a life for yourself in a town or city that speaks to you. I grew up in New York and until I was 35 I lived in Chicago, San Francisco, and Boston—four pretty amazing cities. However, no place I've ever lived or visited has ever felt more like home to me than Boise. I find it easier to recharge my batteries here than any other place I've been. For me, the lack of traffic, incredible access to a multitude of outdoor activities, climate, and quality of life make this the ideal place to live. Does Boise have its shortcomings? Of course, it does—depending on your perspective, there are many. Given that there are only 200,000 people living here, it's obviously not for everyone. Professionally, there are many other places where being a venture capitalist would have been easier for me. However, I believe down to my toes that I'm better at what I do because of where I live, not despite it.

Pam: Twelve years later, moving to Idaho was the best decision we ever made. It's certainly not for everyone, but for us it's just this side of heaven. Twelve months a year, we live an outdoor-centric life, and it's also very gratifying for us to be active participants in our small community of Boise. No matter how successful Mark would have been in Boston, I know we'd never have reached the level of contentment in our lives that we have living in Idaho.

Mark: When I was younger, I never knew how great an impact my geographical surroundings could have on my mental health. For me, Idaho speaks to me as no place else ever has, and I wake each day feeling as if I won the "where do you want to live" lottery. I watch the way my children are growing up knowing that they'll never fully appreciate it until they leave—and hope the gravitational pull will be as strong for them some day as it is for me.

We believe it's important for young people embarking on their lives to realize that geography matters in your happiness quotient and that it can even outweigh the highest-paying job opportunities. Our advice to everyone pondering these important life questions is to figure out where you can best recharge your batteries regularly, whether that's outdoor activities, health and fitness opportunities, museums and other cultural attractions, climate, having local professional sports teams, etc. Then consider things like population challenges, prevailing ideological sentiments, ease (or challenge) of travel, demographics, and other factors important to your life values. Then you can start investigating how to create a life for yourself there. It's never been easier to weave your career aspirations with where you want to live. Brad has written quite a bit about the importance of doing what you're obsessed with, and we couldn't agree more with that notion. However, doing it where you love to be makes life that much richer.

Mark Solon, Highway 12 Ventures, *http://www.highway12ventures.com/*
Pam Solon, Quarterback for Team Solon, @pamsolon

GO ON ADVENTURES BETWEEN COMPANIES

After an entrepreneur has a company acquired, there is often a transition period of a year or two where he works for the acquiring company. Sometimes this transition period is much shorter, and occasionally even abrupt as there is no plan for him to continue with the acquiring company. In other cases, the entrepreneur stays with the acquirer for many years.

When Brad's first company was acquired, the deal closed on a Friday and he got up at 5:00 A.M. Monday morning and went to the office just like he always did. Eighteen months later, when he stopped working full time for the company that had acquired his, he already was actively involved in a numerous other companies as an angel investor. In our case, there was no sabbatical between companies—Brad literally just started the next thing after taking the weekend to relax and celebrate the success.

In hindsight, we regret this. There were several points in time after the sale of Brad's company that we could have taken anywhere from a month to a year off from full-time work. There are many different things we could have done, all of them adventures that as we've gotten older have worked into our lives as part of our Qx vacation or extended trips to different places such as Paris and Tuscany, where we work, but at a totally different tempo than normal.

Tim Miller founded his first business, Avitek, in 1995. He had been working as a consultant commuting from Boulder to San Francisco for the previous two years. At the time, he and his wife, Jerri, had two young children and Jerri's emotions ranged from frustration about why he couldn't just get a "normal" job to relief that he would now be at home with her and their two young children. About a year after he started the business, Jerri joined him as an accountant for the company.

Avitek was acquired in 1999, and shortly after the sale Tim proposed that they take some time off to sail with their daughters, Elizabeth and Sydney, aged 13 and 10. Following is Jerri's story about their adventure.

It's difficult to quantify the effect of our year sailing, but I believe that it had a profound impact on our lives. Tim was sure that I would shut him down, but I was excited about the plan and we embarked on a yearlong sailing adventure in the Mediterranean and Caribbean in May 2001.

Tim spent nearly a year working on the purchase and outfitting of a 58-foot Tayana that we called *Blue Rhapsody*. When we informed people of our plans, there was a common refrain of "I wish I could do something like that". Every time I heard those words I was reminded of one of the benefits and stressors of being married to an entrepreneur. Tim never prefaces "I could do something like that" with an "I wish." There was a lot of family immersion living on a 58-foot sailboat. The four of us were together 24/7 for nearly the entire year. It even surprises me when I reflect on it because that seems like way too much togetherness!

There were several factors that eased our transition. Tim and I had been working together for several years. The first year required adjustments, and we had some contentious conversations regarding our working styles. We were able to resolve our issues and gain greater understanding about our differences and preferences that allowed us to work and live together more harmoniously. We had also always spent a lot of our free time with the kids. For me, knowing where my 10- and 13-year-old were all of the time (within 58 feet) for an entire year was fantastic! I'm not sure they felt quite the same about it, but everything seems to have worked out in the end.

Taking a significant amount of time away from our lives in Boulder gave us the opportunity to develop in new ways. While we were busy mastering the environment of work, kids and their activities, house remodel, social life, and obligations, we were neglecting work on patience, compassion, and humility. Our lives at home and our lives sailing were very different. We changed the oil on the boat, did most of the cleaning, struggled to communicate with people whose language we didn't speak, and were responsible for the girls' education and entertainment There was always something to fix, maintain, clean, or repair. There were times when we'd finished our morning school session and were having a nice peaceful sail to the next harbor, the girls and I would settle somewhere comfortable with a book, and Tim would start talking about the generator or water maker or refrigeration. I would stifle a groan because I knew we'd soon be dismantling and potentially breaking an essential system. Many other times, we were happy and content, or expecting several guests, and something would break of its own accord. We had plenty of challenges and the occasional emergency to avert any undue complacency or boredom.

Another huge difference between life on a sailboat and life in our land-locked home is that at home I'm always thinking of things we need. I have lists on my iPhone, my computer, and various notepads of what we need. On the boat I was primarily focused on what we didn't need due to weight and storage limitations. I still feel kind of bad that the girls were allowed only one carry-on bag for the year, that I didn't allow guests to use beach towels (too hard to dry, they were given sarongs), and that the only person ever allowed ice was my father-in-law, Don, for his evening Jack Daniels! Once again, everything seemed to work out just fine.

What I learned from our year away was how to recognize what is important to me. I had time for reflection, and I was surrounded by people I loved, and who loved me back with full acceptance of both my more appealing and less desirable traits. I became much more comfortable and confident with myself. While busy at home, I was more concerned about filling roles than thinking about what those roles meant. When we returned from sailing, I put more thought into the activities that I chose to participate in.

I learned that it is a joy to meet another person, couple, or family and never ask them what they do for a living, but spend a day or several days with them eating lunch and dinner together, going for hikes, exploring an island, watching the kids swim from boat to boat, or boat to shore, and just shooting the breeze about who we are, not what we are. Then, never expecting to see them again, just to run into them in a completely different part of the world and start back where we left off.

Our year sailing was one of the best decisions that we have ever made. I recently told Tim that if everything goes to hell and we spend the rest of our lives in misery (something that he doesn't worry about, but I'm always on alert), at least we made one good choice, and I will always be extremely grateful that we had that time as a family.

Jerri Miller
Tim Miller, Rally Software, *www.rallydev.com*

RECOGNIZE THAT LIFE IS A MARATHON, NOT A SPRINT

We've been friends with Dave Jilk for almost 30 years. Brad and Dave met on Brad's first day at MIT during fraternity rush; Dave was a senior and Brad was a freshman. Dave met Amy the next year, when Amy was a first-year student at Wellesley and started hanging out at Brad's fraternity. We were friends for seven years, including two where Amy worked for Feld Technologies, and Dave was her boss—before Brad and Amy became romantically involved.

As with long-term friendships, we all have grown together as well as separately over the past 30 years. When we read this contribution from Dave after he emailed it to us, we both recognized it as a powerful approach to thinking about your life and relationship when you are young.

Copyright 2012 David Jilk

Starting and running a company often feels like a sprint. Everything is urgent—there is always limited money, and either you have a fixed runway of investment capital in which to demonstrate viability or you are trying to make payroll twice a month. Even if you are able to think about your company's long-term vision and strategy, it feels distracting and even inane to contemplate your personal career and its structure. If you focus all your energy on your company, you'll achieve success and can think about these things later. Right?

After having started half a dozen companies over the past 28 years, with varying levels of success, I'm here to tell you that it's worth thinking about some of these issues, even in your first company.

Whether you sell your company or it goes out of business, or it achieves success and you have the opportunity to double down—you will eventually have to think about what comes next. As an entrepreneur, you are developing a valuable skill set and powerful knowledge. Further, whether or not you are aware of it, you are incubating a set of attitudes that will make it increasingly difficult to work in a traditional environment. Consequently, your next gig is very likely to be starting another company. That's how it went for me, and it seems like serial entrepreneurship is becoming the rule rather than the exception.

If I could send my younger self a message from the future, it would tell me to treat my career more like a marathon than a sprint.

One area on which I would focus my marathon training is planning and taking real vacations. While I have sometimes had the opportunity to take longer vacations while "between companies," I have generally resisted them while running a company. I have always felt like I needed to put all my energy toward the company, and a vacation takes me away for too long. I have also had the idea that I will have plenty of time off when the company is a success and I can retire or semiretire.

That approach may or may not have worked for me, but it definitely doesn't satisfy my wife, Maureen. She has a more traditional job where she earns substantial vacation time. Indeed, the "upside" in her job is precisely the opportunity to take real vacations. She has been patient, but she wants our vacation plans to be a part of our life now, not merely a fantasy for the future.

We have taken a couple of longer vacations, and they have met with mixed success in my psychology. While I have enjoyed them, it felt like I couldn't allow anything to go wrong because time away is so limited. This makes the vacation more stressful than I'd like—every potential point of failure in the logistics gets out of proportion, and issues that are outside my circle of control (weather, health) create useless worry. Also, although I am pretty good at disconnecting, it puts a lot of stress on the situation that I'll be out of touch for more than a week (typically the places Maureen and I want to go are not well connected). I'm a good delegator, so one week is usually not a problem, but two weeks can be. I also struggle with really getting relaxed during the vacation, because I know I'm going to have to go back. It feels like signing autographs during the sprint.

In contrast, Maureen has unambiguously loved our vacations and travel experiences. She thinks we should travel more, not only because she enjoys it, but also so I can learn to pace myself for the inevitable mishaps of travel as well as those associated with the realities of running a startup. She reminds me that, in the words of John Steinbeck, "A journey is like marriage. The certain way to be wrong is to think you control it."

Had I taken a marathon view from the beginning, I would have put some thought into what reasonable vacations look like for an entrepreneur. I would have taken into consideration what both Maureen and I want and need in vacations. Factors to consider include how much time in a year, how much time away at once, where we want to go and what we want to do, and whether or not to stay "connected." I think it's valuable to come up with an overall framework and try to stick to it. As in a marathon, you have to pace yourself, drink water, and take electrolytes at appropriate intervals.

Dave Jilk, Standing Cloud, *www.standingcloud.com*
Maureen Amundson, Paralegal

SIBLING DYNAMICS

Brad and his brother, Daniel, are both entrepreneurs living in Boulder. While their work
paths cross regularly, they have worked hard
to maintain a separate sibling relationship
that trumps the work dynamics.

The brothers have been partners in a
consulting business, have worked together
at a venture capital firm, and have had several other intersections where Daniel was
an executive of a company in which Brad
was also an investor or board member. While this type of interaction may
be awkward or unthinkable for some siblings, Daniel and Brad have been
clear with each other from the beginning and worked hard to keep separation between their work and personal relationships, with priority placed on
maintaining their personal relationship above all else.

Trust, honesty, and respect for each other are critical components to
Brad and Daniel's success at walking this line. Respecting each other for
their similarities and differences as entrepreneurs, community leaders,
and individuals is a key value for both brothers. This was encouraged
by their parents from childhood and cultivated by the brothers during
adulthood.

One interesting dynamic of the brothers working in similar circles
is the occasional "do you know Brad Feld?" question. As Brad's visibility
has grown over the years, Daniel regularly encounters people who see
him as a way to get access to Brad. While this can be annoying, Daniel and Brad have come up with a very clear way to deal with it. Daniel
is unambiguous when recommending someone to Brad and clear that
when he doesn't, the person should feel free to reach out to Brad at his
easily discoverable email address (brad@feld.com). But neither Brad
nor Daniel plays a game around this, and Daniel is clear about his own
entrepreneurial identity.

To build and maintain their sibling bonds, Brad and Daniel actively
invest time and attention to their relationship. They do this through shared
experiences, regularly scheduled get-togethers, and spontaneous interactions. Ten years ago, the brothers started getting together for an annual
Feld Men's trip. This is typically a short but intense three-day get-together

with Brad and Daniel's father, uncle, and cousins. Additionally, Daniel and Brad schedule dinners together throughout the year, where they can talk about whatever they want to discuss and catch up with each other. Sometimes dinner is about business, relationships, activities, interests, or world events, and sometimes it's about their parents. There's also the occasional quick email, phone call, or hike in the mountains for more spontaneous touch points. These dinners and quick check-ins provide a regular chance for Brad and Daniel to connect and stay grounded in their relationship as brothers.

THE SANDWICH GENERATION

It's inevitable that as you get older, your parents will get older. At some point, you may find yourself confronted with aging parents and the roles and responsibility that can come along with caring for them in the twilight of their life. This situation can be exacerbated by the demands of raising children at the same time as your parents are declining. Being bidirectional caregivers can be emotionally difficult and very stressful. As an entrepreneurial couple, this is made more complex by money, geography, and value systems.

Let's start with money. Brad's parents and Amy's mother have different financial situations. As a result, the conversations we have are very different ones around near-term financial needs and providing financial support. In addition, health care costs and insurance situations are different, and the current health dynamic of each parent impacts this. This is an area where having a good foundation for talking about hard topics will stand you in good stead. What's the money for? How much do you do for one of your families and not the other? Can you trade time with one set of parents against money for the other? What are the roles and responsibilities of your siblings, who may be in a different financial position than you? Make time when you're calm and well rested to discuss these hard topics with your partner.

Geography is another challenging issue. Brad's parents have lived in the same house in Dallas for our entire relationship. Amy's mom lived alone in Pittsburgh after moving from Alaska until it made more sense for her to be physically closer to her three daughters for care and support, at which time she moved to the Boulder area. If your aging parent lives far away, additional travel on top of the often-demanding startup company travel schedule can add to an already stressful situation. Deciding how to compromise on who provides child care while one of you travels to your parent's city, how much time to spend apart, and whether to try to provide plane tickets for other siblings can all be complicated. Our actions toward and relationship with each parent doesn't have to be exactly equivalent, but we have do need to be aligned in our view of how we offer support to each.

Talk together regularly to make sure you are in alignment on your decisions. Offer support and show extra kindness above and beyond your regular daily quotient to your partner who is dealing with an aging parent. Acknowledging and accepting the mortality of your parents is another benchmark of adulthood that's not very pleasant. Having the presence of your partner beside you can help ease this difficult reality.

CHAPTER THIRTEEN

SEX AND ROMANCE

I f you and your partner are young and energetic, you may think that sex and romance aren't things you need to think about; but like many areas of life, the effort that you put in creates increasing returns. Sex and romance are areas where actions speak much more loudly than words and often get overlooked as a relationship matures, especially in the chaos of an entrepreneurial life.

Sex is the thing that you do with your partner that you don't do with anyone else. If you have unresolved issues or uncommunicated emotions, particularly negative ones like resentment, anger, or frustration, your sex life can be impacted or can become an arena where unresolved tensions are played out. Instead of being a playground of intimacy, connection, and good feelings, your sex life can become a battleground. It can be fun. It can be complicated. It can be a tool. It can be a weapon. It can be an emotional and physical release. Ideally, it's wonderful.

Romance is a key part of the intimacy of a committed relationship. It's also one of the first things to be tossed out the window or ignored in the cadence of a busy life. Gender dynamics around romance fill volumes of self-help books, and one partner's definition of romance is often mysterious and confusing to the other partner. Like sex, romance requires effort over time, and the patterns developed early in a relationship pay off throughout the life of the relationship.

COMMUNICATION AROUND SEX

We think of sex as a very special form of communication. Many of the same guidelines for other types of communication we've discussed earlier apply here. Gender dynamics often play a big role in sex, and this can be accentuated by the intensity of the entrepreneurial life. In Brad's first marriage, sex was clearly a weapon that accelerated the demise of his relationship. From the beginning of our relationship, we've worked hard to make it a special, magical shared experience.

While we each brought previous sexual experiences to our relationship, we were sensitive to each other's emotional dynamics around sex. Brad had been hurt by sexual infidelity on the part of his first wife; Amy had been in a long relationship with a partner who was HIV-positive, so she felt danger around the edges of her sexual experience. While our early sex was mind-blowingly incredible, we were both careful to talk not just about the sex itself, but how it made us feel, both good and bad.

Talking about sex wasn't a burden. In many cases, merely talking about it led to more sex. Or better sex. And it established a deep intimacy around our conversational patterns early in our relationship. We were sensitive about the timing of the discussion—each of us were aware that the best time to talk about sex was when we were both rested, relaxed, and ready, and usually not in the bedroom.

We laugh a lot and made sure that humor was part of our sexual experience. While we have moments of deep, slow, quiet, serious sex, we also have plenty of giggling, laughing, and lying in bed afterwards making funny noises and teasing each other about something completely random.

Twenty years into our relationship we still periodically talk about sex. We don't have crazy monkey sex as often as we did the first few years of our relationship, but when we do we both acknowledge that we've still got it, often with a whoop and a high five when we've caught our breath after a bout of lovemaking that alarms the dogs.

Having an active and healthy sex life is a great way of taking care of your physical self, emotional self, and your partner. The emotional intimacy that comes from it transcends and helps heal many of the struggles of everyday life and provides mutual strength in the face of the pressure of an entrepreneurial life.

Each of you is responsible for figuring out what you need and communicating that to your partner. It can be hard to express feelings about sex or to give constructive feedback about things that don't work for you. Honesty isn't just the best policy here; it's the only way to be.

THE WORK OF ROMANCE

While "the work of romance" might sound like an oxymoron, we've found that there are some tactics you can practice to keep romance alive while working on your company and traveling, emailing, and taking care of a million other things. While some of the tactics we list here may seem small, the cumulative impact of doing them on a regular basis shows your partner that she matters to you.

First, always answer her calls, no matter what you are doing. Brad let Amy choose her ringtone for his phone; she chose "The Imperial March" from *Star Wars*. Whenever it goes off, Brad politely tells whomever he is with that his wife, Amy, is calling and he needs to take the call. This might be in front of 500 people when Brad is giving a talk on Startup Communities or in front of one of Brad's investors in a one-on-one meeting. Brad always apologizes after for the interruption but explains that we have an agreement that he will answer the phone anytime Amy calls. To date, no one has ever objected or been offended by this, and we know of many people who have adopted this. Amy also is sensitive when Brad is with other people and makes her calls brief.

When Brad is on the road, he tries to send Amy something every day. Sometimes it's a quick postcard from wherever he is, such as one that says "Seattle with love." In the airport, Brad swings through one of the gift shops, grabs a few cute local postcards—one for each day—and puts them by the bed at night. Upon waking, he fills it out quickly and drops it off at the front desk to be sent to Amy at home. Sometimes he substitutes flowers for a postcard, or does this in addition to the postcard.

We each make small gestures along with our grand gestures. We each regularly and deliberately say "thank you" and "I love you." We say nice things about what the other has done. We say nice things to each other about our friends and family, reinforcing that we are good spirited. These aren't forced or artificial; after 20 years together, they are at the core of the way we communicate and reinforce our fondness for each other.

We have two giant golden retrievers who give us their undivided attention, especially when we have food in our hands. We call this "golden retriever eyes," and Brad has learned that Amy loves being on the receiving end of golden retriever eyes. So when we listen, we use both our ears and our eyes.

Different people have different ideas of what constitutes romance. If she thinks cut flowers are wasteful and useless, don't send them. If he doesn't enjoy haute cuisine, don't book a table at the fanciest place in town for date night. Don't try to force your view of what you think is romantic on your partner. Instead, turn it around and lead with what your partner thinks is romantic. While doing this, work on expanding your gratitude for the attempts your partner makes, even if those attempts sometimes fall short. Effort does count, and partial credit should be given when grading on this particular scale.

The work of romance can and should be fun. Don't be afraid to mix sex with the romance; give your partner a coupon book for certain sexual favors. But don't force the linkage between romance and sex—nothing is a buzz kill like feeling obligated to have sex because of a romantic gesture from your partner.

You and your partner will inevitably be disappointed by the other, especially in a romantic context. A missed anniversary or birthday, a distracted evening out together, or a last-minute call that interrupts a planned event will unfortunately occur. We've had this happen to each of us, and have learned that there is no value in becoming attached to being the injured party. Instead of using your partner's remorse and guilt over blowing a romantic moment, be quick to forgive, and communicate your forgiveness. Your partner will appreciate it and will try harder the next time.

GOAL ORIENTATION

You may disagree about whether to bring goal orientation into your sex life or whether you need a spreadsheet to track your data, but subjective emotions can be tempered by objective information. If you can agree on the amount, frequency, and type of actions that matter, then you can see whether the entrepreneurial partner is meeting those targets. It's also a way to forestall feeling nagged or being falsely accused of being neglectful.

Early in our relationship, we made a list of what each of us enjoys, from the tiny, daily, incremental, cumulative things like saying "I love you" to surprise weekend getaways. We used this list to build basic patterns into our romantic efforts and evolved them over time. We still sit down every now and then with a blank piece of paper and talk about what we haven't done together that we'd love to.

For a few years we kept a jar in the kitchen with dollar bills in it. Each time we had sex, we put another dollar in the jar. If it was really amazing sex, we put a five dollar bill in the jar. At the end of the year, we went out to a fancy dinner with the money in the sex jar. We did this to have fun with the objective measure and, after we'd done it for a few years, stopped to play around with a different fun measure, such as the hearts that Amy puts in her day timer every time we knock boots.

If one of you doesn't feel like you are having enough sex, talk about it. Recall the scene in Annie Hall:

> [Alvy and Annie are seeing their therapists at the same time on a split screen]
> Alvy Singer's therapist: How often do you sleep together?

Annie Hall's therapist: Do you have sex often?
Alvy Singer: [*lamenting*] Hardly ever. Maybe three times a week.
Annie Hall: [*annoyed*] Constantly. I'd say three times a week.

Once again, communicate. With each other. Often.

CONFLICT AROUND SEX

Sex can be the source of some of the biggest conflicts in any relationship. Over the years, we've experienced many different conflicts around sex. Our ability to discuss them openly and work through them is an important part of the success of our relationship.

Early in our relationship we had to deal with the issue of infidelity given that this was the trigger that ended Brad's first marriage. We agreed early on that infidelity—both physical and emotional—was an unforgivable act. By agreeing on this early, it made the time apart, which is impossible to avoid in an entrepreneurial relationship, easier to deal with because there was never a concern where, or with whom, one of us was sleeping.

We brought different sexual experiences into our relationship. Each of us had a different tolerance and desire to try certain things. When one of us was uncomfortable or uninterested in something, we acknowledged it, discussed it, and decided whether or not it should exist in our shared sexual repertoire. If we decided it didn't, which was the occasional outcome, there was no resentment, just a mutual understanding that it was okay not to want to try something.

Our close friend Warren Katz adds some thoughts on committing to the long term.

Well, this is quite an interesting topic for entrepreneurs, something that is constantly debated, revisited, and ruminated over and over again.

The easier "sticking with it" question is often targeted at the company or business opportunity in which the entrepreneur is engaged. Usually, the emotional ties are eclipsed by financial return on investment (ROI) concerns and liquidation paths, and there are often a significant number of parties involved. One can relatively easily compute whether staying is better than going, and often others make the decision.

The tougher relationship to evaluate is your spousal/family situation. Entrepreneurs have all the regular problems every other couple has, compounded by a few overriding stresses:

- Entrepreneur is usually a Type-A workaholic.
- Even if not a Type-A workaholic, entrepreneur is usually expected to work more than everyone else around him.
- Expectation that a spouse will relieve workday stress, not add to it.
- Excessive single point of failure for financial future of family (whether in deep debt to fund the company or too much net worth wrapped up in one place).
- Ego and financially driven sense of entitlement for entrepreneur (why can't I have a family and a bunch of 20-something mistresses as well).
- Financially driven sense of entitlement for spouse (if that SOB is going to spend all his time on the road, I'm going to drown my boredom in jewelry, cars, fur coats, etc.).

Well, I've seen every possible variation of outcome from my entrepreneur friends, from the dedicated long-term monogamous partnership that is unwavering, to the self-centered cooling, distanced permanent détente, to the surface show marriage accompanied by secret partners on both sides, to eventual divorce after a long protracted show for the benefit of kids or business appearances, to the quick violent separation followed by bitter protracted warfare over assets, to the remarriage to trophy arm-candy.

There isn't enough space here to go through every one of these perturbations, and I'm only qualified to describe my own situation, but let me first observe one overriding common characteristic of entrepreneurs that often plays a strong role in their selected paths. Entrepreneurs who have found themselves in managerial roles (a large percentage) are indoctrinated over time to understand that bad employment situations get worse much more often than they get better. After attempting time and time again to salvage bad personnel situations and being burned over and over, an instinct of objectively assessing likely futures and acting on them sooner rather than later is something most entrepreneurs develop. An oft-quoted entrepreneur's adage is "I never fired too soon." One can easily see how an entrepreneur might then apply this objective eye and faster trigger to their personal lives, despite the emotional implications (which also exist in the corporate environment). Most entrepreneurs are just less prone to let chronic situations drag on.

Now, on to my situation: I met my lovely wife, Ilana, in 1988, before I started my company, one year out of college, while I still had a negative net worth. I started my company in 1990, and we married in 1993. She was supportive throughout the process, and considering we never had kids, was not very selfish regarding my time. When wondering whether she loves me for me, or loves me for my money, I just think back to the time we drove around in my 1983 rusted-out Dodge Colt. She loved me then, and I am comforted. As the demands on my time increased, and my net worth rose, Ilana remained down-to-earth and never developed any expensive habits or hobbies. Though watching her spend 20 minutes of my time arguing over a 10-cent coupon in the grocery store was an amusing waste of pricey C-level labor, I vastly prefer that ingrained instinct to any of the likely alternatives. Ilana's biggest angst about money is that her husband has developed some expensive habits and she's concerned about my expenditures getting out of hand. I view that as a good counterforce in my life.

The biggest problem in our relationship was probably my Type-A egocentric sense of entitlement regarding women. Though I kept Ilana apprised and involved as much as she could handle as I have a problem with lying or keeping secrets, ultimately this was a choice I had to make. After many ups and downs, I finally admitted that I'm not likely to be a porn star any more and any attractive women that were interested in me at that point were interested in things other than my irresistible manliness. So my entitlement to wild sexual experiences had to go. Though disappointed by that realization and decision I was forced into, I have become more and more at peace with it as time goes on, and the benefits have clearly outweighed the sacrifice.

Ilana herself is sexy and funny as shit. I don't ever want to do a mind-meld with her, as her mind is a dangerous and scary place to go wandering around, but what comes out of her mouth makes you pee in your pants. Overall, every day I came home from a hard day of work I received support (sometimes unwelcome when I needed just to go into my cave), a hot meal or the offer to make one, and some funny repartee. I have to pay a price by spending some energy picking up her sometimes-fragile ego, but toughness in those areas is something I think she's picked up from me so even that has been getting pretty reasonable these days.

Yeah, I stuck with it and I'm happy with that decision.

Warren Katz, Mak Technologies, *www.mak.com*
Ilana Katz, Novelist and Boston Subway Fiddler, *www.ilanakatz.com*

We have different styles around privacy, some gender based and some personality based. Early on, we discovered that it was easy to criticize the other in public using a nasty comment about sex, or lack thereof, and decided to keep our sex life private. At the same time, we decided it was okay to talk to close friends about positive aspects of our sex life, especially if it came up in the context of a struggle a friend was having with their own sex life. Every now and then one of us will say something publicly that hurts the other; whenever this happens, the injured partner brings it up the next time we are alone together and clearly expresses what was said that hurt. The person who said it acknowledges the statement, apologizes, and we move on.

Timing and fatigue is another source of conflict. When we find ourselves out of a rhythm, because Amy's hormones are alive and kicking in the afternoon when Brad is at work and Brad is thinking about a quickie before bedtime when Amy is tired and doesn't feel like anything other than going to sleep, we listen to the other and put effort into getting into sync and making time for sex, rather than defaulting into it when we are getting into bed to go to sleep at night. While Brad's 14-year-old inner self could never imagine a situation where he'd be lying naked next to a woman yet be uninterested in sex, it happens, and it's okay, rather than a being source of anger, frustration, or disappointment for us.

KEEPING THE MAGIC ALIVE

We aren't going to pretend to be your sex therapists, but we've got a few hints that we'll end on about keeping the magic alive.

If you haven't had sex for a while, or are finding that it's never satisfying, carve out time to talk about it in a safe place. We've gone through dry spells in our relationship and have learned that if more than a month goes by without some adult entertainment, something might be going on. Often, nothing is, and by merely talking about it we reignite the flame. But sometimes something has been bothering one of us, even if we haven't been able to figure out what it specifically is, and the conversation brings it to the surface. Usually, this is around our specific priorities at a particular moment in time, and it helps us bring each other and our partnership back into focus as the ultimate priority.

We surprise each other constantly with humorous little hints. The other day Brad came home to a *New Yorker* cartoon on the keyboard on his desk titled "The Married Kama Sutra." After reading the caption that said "When the man is loading the dishwasher, and the woman must come over, because he is loading it wrong, it is called 'the dishwasher position.'" (*The New Yorker*, 9/24/12, p. 74) After two decades together, we've still never really resolved the dishwasher loading algorithm, but having a sense of humor, and a cartoon that validates that we're not alone in this struggle, really helps.

As we've gotten older, we've explored different tempos. Unlike the movies, we don't often rush into the house, tear each other's clothes off, and do it in the middle of the living room like we used to early in our relationship when we lived in a one-room loft apartment. Instead, we come home, let the dogs out, go through our evening routines, draw a bath, and sit together for a while as the dirt of the day gets washed away. These moments are quiet and intimate, even if they don't result in a mutual orgasm leaving us both breathless. As we crawl into bed and cuddle, we know the magic is there.

CHAPTER FOURTEEN

ENOUGH

The idea of "enough" is not a common notion in American culture. From an early age we are taught to strive for, accomplish, and acquire more. Endless comparisons to our neighbors are rampant, and we are always trying to "keep up with the Joneses." Our successes are never enough—"I sold my company but only made $1 million from it—I've really got to go for it the next time." Our cars are not fancy enough; our toys are not the newest, best ones; and our house can always use a bigger something.

The first entrepreneurial success is a defining moment for many entrepreneurs and their partners. While some entrepreneurs grew up with financial resources from their families, many didn't. They start their first company with no money, sleep on a mattress, drive a car that barely works, and save every dime they can for when they might need it if things don't go well. A first-time entrepreneur's life is exciting and intense, but rarely extravagant.

While many entrepreneurs toil away for many years before having a financial success, when it happens, it often happens fast. One day you have no money in your bank account, have plenty of debt, and are often shuffling around small bits of money to make ends meet. Then your company is acquired, and overnight you have a bank account with seven, eight, or even nine figures in it.

It's disorienting. Previously, you spent no time with money managers—even going to an ATM generated some anxiety that there wouldn't be any money available, and credit card offers that came in the mail were actually opened in the hope that this one would contain an offer with an interest rate that actually was reasonable. Now you get daily calls from money managers, investment advisers, and family offices to help you out.

GO SLOW

Our first advice to entrepreneurial couples who call us after they've had some success is "go slow." Don't make any decisions about money for the first 90 days. There will be urgency and pressure on you to "put the money to work," "sign up with money managers," or "figure out a strategy." In the grand scheme of things, 90 days won't matter. Take a deep breath, have a few nice dinners, but take it slow. Don't make any commitments, to anyone.

THE 10 PERCENT RULE

Financial entrepreneurial success can't be timed. We describe it as "a big bag of money fell out of the sky and hit us on the head." Sure, Brad works incredibly hard as an entrepreneur and investor, but the timing of the exit is completely unpredictable. We live within our cash flow means on a daily basis, but when a big bag of money falls out of the sky, we follow something called the 10 percent rule.

We spend 10 percent of what we just got on something extravagant. Early on, these numbers often translated into a new car, a piece of art that was outside of our reach, or a house. By bounding the number to 10 percent, we didn't have to struggle with what we would spend—it was a fixed, predetermined amount. The first few times we did this were an awesome celebration of the success we'd just had and a way for us to share in the results of the hard work. Since we had preallocated 10 percent to this, there was no guilt around the purchase. There was no personal baggage around money to mess us up about what we wanted to do. We just did it.

The fact that we had a 10 percent upper bound was also helpful. We simply viewed our after-tax income as being reduced by 10 percent—the deal included 90 percent cash and 10 percent a special magic thing we wanted. We'd name these things—the house AmeriData built, the NetGenesis car—and remember them long into the future.

DO YOU HAVE TO BE FRUGAL IN YOUR NEXT STARTUP?

Most entrepreneurs aren't done after their first successful company. While some run their company their entire adult lives, most end up leaving, especially if their company is acquired. Entrepreneurs are wired to create companies—that's what they do—and it often isn't long before the next startup idea starts germinating.

By now you are sleeping in a comfortable master bed in a big house. You drive a fancy car. You eat out at nice restaurants whenever you want. You fly first class. You don't think twice about staying at a $500-per-night hotel when you travel. As a couple, you are used to the comforts that come from making a sizable amount of money.

As you walk into the dark, cramped office you've subleased for your new company, you realize the intellectual dissonance that exists between the beautiful office you have at home and the shithole you are camping out in as you work to get company number two off the ground. The difference is disorienting but powerful.

A startup is still a startup. Every dime matters, even if you have plenty of them to waste. The culture you set at the beginning—how you spend money as a startup—will get amplified quickly throughout your organization as it grows. While you may have more resources this time around, your goal with your startup is still to invest the least amount of money to make the most progress as quickly as possible. But more important than being frugal, recognize that you are setting a tone.

You can disconnect this from your personal life. There's no reason to scale down your house or your living expenses just for show for your future employees. You were successful and made a lot of money on your last business—enjoy that. But separate the personal extravagance from the business context.

The best entrepreneurs are thoughtful about this, not because they are being judged, but because it helps eliminate the dissonance. If you are used to flying first class but you want everyone in your company to fly coach, have the company pay for the coach portion of your ticket while you personally cover the first-class segment. Or take your chances by buying coach and relying on an upgrade. Stay in the same hotels your employees do. Use a simple rule: if you don't want the company to cover something for all employees but you want to do it for yourself, simply pay for the difference.

HOW MUCH IS ENOUGH?

Many years ago we were sitting at dinner with another entrepreneurial couple. The husband was on his second startup; his first had gone public. He was working as hard as ever flying around the world. Over dinner the topic of enough came up. Brad started by saying, "I've always had enough money—I'm in this for other things." Our friend countered by saying, "Once I have $10 million in the bank, I'll have enough." At the time we had nowhere near $10 million in the bank, so we remember jumping out of our chairs a little and then having a very deep conversation about what "enough" meant.

Several years later we were together with this couple again. He was on his third company—the one he had been part of was on a success path even though he was no longer part of it. The same conversation came up. This time the magic number was $20 million. "What changed from the $10 million number," asked Brad? "I decided $10 million wasn't enough," said our friend. We talked for a while but never really got to the root cause of the change in number.

Our friend had continued success and blew through his $20 million number. But he kept starting companies. He had an incredible track record of success and was in demand as a board member and angel investor in addition to being a full-time CEO. He had a growing family, several beautiful houses, was in great health, and had an awesome relationship.

One day he had a fluke accident and broke his back. He was lucky and had a full recovery within a year. This was an accident of inches—a few in one direction and he would have been crippled for life or possibly dead.

He came out of the accident realizing he had enough. He decided to retire to raise his kids, spend more time with his wife, travel more, and work on things with people he was passionate about. Through facing a potential life-threatening tragedy, he realized that enough had nothing to do with money.

WHAT DOES RETIREMENT MEAN?

The historical American notion of a gold watch at retirement doesn't apply to entrepreneurs. For starters, if they want a gold watch, most entrepreneurs will have bought themselves one much earlier in their lives. Entrepreneurs also rarely wait for other people to give them things, other than the regular awards they get for being entrepreneurs, which are usually received with humility and a touch of amusement or embarrassment. In an entrepreneurial context, retirement is a foreign concept.

Brad will be 47 when this book is published. He's been working hard as an entrepreneur since he was 19. We expect he'll work hard at something until the lights go out given his deep intrinsic motivation for learning. But we've talked often about what this means. Will it be software and Internet startups? Or will it be a second career in metal sculpture or the practice of bonsai?

We consciously decided not to wait until retirement to enjoy all the things we would otherwise do in retirement. We've woven into our daily life the notion of sabbaticals, extended trips together for a month or more, time completely disconnected from work, and experiments living in different cities for stretches of time.

Other entrepreneurial friends of ours have retired for periods of time after they sold a company. One took a year off and sailed around the world with his wife and teenage daughters. Another took the summer off and read a bunch of the great books. Yet another took several years off, moved to a foreign country, and studied a new language while experiencing life in a different culture with his family.

Retirement for an entrepreneur is a very different concept. The mistake isn't "not retiring"; it is not understanding that it means something entirely different. And the deeper mistake is not discussing it as a couple and understanding what each of your expectations are.

ARE YOU AND YOUR PARTNER IN DIFFERENT PLACES?

We both agree that we're not envisioning a life where Brad plays golf and canasta all day, but we do have different ideas of when a time would come that Brad's calendar wasn't already full an entire year in advance. Amy would like it to come sooner than Brad. The discussions we started having several years ago highlighted that we were in very different places as a couple on the topic.

Brad approached it without a clear commitment to an end point. While consistent with his personality and belief that life is over when the lights go out, it highlighted a key difference in perspective. Amy shares the same belief but wasn't willing to defer a set of activities indefinitely in the context of this belief system. More important, the lack of certainty of what and when retirement meant reinforced a workaholic concern that Amy had.

Specifically, work is a central part of Brad's life. At times, it's hard to tell whether it is ambition, workaholism, or a psychological dynamic—either to be needed or to avoid dealing with all the other things in life. For Amy, this isn't an acceptable dynamic, especially in the context of either defaulting into endlessly behaving the same way or creating an inflexible singular entrepreneurial identity for Brad.

We've addressed this by talking about it. Every year, we look a year forward and discuss what the tempo of the next 12 months will be. We also talk about a time where there will be a conclusion of a gradual mode shift into fewer work commitments. We've arbitrarily decided that this is when

Brad turns 60 years old. It's not that on Brad's 60th birthday he will suddenly retire; rather, over the next 13 years we will continue to tune the way we spend our time, especially around work, so that when Brad turns 60 it will be natural to be in a totally different head space around work.

As with many things we've discussed in this book, this is complicated and ever changing. We could easily change the age to 55 just as we could extend it out to 65. Or we could redefine the overall context, accelerating focus on certain activities while letting others that we think are important to us today fade into the background. As always, it's important that we talk openly and regularly about this, recognize when we are in different places, and work hard to be in a similar place.

We've also done some things that people might ordinarily save for their retirement years, like spend eight weeks in Europe where Brad was still working, but maybe only 40 hours a week or some similarly small and manageable amount. Several friends joined us at the place we rented in Italy and made our midlife mini-sabbatical extra special. We make his birthday celebration last at least a week and invite 15 to 20 friends to join us in some fun place like Scottsdale or Mexico. We make Amy's birthday celebration equally celebratory and social.

It can be hard to keep your focus on the values and goals that really matter to you, which we're hoping are a happy life, happy work, and happy love.

PRACTICE, PRACTICE, PRACTICE

Throughout this book we've given you lots of things to think about and try. Some of these might not work for you and your partner. You will have new ideas we haven't thought about, or variations on ideas that dramatically improve our suggestions. Hopefully you've gotten the sense that a willingness to try, an openness to exploring what works and what doesn't, and a desire to continue to improve your partnership results in a long-lasting and happy relationship over time.

We've found that practice may not make perfect, but it helps keep the love alive. We hope this helps you during your journey together.

BIBLIOGRAPHY

Communication and Gender

Tannen, Deborah, PhD. *You Just Don't Understand: Women and Men in Conversation.* New York: Ballantine, 1990; Quill, 2001.
Tannen, Deborah, PhD. *Talking from 9 to 5: Women and Men at Work.* Avon, 1994.

Entrepreneurship

Feld, Brad, and David Cohen. *Do More Faster: TechStars Lessons to Accelerate Your Startup.* Hoboken, NJ: John Wiley & Sons, 2010.
Hirshberg, Meg Cadoux. *For Better or for Work: A Survival Guide for Entrepreneurs and Their Families.* An Inc. Original, 2012.
Roberts, Ed. *Entrepreneurs in High Technology: Lessons from MIT and Beyond.* Oxford University Press, 1991.

Marriage

Gray, John. *Men Are from Mars, Women Are from Venus: A Practical Guide for Improving Communication and Getting What You Want in Your Relationships.* New York: Harper Collins, 1992.
Pope, Tara Parker. *For Better: How the Surprising Science of Happy Couples Can Help Your Marriage Succeed.* Dutton Adult, 2010.
Szuchman, Paula, and Jenny Anderson. *Spousonomics: Using Economics to Master Love, Marriage, and Dirty Dishes.* New York: Random House, 2011.

Meditation

Brantley, Jeffrey, and Wendy Millstine. *Five Good Minutes with the One You Love: 100 Mindful Practices to Deepen and Renew Your Love Every Day.* New Harbinger Publications, 2008.

Brantley, Jeffrey and Wendy Millstine. *Five Good Minutes: 100 Morning Practices to Help You Stay Calm and Focused All Day Long.* New Harbinger Publications, 2005.

Brantley, Jeffrey, and Wendy Millstine. *Five Good Minutes at Work: 100 Mindful Practices to Help You Relieve Stress and Bring Your Best to Work.* New Harbinger Publications, 2007.

Brantley, Jeffrey, and Wendy Millstine. *Five Good Minutes in the Evening: 100 Mindful Practices to Help You Unwind from the Day and Make the Most of Your Night.* New Harbinger Publications, 2006.

Brantley, Jeffrey, and Wendy Millstine. *Five Good Minutes in Your Body: 100 Mindful Practices to Help You Accept Yourself and Feel at Home in Your Body.* New Harbinger Publications, 2009.

Chodron, Pema. *Comfortable with Uncertainty: 108 Teachings on Cultivating Fearlessness and Compassion.* Shambhala, 2008.

Chodron, Pema. *When Things Fall Apart: Heart Advice for Difficult Times.* Shambala Classics, 2000.

Chodron, Pema. *The Places that Scare You: A Guide to Fearlessness in Difficult Times.* Shambala Classics, 2008.

Hanh, Thich Nhat. *Happiness: Essential Mindfulness Practices.* Parallax Press, 2009.

Hanh, Thich Nhat. *Peace Is Every Step: The Path of Mindfulness in Everyday Life.* Bantam, 1992.

Kabat-Zinn, Jon. *Mindfulness for Beginners: Reclaiming the Present Moment—and Your Life.* Sounds True, 2011.

Kabat-Zinn, Jon. *Full Catastrophe Living: Using the Wisdom of Your Body and Mind to Face Stress, Pain, and Illness.* Delta, 1990.

Mortality

O'Kelly, Eugene. *Chasing Daylight.* New York: McGraw-Hill, 2005.

Pausch, Randy. *The Last Lecture.* New York: Hyperion, 2008.

Personal Finance

Orman, Suze. *The 9 Steps to Financial Freedom: Practical and Spiritual Steps So You Can Stop Worrying.* New York: Crown, 1997.

Orman, Suze. *Suze Orman's Action Plan, New Rules for New Times.* Spiegel & Grau, 2010.

Philosophy

Ariely, Dan. *Predictably Irrational: The Hidden Forces that Shape Our Decisions.* New York: Harper, 2009.

Bok, Sissela. *Secrets: On the Ethics of Concealment and Revelation.* Pantheon, 1983.

Bok, Sissela. *Exploring Happiness: From Aristotle to Brain Science.* Yale University Press, 2010.

Cain, Susan. *Quiet: The Power of Introverts in a World that Can't Stop Talking.* New York: Crown, 2012.

Conniff, Richard. *The Ape in the Corner Office: How to Make Friends, Win Fights and Work Smarter by Understanding Human Nature.* New York: Crown Business, 2005.

Duhigg, Charles. *The Power of Habit.* New York: Random House, 2012.

Gilbert, Daniel. *Stumbling on Happiness.* Vintage, 2007.

Lyubomirsky, Sonja. *The How of Happiness: A New Approach to Getting the Life You Want.* Penguin Press, 2007.

Rubin, Gretchen. *The Happiness Project: Or, Why I Spent a Year Trying to Sing in the Morning, Clean My Closets, Fight Right, Read Aristotle, and Generally Have More Fun.* New York: Harper, 2009.

Rubin, Gretchen. *Happier at Home: Kiss More, Jump More, Abandon a Project, Read Samuel Johnson, and My Other Experiments in the Practice of Everyday Life.* Crown Archtype, 2012.

Sandel, Michael. *What Money Can't Buy: The Moral Limits of Markets.* Farrar, Straus and Giroux, 2012.

Schwartz, Barry. *The Paradox of Choice: Why More Is Less.* Harper Perennial, 2005.

Seligman, Martin. *Learned Optimism: How to Change Your Mind and Your Life.* New York: Knopf, 1991.

Seligman, Martin. *Authentic Happiness: Using the New Positive Psychology to Realize Your Potential for Lasting Fulfillment.* Free Press, 2002.

Seligman, Martin. *Flourish: A Visionary New Understanding of Happiness and Well-Being.* Free Press, 2011.

Positive Psychology

Dweck, Carol. *Mindset: The New Psychology of Success.* New York: Random House, 2006.

Zolli, Andrew, and Ann Marie Healy. *Resilience: Why Things Bounce Back.* Free Press, 2012.

Romance

Godek, Gregory J. P. *1001 Ways to Be Romantic.* Casablanca Press, 1992.
Godek, Gregory J. P. *1001 More Ways to Be Romantic.* Casablanca Press, 1993.
Godek, Gregory J. P. *10,000 Ways to Say I Love You.* Casablanca Press, 1999.
Godek, Gregory J. P. *264 Outrageous, Sweet, and Profound Questions.* Casablanca Press, 2005.

ABOUT THE AUTHORS

Brad has been an early-stage investor and entrepreneur since 1987. Prior to co-founding Foundry Group, he co-founded Mobius Venture Capital and, prior to that, founded Intensity Ventures, a company that helped launch and operate software companies. Previously, Brad was an executive at AmeriData Technologies after it acquired Feld Technologies, a firm he co-founded in 1987 that specialized in custom software applications. Brad is also a co-founder of TechStars.

Brad currently serves on the board of directors of BigDoor, Cheezburger, Fitbit, Gnip, MakerBot, MobileDay, Oblong, Orbotix, SEOMoz, Standing Cloud, and Yesware for Foundry Group.

In addition to his investing efforts, Brad has been active with several nonprofit organizations and currently is chair of the National Center for Women & Information Technology, co-chair of Startup Colorado, and on the board of Startup Weekend.

Brad is a nationally recognized speaker on the topics of venture capital investing and entrepreneurship. He writes the widely read blogs "Feld Thoughts," "Startup Revolution," and "Ask the VC." He has written four previous books: *Do More Faster: TechStars Lessons to Accelerate Your Startup; Venture Deals: Be Smarter Than Your Lawyer and Venture Capitalist; Burning Entrepreneur: How to Launch, Fund, and Set Your Start-Up on Fire!;* and *Startup Communities: Building an Entrepreneurial Ecosystem in Your City.*

Brad holds bachelor of science and master of science degrees in management science from the Massachusetts Institute of Technology. Brad is also an avid art collector and long-distance runner. He has completed 23 marathons as part of his mission to run a marathon in each of the 50 states.

my is a managing director of the Anchor Point Fund, which makes grants to nonprofit organizations in the arts, education, entrepreneurship, conservation and the environment, health and human services, women's and human rights, international development, capacity building, and progressive public policy. She is a co-founder and partner of Social Venture Partners Boulder County (*www.svpbouldercounty.org/*), which strengthens nonprofits through investments of cash grants and pro bono consulting and emphasizes building the capacity and sustainability of organizations.

Amy currently serves on the Board of Trustees at Wellesley College (since 2009). The Anchor Point Internships in Global Leadership at Wellesley College provide funds for four students to participate in 10-week internships in Africa each summer. A collector of contemporary art, she has been a trustee of the Boulder Museum of Contemporary Art since 2000, and also serves on the Visual Arts Curatorial Committee at the Dairy Center for the Arts in Boulder. Amy served as a trustee of the Community Foundation serving Boulder County from 2000 to 2005. She is currently a member of the Dean's Leadership Council at the Harvard Graduate School of Education.

Amy blogs at *http://anchorpoint.blogs.com/* and can be found on Twitter (@abatchelor) and Facebook (amy.batchelor). She is working on two novels, *The North Side of Trees*, and *Epicenter*, about the 1964 Alaska earthquake.

Amy graduated from Wellesley College in 1988 with a BA in Political Philosophy. Amy lives in Boulder, Colorado, and has homes in Keystone, Colorado, and Homer, Alaska, where she was born. Amy travels extensively and has spent time on every continent except Antarctica.

Brad and Amy have been together for 22 years, through lots of ups and downs, and are having an amazing time being together.

INDEX

CHAPTER THREE

PRINCIPLES OF A VIBRANT STARTUP COMMUNITY

Now that you've had an introduction to Boulder and its history from my point of view, I'd like to describe the principles that drive the Boulder startup community, which I'll call the Boulder Thesis. First, however, I'll discuss the three historical frameworks that have been used to describe why some cities become vibrant startup communities.

HISTORICAL FRAMEWORKS

The investigation into startup communities is among the most important inquiries of our time. Why do some places flourish with innovation while others wither? What are the determinants that help a startup community achieve critical startup mass? Once under way, how does a startup community sustain and expand entrepreneurship? Why do startup communities persist, despite often having higher real estate costs and wages than other areas? At stake is nothing less than the continued economic vitality, and even the very existence of towns, cities, and regions.

Studies show that the geography of innovation is neither democratic nor flat. This may be surprising since you might think that location should matter less than ever in today's society. Information can be quickly sent and received by anyone from almost anywhere. In theory, expanding access to resources and information from anywhere might decouple the relationship between place and innovation.

Economic geographers, however, observe the opposite effect. Evidence suggests that location, rather than being irrelevant, is more important than ever. Innovation tilts heavily toward certain locations and, as scholar Richard Florida (professor at Rotman School of Management, at the University of Toronto and author of *The Rise of the Creative Class* (2002)) says, is "spiky" with great concentration of creative, innovative people in tightly clustered geographies. Location clearly matters.

Three prominent frameworks explain why some locales are hotbeds of entrepreneurship whereas others are the innovation equivalent of a twenty-first century economic mirage. Each explanation of regional entrepreneurial advantage comes from a different discipline—one from economics, another from sociology, and a third from geography. These explanations are, for the most part, nonexclusive and complementary.

The first explanation, *external or agglomeration economies*, comes from economics. This line of analysis reaches back to the research of economist Alfred Marshall, and, in recent decades, Michael Porter, Paul Krugman, and Paul Romer have deepened this account. External economies focus on the benefits of startup concentration in an area. This explanation focuses on economic concepts as they apply to location. One is that companies co-located in an area benefit from "external economies of scale." Emerging companies need certain common inputs—for example, infrastructure, specialized legal and accounting services, suppliers, labor pools with a specialized knowledge base—that reside outside the company. Companies in a common geographic area share the fixed costs of these resources external to the company. As more and more startups in an area can share the costs of specialized inputs, the average cost per startup drops for the specialized inputs. This provides direct economic benefit to companies located within a startup community.

Another economic concept, *network effects*, explains why geographic concentration yields further advantage. Network effects operate in systems where the addition of a member to a network enhances value for existing users. The Internet, Facebook, and Twitter are examples in which network effects operate powerfully. These services may have some value to you if there are just 100 other users. However, these networks are immensely more useful if there are 100 million other users that you can connect with. Startup communities similarly feature strong network effects. For example, an area with 10 great programmers provides a valuable pool of labor talent for a startup. However, an additional 1,000 amazing programmers in the same area is vastly more valuable to startups, especially if programmers share best practices with other programmers, inspire one another, or start new companies. External economies of scale lower certain costs; meanwhile, network effects make co-location more valuable.

The second explanation of startup communities, *horizontal networks*, comes from sociology. In her PhD work at MIT, AnnaLee Saxenian (currently Dean of the UC Berkeley School of Information) noticed that external economies do not fully explain the development and adaptation of startup communities. In particular, in her seminal book *Regional Advantage: Culture and Competition in Silicon Valley and Route 128* (1994) Saxenian noted that two hotbeds for high-tech activity—Silicon Valley and Boston's Route 128—looked very similar in the mid-1980s. Each area enjoyed agglomeration economies associated with the nation's two high-tech regions. Yet just a decade later, Silicon Valley gained a dominant advantage over Route 128. External economies alone did not provide an answer. Saxenian set out to resolve the puzzle of why Silicon Valley far outpaced Route 128 from the mid-1980s to mid-1990s.

Saxenian persuasively argues that a culture of openness and information exchange fueled Silicon Valley's ascent over Route 128. This argument is tied to network effects, which are better leveraged by a community with a culture of information sharing across companies and industries. Saxenian observed that the porous boundaries between Silicon Valley companies, such as Sun Microsystems and HP, stood in stark contrast to the closed-loop and autarkic companies of Route 128, such as DEC and Apollo. More broadly, Silicon Valley culture embraced a horizontal exchange of information across and between companies. Rapid technological disruption played perfectly to Silicon Valley's culture of open information exchange and labor mobility. As technology quickly changed, the Silicon Valley companies were better positioned to share information, adopt new trends, leverage innovation, and nimbly respond to new conditions. Meanwhile, vertical integration and closed systems disadvantaged many Route 128 companies during periods of technological upheaval. Saxenian highlights the role of a densely networked culture in explaining Silicon Valley's successful industrial adaptation as compared to Route 128.

Finally, the third explanation of startup communities, the notion of the *creative class*, comes from geography. Richard Florida describes the tie between innovation and creative-class individuals. The creative class is composed of individuals such as entrepreneurs, engineers, professors, and artists who create "meaningful new forms." Creative-class individuals, Florida argues, want to live in nice places, enjoy a culture with a tolerance for new ideas and weirdness, and—most of all—want to be around other creative-class individuals. This is another example of network effects, because a virtuous cycle exists where the existence of a creative class in an area attracts more creative-class individuals to the area, which in turn makes the area even more valuable and attractive. A location that hits critical mass enjoys a competitive geographic advantage over places that have yet to attract a significant number of creative-class individuals.

Each of the three explanations just outlined provides a useful lens to understand why the entrepreneurial world has concentrations of

startup communities in specific geographies. They are incomplete, however, concerning how to put a startup community into motion. There is a
serious chicken and egg problem; although it is not difficult to see why innovation havens have an advantage, it is more challenging to explain how to
get a startup community up and running.

THE BOULDER THESIS

I suggest a fourth framework based on our experience in Boulder. Let's call
it the Boulder Thesis. This framework has four key components:

1. Entrepreneurs must lead the startup community.
2. The leaders must have a long-term commitment.
3. The startup community must be inclusive of anyone who wants to
   participate in it.
4. The startup community must have continual activities that engage
   the entire entrepreneurial stack.

LED BY ENTREPRENEURS

The most critical principle of a startup community is that entrepreneurs
must lead it. Lots of different people are involved in the startup community
and many nonentrepreneurs play key roles. Unless the entrepreneurs lead,
the startup community will not be sustainable over time.

In virtually every major city, there are long lists of different types of
people and organizations who are involved in the startup community including government, universities, investors, mentors, and service providers.
Historically, many of these organizations try to play a leadership role in the
development of their local startup community. Although their involvement
is important, they can't be the leaders. The entrepreneurs have to be leaders.

I define an entrepreneur as someone who has co-founded a company. I differentiate between "high-growth entrepreneurial companies" and "small businesses." Both are important, but they are different things. Entrepreneurial companies have the potential to be or are high-growth businesses whereas small businesses tend to be local, profitable, but slow-growth organizations. Small-business people are often "pillars of their community" as their businesses have a tight co-dependency with their community. By contrast, founders of high-growth entrepreneurial companies generally are involved in the local community as employers and indirect contributors to small businesses and the local economy, but they rarely are involved in the broad business community because they are extraordinarily focused on their companies.

Because of this intense focus, it's unrealistic to think that all entrepreneurs in a community will be leaders. All that is needed is a critical mass of entrepreneurs, often less than a dozen, who will provide leadership.

LONG-TERM COMMITMENT

These leaders have to make a long-term commitment to their startup community. I like to say this has to be at least 20 years from today to reinforce the sense that this has to be meaningful in length. Optimally, the commitment resets daily; it should be a forward-looking 20-year commitment.

It's well understood that economies run in cycles. Economies grow, peak, decline, bottom out, grow again, peak again, decline again, and bottom out again. Some of these cycles are modest. Some are severe. The lengths vary dramatically.

Startup communities have to take a very long-term view. A great startup community such as Silicon Valley (1950–today) has a long trajectory. Although they have their booms and busts, they continued to grow, develop, and expand throughout this period of time.

Most cities and their leaders get excited about entrepreneurship after a major economic decline. They focus on it for a few years through a peak.

When the subsequent decline ultimately happens, they focus on other things during the downturn. When things bottom out, most of the progress gained during the upswing was lost. I've seen this several times—first in the early 1990s and again around the Internet bubble. All you have to do is think back to the nickname of your city during the Internet bubble (Silicon Alley, Silicon Swamp, Silicon Slopes, Silicon Prairie, Silicon Gulch, and Silicon Mountain) to remember what it was like before and after the peak.

This is why the leaders have to first be entrepreneurs and then have a long-term view. These leaders must be committed to the continuous development of their startup community, regardless of the economic cycle their city, state, or country is in. Great entrepreneurial companies, such as Apple, Genentech, Microsoft, and Intel, were started during down economic cycles. It takes such a long time to create something powerful that, almost by definition, you'll go through several economic cycles on the path to glory.

If you aspire to be a leader of your startup community, but you aren't willing to live where you are for the next 20 years and work hard at leading the startup community for that period of time, ask yourself what your real motivation for being a leader is. Although you can have impact for a shorter period of time, it'll take at least this level of commitment from some leaders to sustain a vibrant startup community.

FOSTER A PHILOSOPHY OF INCLUSIVENESS

A startup community must be extremely inclusive. Anyone who wants to engage should be able to, whether they are changing careers, moving to your city, graduating from college, or just want to do something different. This applies to entrepreneurs, people who want to work for startups, people who want to work with startups, or people who are simply intellectually interested in startups.

This philosophy of inclusiveness applies at all levels of the startup community. The leaders have to be open to having more leaders involved, recognizing that leaders need to be entrepreneurs who have a long-term view of building their startup community. Entrepreneurs in the community need to welcome other entrepreneurs, viewing the growth of the startup community as a positive force for all, rather than a zero-sum game in which new entrepreneurs compete locally for resources and status. Employees of startups need to recruit their friends and open their homes and city to other people who have moved into the community.

Everyone in the startup community should have a perspective that having more people engaged in the startup community is good for the startup community. Building a startup community is not a zero-sum game in which there are winners and losers; if everyone engages, they and the entire community can all be winners.

ENGAGE THE ENTIRE ENTREPRENEURIAL STACK

Startup communities must have regular activities that engage the entire entrepreneurial stack. This includes first-time entrepreneurs, experienced entrepreneurs, aspiring entrepreneurs, investors, mentors, employees of startups, service providers to startups, and anyone else who wants to be involved.

Over the years, I've been to many entrepreneurial award events, periodic cocktail parties, monthly networking events, panel discussions, and open houses. Although these types of activities have a role, typically in shining a bright light on the people doing good things within the startup community, they don't really engage anyone in any real entrepreneurial activity.

The emergence of hackathons, new tech meetups, open coffee clubs, startup weekends, and accelerators like TechStars stand out in stark contrast. These are activities and events, which I will cover in depth later in this book, that last from a few hours to three months and provide a tangible, focused, set of activities for the members of the startup community to engage in. By being inclusive of the startup community, these activities consistently engage the entire entrepreneurial stack.

Some of these activities will last for decades; others will go strong for a few years and then fade away; others will fail to thrive and die quickly. This dynamic is analogous to startups—it's okay to try things that fail, and the startup community must recognize when something isn't working and move on. The leaders of the failed activity should try again to create things that engage the entire entrepreneurial stack, and participants in failed activities should keep on engaging in stuff, recognizing that they are playing a long-term game.